Civil War Congress and the Creation of Modern America

Perspectives on the History of Congress, 1801–1877

Donald R. Kennon, Series Editor

Congress and the Emergence of Sectionalism: From the Missouri Compromise to the Age of Jackson, edited by Paul Finkelman and Donald R. Kennon

In the Shadow of Freedom: The Politics of Slavery in the National Capital, edited by Paul Finkelman and Donald R. Kennon

Congress and the Crisis of the 1850s, edited by Paul Finkelman and Donald R. Kennon

Lincoln, Congress, and Emancipation, edited by Paul Finkelman and Donald R. Kennon

Congress and the People's Contest: The Conduct of the Civil War, edited by Paul Finkelman and Donald R. Kennon

Civil War Congress and the Creation of Modern America: A Revolution on the Home Front, edited by Paul Finkelman and Donald R. Kennon

Civil War Congress and the Creation of Modern America

A Revolution on the Home Front

Edited by Paul Finkelman and Donald R. Kennon

Published for the
United States Capitol Historical Society
by Ohio University Press • Athens

Ohio University Press, Athens, Ohio 45701
ohioswallow.com

Printed in the United States of America
Ohio University Press books are printed on acid-free paper ∞™

Cover art: Lincoln and Congress considered the continuing construction of the United States Capitol during the Civil War as "a sign that the Union would go on." Just as the completion of the innovative cast-iron dome altered and enhanced the Capitol, the war forever changed the American nation, bringing it closer to the "new birth of freedom" Lincoln promised in his Gettysburg Address. *Courtesy Architect of the Capitol*

28 27 26 25 24 23 22 21 20 19 18 5 4 3 2 1

Library of Congress Cataloging-in-publication data available upon request.
Names: Finkelman, Paul, 1949- editor. | Kennon, Donald R., 1948- editor.
Title: Civil War Congress and the creation of modern America : a revolution on the home front / edited by Paul Finkelman and Donald R. Kennon.
Description: Athens : Published for the United States Capitol Historical Society by Ohio University Press, [2018] | Series: Perspectives on the history of Congress, 1801/1877 | Includes bibliographical references and index.
Identifiers: LCCN 2018031921| ISBN 9780821423387 (hc : alk. paper) | ISBN 9780821446454 (pdf)
Subjects: LCSH: United States--Politics and government--1861-1865. | United States. Congress--History--19th century. | Federal government--United States--History--19th century. | United States--History--Civil War, 1861-1865--Social aspects. | Civilians in war--United States--History--19th century. | Social change--United States--History--19th century.
Classification: LCC E459 .C595 2018 | DDC 973.7/1--dc23
LC record available at https://lccn.loc.gov/2018031921

Contents

Paul Finkelman

Introduction

The Congress, the Civil War, and the Making of Modern America

THE CIVIL WAR remains the central moment of American history. The ordeal by fire kept the Union together at the cost of some 630,000 deaths by bullets, disease, exposure, and the horrid conditions in both United States and Confederate prisoner of war camps. It was not merely America's bloodiest war, but as bloody as all other American wars combined. Wounded and maimed veterans came home bearing the outward scars of battle and carrying inner scars.

Our memory of the Civil War is mostly about warfare and battles, the carnage made glorious and meaningful by emancipation. Certainly the central meaning of the war is national unity and national freedom, followed by a critical (although incomplete) restructuring of the Constitution and the nature of the national government. But as the essays in this volume show, the war changed the nation in other ways as well. Indeed, beyond emancipation and the constitutional changes of the Thirteenth, Fourteenth, and Fifteenth amendments, the war permanently altered the American nation. The war forced Congress to expand the size of the government beyond anything imaginable before 1861. At the same time, the absence of senators and representatives from most of the slave states enabled Congress to pass legislation that allowed for internal improvements, expanded foreign policy initiatives, stimulated western settlement, and supported the general welfare of the nation. Southerners had blocked such laws, arguing that they helped the North and the free states, threatened slavery, harmed the South, or overly expanded the national government.

The war effort fundamentally and permanently changed the nation in many ways. About two million Northern men served in the United States Army and Navy during the war.[1] These men constituted about 10 percent of the entire population of the North. The absence of so many men naturally affected day-to-day life, as did the more than 300,000 Northern men who died while in the military. Recruitment of troops also affected the home front, the nation, and the future of the nation. Initially the United States Army was made up of members of state militias, who were mobilized at the very beginning of the war, after a proclamation from President Lincoln.[2] After the Confederate attack on Fort Sumter, Lincoln called for 75,000 troops, thinking this would be sufficient to suppress the rebellion. But the war lasted longer and was more costly than anyone could imagine. By mid-1862 the United States had suffered more than 75,000 casualties (killed, wounded, captured, or missing). In the Militia Act of 1862, Congress opened military service to African American men,[3] reversing seven decades of discrimination and ultimately paving the way for black suffrage on the same basis as whites. Its immediate consequence was to alter Northern society, especially in black communities, as tens of thousands of African American men enlisted.

The recruitment and movement of troops affected daily life in many places. As Guy Gugliotta notes, "Housing in wartime Washington was at a premium." Living conditions were crowded and stressful. "Civility" had all but disappeared as people "routinely dumped garbage in the vacant lot[s]" and unruly children threw rocks at windows. The nation's capital was filled with civil servants, politicians, contractors, fugitive slaves, tens of thousands of soldiers, and all manner of other people. In the summer of 1862 Congress ended slavery in the District of Columbia, which dramatically altered

---

[1]At least 300,000 Union servicemen were Southerners, including about 150,000 former slaves.

[2]Abraham Lincoln, "Proclamation Calling Militia and Convening Congress (Apr. 15, 1861)," in Roy P. Basler ed., *The Collected Works of Abraham Lincoln*, 9 vols. (New Brunswick, N.J., 1953–55), 4:331.

[3]"Act to Amend the Act Calling Forth the Militia to Execute the Laws of the Union, Suppress Insurrections, and Repel Invasions, Approved February Twenty-Eight, Seventeen Hundred and Ninety-Five, and Acts Amendatory Thereof, and for Other Purposes [Militia Act of 1862]," Act of July 17, 1862, 12 Stat. 597 (1863).

social life in the capital.[4] Congress later provided civil rights protections for former slaves and began to provide them with schools and other benefits of freedom.[5]

In March 1863 Congress more dramatically altered American culture and society by establishing the nation's first system of military conscription.[6] This law gave vast powers to the national government. Ironically, the secessionists claimed that a powerful national government threatened their way of life and states' rights, but their acts of secession and treason facilitated and necessitated the enhancement of national power. Even more ironic, the Confederacy had implemented conscription in April 1862, thus for more than a year the Confederate government had more power than the United States government.[7] Conscription was a major change in American policy and national culture. Military service was no longer tied to patriotism and a desire to serve the nation. It was now becoming mandatory. In her essay "Conscription and the Consolidation of Federal Power during the Civil War," Jennifer L. Weber outlines the mechanics of conscription, noting that the law "resulted in a tectonic shift in the relationship between federal and state governments and between the nation and its people." Indeed, much of this book tracks this theme, as we see the exigencies of war giving Congress powers it never would have imagined using before the war.

Similarly, the sheer magnitude of the war—the expense in blood and treasure—forced other changes. The war effort required a vast industrial expansion—the war transformed the nation from one that was overwhelmingly agricultural to one that was increasingly industrial. While there were factories and some industry in the North before 1861, the war was the engine that truly brought the Industrial Revolution to the United States. In

---

[4]"An Act for the Release of Certain Persons Held to Service or Labor in the District of Columbia," Act of Apr. 16, 1862, 12 Stat. 376 (1863). See Kate Masur, *An Example for All the Land: Emancipation and the Struggle over Equality in Washington, D.C.* (Chapel Hill, N.C., 2010).

[5]See Paul Finkelman, "The Summer of '62: Congress, Slavery, and a Revolution in Federal Law," in Paul Finkelman and Donald R. Kennon, eds., *Congress and the People's Contest: The Conduct of the Civil War* (Athens, Ohio, 2017).

[6]"An Act for Enrolling and Calling Out the National Forces, and for Other Purposes [The Enrollment Act]," Act of Mar. 3, 1863, 12 Stat. 731 (1863).

[7]Act of Apr. 16, 1862, *Statutes at Large of the Provisional Government of the Confederate States of America*, 1st sess., chap. 31, pp. 29–32; William Alan Blair, *Virginia's Private War: Feeding Body and Soul in the Confederacy, 1861–1865* (New York, 1998). See also Susanna Michele Lee, "Twenty-Slave Law," in Virginia Foundation for the Humanities, *Encyclopedia Virginia*, May 31, 2012, http://www.EncyclopediaVirginia.org/Twenty-Slave_Law.

addition to the obvious expansion of the production of military hardware, the nation had to produce vast quantities of preserved and canned food, boots, uniforms, bugles, drums, saddles and reins, and other equipment and accoutrements. Nonmilitary industrial production that was used for the war effort, such as rails for train tracks, engines for trains, and wire for telegraph lines, further changed and modernized the nation by creating new jobs, new factories, investments, and profits.

Similarly, the war cost money. Paying for the war was enormously complicated, as Jenny Bourne shows in "To Slip the Surly Bonds of States' Rights and Form a More Perfect (Financial) Union: One Legacy of the Thirty-Seventh Congress." Among other things, the war led Congress to pass the nation's first income tax and to print paper money for the first time since the Revolution. As Bourne notes: "Congress resorted to innovative schemes, including the first-ever income tax, widespread use of fiat money issued via newly created national banks, massive amounts of government borrowing, and debt sold directly to the public." The war allowed Congress to remake the national economy, in part because of necessity. Secession also made it possible. With the demise of the Bank of the United States in the 1830s, opposition to national economic policy—and even a national currency—had been a mantra of the Democratic Party, which usually controlled Congress and the White House in this period.[8] But with the absence of Southern states' rights legislators and the resulting huge Republican majority in Congress, nationalizing economic legislation was possible. The nation now had paper currency—greenbacks—that was backed not by gold or silver but by only the full faith and credit of the United States. Today we take such currency for granted, as we spend and receive Federal Reserve notes. But in 1862 and 1863 the laws creating this currency—the Legal Tender Acts—were revolutionary,[9] and we still live under the currency regime they helped create.

---

[8]The only exception to control of the White House was the four years of the Taylor–Fillmore presidencies (1849–53) and the first month of William Henry Harrison's presidency in 1841. Harrison's successor, John Tyler, was a states' rights slaveholder from Virginia and a lifelong Democrat who generally opposed Whig economic policies.

[9]"An Act to Authorize the Issue of United States Notes, for the Redemption or Funding Thereof, and for Funding the Floating Debt of the United States [First Legal Tender Act]," Act of Feb. 25, 1862, 12 Stat. 345 (1863); "An Act to Authorize an Additional Issue of United States Notes, and for Other Purpose," Act of July 11, 1862, 12 Stat. 532 (1863); and "An Act to Provide Ways and Means for Support of the Government," Act of Mar. 3, 1863, 12 Stat. 709 (1863).

In 1862 Congress created the Internal Revenue Service, and of course we live under that regime as well.[10] We live under a tax system created by the war.

The military's insatiable appetite for manpower, the use of greenbacks as a national currency, and the general expansion of the federal government in Washington led to another dramatic change in national culture: the employment of women. The diversion of more than two million men into the military forced Americans to rethink gender roles, and pointed the way toward a postwar world where women would be working outside their homes as never before. All of the war production affected the labor market and who worked. For the first time in American history the federal government hired women in large numbers, as Daniel W. Stowell explains in "Abraham Lincoln and 'Government Girls' in Wartime Washington." The "employment of female clerical workers in the federal government dates to the fall of 1861, when Francis E. Spinner, treasurer of the United States, began to employ women to cut and count treasury notes." As Stowell tells us, Spinner was appalled to find healthy young men cutting newly printed sheets of currency into individual bills. Spinner believed "these young men should have muskets instead of shears placed in their hands," and with these men fighting the Confederates, Spinner would hire women (at lower wages) to do what, to nineteenth-century men, appeared to be women's work—cutting things with shears. After the war, the nation realized that this single move led to a permanent change in the American labor market. Women could now be employed as clerks for the government. Paid less than men, women nevertheless realized that wielding scissors and working for the Treasury Department put food on their tables, allowed them to make an important and meaningful contribution to the war effort, and put more soldiers in the field to defeat the Southern traitors. It also set the stage for a far greater expansion of women workers after the war.

Legislation passed during the war for nonmilitary purposes promised to further alter Northern society. During the war, Congress passed a plethora of laws that reshaped the nation but had nothing to do with the military.[11]

---

[10] "An Act to Provide Internal Revenue to Support the Government and to Pay Interest on the Public Debt," Act of July 1, 1862, 12 Stat. 432 (1863).

[11] See Finkelman, "The Summer of '62."

Thus, Congress created the Department of Agriculture,[12] passed the Homestead Act,[13] upgraded public education in the District of Columbia,[14] and passed laws for the creation of the transcontinental railroad[15] and land-grant colleges.[16]

While the war slowed down America's relentless westward expansion, it also stimulated it. The Pacific Railroad Act promised that those who moved west would be increasingly less isolated from their families and friends in the East, and the goods they grew, raised, mined, and produced would be more likely to reach favorable markets. The Land-Grant College Act, as Peter Wallenstein explains, also tied the East to the West during the war. By allocating western lands to provide money for eastern (and in the future, western) public colleges, the law gave easterners a reason to support western settlement. The new colleges would benefit the whole nation.

The West had of course always been a place of warfare. Before the Civil War the main occupation of the army had been to threaten or fight Indians, to force them to move farther west, and sometimes to protect them (however briefly) from overreaching white settlers. With the Civil War raging, the government had fewer resources to support a frontier army and less need. Thus, during the war, the United States was certainly not pushing for western migration or an aggressive policy toward Indians. But, as my own chapter on the Dakota War in Minnesota shows, white-Indian relations did not come to a standstill during the Civil War. The brief war ended in defeat for the Dakota and a forced migration out of Minnesota. After the war the military sought to execute more than 300 Dakota soldiers in a

---

[12]"An Act to Establish a Department of Agriculture," Act of May 15, 1862, 12 Stat. 387 (1863).

[13]"An Act to Secure Homesteads to Actual Settlers on the Public Domain [The Homestead Act]," Act of May 20, 1862, 12 Stat. 392 (1863).

[14]"An Act to Provide for the Public Instruction of Youth in Primary Schools throughout the County of Washington, in the District of Columbia, without the Limits of the Cities of Washington and Georgetown," Act of May 20, 1862, 12 Stat. 394 (1863). It is worth noting that only North Carolina had even a rudimentary system of public schools in the South.

[15]"An Act to Aid in the Construction of a Railroad and Telegraph Line from the Missouri River to the Pacific Ocean, and to Secure to the Government the Use of the Same for Postal, Military, and Other Purposes [The Pacific Railroad Act]," Act of July 1, 1862, 12 Stat. 489 (1863).

[16]"An Act Donating Public Lands to the Several States and Territories Which May Provide Colleges for the Benefit of Agriculture and Mechanic Arts [The Morrill Land-Grant College Act]," Act of July 2, 1862, 12 Stat. 503 (1863).

grotesque attempt at racist vengeance. Lincoln commuted (and effectively pardoned) 87 percent of those sentenced to die, just as he reprieved countless soldiers sentenced to the firing squad for failing to stay awake on guard duty, succumbing to their fears in battle, or believing, in an almost premodern view of military service, that they needed to return home for the funeral of a parent. The Dakota War was a reminder, in the middle of the War for the Union, that on the home front racism and oppression of Indians remained common and palpable. It is also a reminder of Lincoln's ability, in the midst of the awful carnage of the war, to prevent unnecessary killing wherever he could. Finally, the trials after the war and Lincoln's willingness to prevent the vast majority of the proposed executions, pointed to an age when the law of war would become part of military and political policy.

Emblematic of how the war changed the nation and the home front are the last two essays in this book. Jean H. Baker takes us into the Executive Mansion—what today we call the White House. Here the war and the home front intersected every day, all day long. President Lincoln lived his life, struggled with marriage and family issues, and tried to raise one young son and guide another who was on the cusp of adulthood. He also faced the war, every day, every night. As Baker writes: "The White House, with its multiple functions as a family residence, an executive office, and the location of endless ceremonies and rituals, complicated the sixteenth president's tenure in many, not always positive, ways." Lincoln met dignitaries, generals, and individual citizens in the White House. He invited Frederick Douglass to discuss policy with him, thus rewriting the rules of racial etiquette in America, as a president sought the advice of a black man. He considered political strategy and military strategy. He slept, often fitfully, worrying about the carnage of the war and the future of a nation "dedicated to the proposition that all men are created equal." It was there he drafted the Emancipation Proclamation, to finally end slavery, and promised the nation a new birth of freedom.

Just as Lincoln drafted the language of liberty and freedom at his home—the White House—during the war, Congress helped provide a symbolic message of freedom to the nation through the architecture of the Capitol. As Guy Gugliotta teaches us in this volume, with most Southerners no longer in Congress, the Capitol dome could now be completed. In the 1850s, Southerners in Congress had prevented the design of the iconic statue

"*Freedom*—a gorgeous, wraithlike figure wearing a 'liberty cap,'" sitting on top of the building. Powerful Southerners in Congress backed former Senator Jefferson Davis of Mississippi, who, as secretary of war, was able to prevent the national government from crowning Congress with an icon of "freedom" and a "liberty cap," because the cap was a cultural condemnation of slavery. He pushed for a new design of *Freedom* that Congress accepted, but the proslavery Buchanan administration and the Southern Democrats in Congress still prevented completion of the dome. But in 1861 Davis had embraced treason as the president of the Confederacy. Although he was a graduate of West Point, Davis had ordered his troops to fire on the United States Army at Fort Sumter and continued to make war on his former comrades-in-arms. But he could no longer stop the nation from embracing freedom with an icon to liberty at the top of Congress.

Thus, as Guy Gugliotta notes in his chapter, the symbol of the home front finally sat atop the Capitol dome in 1863—"a robust nineteen-foot Indian princess–Roman goddess with a buckskin skirt, classical drapery above the waist, European features, and a bird purporting to be an American eagle sitting on her head with its mouth open." The statue, called *Freedom Triumphant in War and Peace*, was "bolted in place atop the Capitol dome during the depths of the Civil War."

The message was clear: the American nation, backed by the Emancipation Proclamation, now stood for freedom. This freedom was being implemented by a gigantic army that included former slaves, free black volunteers, and conscripted whites, all paid in greenbacks. The war had permanently changed the nation, and these changes in turn made a victory for *Freedom* possible. As we know, in hindsight, it was an incomplete and imperfect victory, but it still brought the nation many steps closer to the "new birth of freedom" Lincoln promised in the Gettysburg Address.

Jennifer L. Weber

Conscription and the Consolidation of Federal Power during the Civil War

In March 1863, an increasingly desperate Union Congress passed a new law called the Enrollment Act to encourage more men to volunteer for military service. In theory, it was a carrot-and-stick sort of arrangement: enlist honorably and receive a healthy incentive for doing so, or undergo the shameful act of being drafted and pass on any bonus. In practice, the arrangement was more complicated because of the various legal options it provided for men to avoid service altogether. And, as it turned out, the law had far-reaching consequences for Americans. The bland legal language of the Enrollment Act belied the changes that it set in motion, changes that resulted in a tectonic shift in the relationship between federal and state governments and between the nation and its people. The transformation that Americans experienced as a result of the draft act fell into three categories: who would raise troops, the degree to which federal government could use coercion, and the ability of the federal government to gather and keep information on its citizenry.[1]

The United States Army had a mere 16,000 members as of 1860, and they were spread widely across the West. About a third of the officers, along with a handful of enlisted men, resigned to join the Confederacy. Clearly, the Union army did not have the manpower to bring the rebels in line. The day

[1]"An Act for Enrolling and Calling Out the National Forces, and for Other Purposes," 1863, 37th Cong., 3d sess., S.Misc.Doc. 41 (hereafter referred to as the Enrollment Act).

after the Confederates took Fort Sumter, President Abraham Lincoln issued a proclamation asking for 75,000 militiamen to suppress them. In the early days of the conflict, war fever gripped the North, and so many men volunteered that the states in charge of enlisting them turned them away. Rebels and Yankees alike predicted the war would last a mere ninety days. South Carolina Senator James Chesnut had offered to drink all the blood that would be spilled, and Southerners assured each other that "a lady's thimble will hold all the blood that will be shed." In the North, loyal men continued to step forward enthusiastically well after ninety days had come and gone. For the next year or so, volunteers—the term "militiaman" had been rapidly replaced—were rewarded for their efforts with a hundred-dollar bounty payable upon their being mustered out at the end of their three-year term. Northern recruitment efforts hummed along until the spring of 1862, when enlistments started to drop off.[2]

Over the course of that season, two great realizations seeped into the Northern consciousness. First, Americans began to understand that many, many men would die in the war. The Battle of Shiloh in early April was the deadliest fighting ever seen on the continent to that time, and it helped drive the point home. Seven Pines at the end of May, the biggest fight yet in the East, seconded the notion. The sobering reality of war withered many young men's visions that the war would be exciting, a lark. Second, the people of the North came to realize that not only would the war be bloody, but it would also be long. Robert E. Lee in particular was responsible for this somber new reality. Before his appointment on June 1 to command the Army of Northern Virginia, Americans could still believe they would win the war in rather short order. His rapid string of successes in the spring and summer of 1862 forced Northerners to come to terms with a far more grinding war than they had expected. As these two truths settled around the shoulders of Union loyalists like one of Lincoln's shawls, even patriotism shriveled as a motivation to join the ranks. As ideological reasons to enlist vanished, practical reasons not to serve grew. The army could not pay its men on time. The federal government shuttered all its recruiting offices and sold the public property that went with them. Secretary of War

[2]Herman Hattaway and Archer Jones, *How the North Won: A Military History of the Civil War* (Urbana, Ill., 1983), p. 10; Roy P. Basler, ed., *The Collected Works of Abraham Lincoln*, 9 vols. (New Brunswick, N.J., 1953–55), 4:331–32; E. Merton Coulter, *The Confederate States of America, 1861–1865: A History of the South* (Baton Rouge, La., 1950), p. 15.

Edwin Stanton said they were too expensive to maintain. Besides, the public was so flush with recent victories that the ranks would easily be refilled. Two months later, in mid-June, he was begging governors for troops.[3]

On July 1, just as Union Major General George McClellan was wilting before Lee's army at the Seven Days Battles, Lincoln issued a call for 300,000 three-year men. As had been the case to this point in the war, states had the constitutional responsibility to raise troops. The men were considered citizen-soldiers rather than part of the permanent army, which remained a separate entity, and volunteer regiments were designated by state. The governor usually appointed regimental commanders—a political boon since the posts offered more opportunity for patronage—though in some instances soldiers would elect their own officers. These units were under state control and subject to the laws of the state militia until they were mustered into federal service.[4]

The president hoped that pride and patriotism were still powerful enough to replenish the army, a hope articulated in a song that would become famous, "We Are Coming, Father Abraham, 300,000 More." Reality overrode the optimism of the title. Men were dribbling into recruiting offices, not flooding them. Support for the war softened with each of the keen blows the Union suffered in the summer of 1862. On July 17, Lincoln signed the Militia Act, which allowed black men to serve in the army. This was the first time since 1792 that African Americans had been allowed to serve legally, an indication of both how stretched the army was becoming and congressional Republicans' commitment to emancipation. The Militia Act also allowed the administration to call on the states for an additional 300,000 men who would serve a term of nine months, an option Stanton exercised two and a half weeks after the law went into effect. States that did not fill their quotas by August 15 would have to hold drafts.[5]

---

[3]Reid Mitchell, *Civil War Soldiers* (New York, 1988), pp. 1–23; James W. Geary, *We Need Men: The Union Draft in the Civil War* (DeKalb, Ill., 1991), pp. 15–16; Allan Nevins, *The War for the Union: War Becomes Revolution, 1862–1863*, 4 vols. (New York, 1959), 2:105, 143; United States War Department, *The War of the Rebellion: A Compilation of the Official Records of the Union and Confederate Armies* (Washington, D.C., 1880–1901), ser. 3, vol. 2, pp. 2–3 (hereafter referred to as *O.R.*).

[4]Basler, *Collected Works*, 5:296–97.

[5]"We Are Coming, Father Abraham, 300,000 More," J. A. Getze, arranger (Philadelphia, 1862); *O.R.* ser. 3, vol. 2, pp. 280–82.

Officials struggled to meet the demands of the president and the Militia Act. First, they struggled to determine who was responsible for what. Only the War Department could top up existing regiments with new men, and only the states could form new regiments. Second, they discovered stiff resistance to military service, even under the threat of conscription. The hope had been that the specter of drafting would prompt men to volunteer in greater numbers—conscription being deemed a cowardly way to wind up in the army. Much has been written about the honor culture of the South, but it extended north of the Mason-Dixon Line as well.[6] The failure to volunteer brought shame not only on individual men but also on their communities. A supervisor in Cook County, Illinois, said that he would pay any sum of money to find recruits rather than have his county "submit to the disgrace" of a draft. Nevertheless, enlistments nationally fell short. Parts of the North would now experience conscription, though in truth the efforts in the fall of 1862 were more of a protodraft.[7]

During the American Revolution, states had resorted to conscription to fill the ranks of their militia. The effort did not go particularly well then, and time had not improved the states' abilities. The effort in the fall of 1862 was beset with troubles. Some governors dragged their feet in putting together the bureaucratic machinery to carry off a draft. Others spent months haggling with the administration about how many men their states already had sent into the service and how many more they were now expected to send. Rioting broke out in Ozaukee County, Wisconsin, and in the coal fields of Pennsylvania. Meanwhile, various forms of fraud and deceit began to creep into the system. Because drafted men could buy substitutes, brokerages sprang up offering significant sums to attract men who would hire themselves out in this capacity. Brokers paid better than bounties, and volunteer enlistments suffered as a result. Draft dodgers headed for Canada or the West or bribed doctors for certificates of disability. Some men enlisted, accepted whatever bounty they might be paid up front, then deserted. Throughout the fall, the general approach to military manpower seemed to be one of dillydallying, nit-picking, bickering, and evasion, even as the Union forces continued to suffer huge losses at Second Bull

[6]The best work on this remains Bertram Wyatt-Brown, *Southern Honor: Ethics and Behavior in the Old South*, 25th anniversary ed. (New York, 2007).

[7]Aretas A. Dayton, "The Raising of Union Forces in Illinois during the Civil War," *Journal of the Illinois State Historical Society* 34 (1941):413.

Run, Fredericksburg, and, most notably, Antietam, the deadliest day in American history. Despite the many obstacles and frustrations, though, Lincoln's calls yielded 421,000 three-year volunteers and 87,000 nine-month militia members.[8]

By early 1863, multiple factors suggested that the Union would have to resort to a true draft, not the militia draft that had recently concluded. The enlistment period for men who had signed up for two years in 1861 would be over in a few months. So would the terms of the nine-month men who had joined in the summer and fall of 1862. Most importantly, volunteer recruitment had dried up. Congress had to take steps to ensure the army could continue. Under the Constitution, Congress has the authority to raise armies and call out the state militias. The states have the responsibility of organizing, training, arming, and disciplining those militias. The Founders dealt out authority this way because they worried about what an unscrupulous commander in chief would do with a large standing army at his disposal. In addition, their military experiences involved local militias that supplemented either the Royal or the Continental army. Dividing power this way kept primary responsibility for the nation's military policy in state hands and for the most part avoided the threat of a standing army. This approach had worked during the Seven Years' War and the American Revolution. Later, the Constitution said nothing about conscription, which apparently did not come up in the Constitutional Convention or the state ratifying conventions. During the War of 1812 James Madison and the Federalists had wanted to draft militiamen into the regular army, but the conflict ended before anything like that could be put in place. The Civil War was larger, more complex, and more violent than America's previous wars, and the piecemeal, state-level efforts proved utterly inadequate to the task.[9]

---

[8]Gary Wamsley, *Selective Service and a Changing America: A Study of Organizational Environmental Relationships* (Columbus, Ohio, 1969), p. 18; Jack Furniss, "Civil Wars: Union Governors and Federal–State Conflict in the North" (paper presented at the biennial meeting of the Society for Civil War Historians, Chattanooga, Tenn., June 2016), pp. 3–7; Lawrence H. Larsen, "Draft Riot in Wisconsin, 1862," *Civil War History* 7 (1961):421–26; Grace Palladino, *Another Civil War: Labor, Capital, and the State in the Anthracite Regions of Pennsylvania, 1840–68* (Urbana, Ill., 1990), chap. 5; Nevins, *War for the Union*, 2:164.

[9]U.S. Constitution, Art. I, Sec. 8; Wamsley, *Selective Service*, pp. 22–23. Gordon Wood, *The Creation of the American Republic, 1776–1787* (Chapel Hill, N.C., 1969) remains an excellent study of republican ideology in the Revolutionary War period.

In March 1863, Congress passed the Enrollment Act, a law that one modern legal scholar termed "desperate and problem-laden." It marked a radical departure from what Americans understood as normative. During the Revolutionary War, some states had resorted to a draft, and five state constitutions explicitly allowed conscription. Under the law, states would no longer be conscripting—only the federal government would. The Enrollment Act created an agency within the War Department, the Provost Marshal General's Bureau, to administer and enforce any draft. The law required that the bureau have at least one office in every congressional district in the North. The provost marshal's agents would take a census of men between the ages of twenty and forty-five and enroll them for the draft. If the area fell short in meeting its quota, the bureau would hold a draft, which generally meant blindfolded men pulling names written on slips of paper out of a draft wheel (fig. 1). If the agents could recruit a local blind man for the job, all the better. After being drafted, a man had several days to report before his local draft board and take a physical. In the interim, he could avoid service by hiring a substitute or paying a $300 commutation fee, or he could enlist voluntarily. As if the Enrollment Act had not encroached enough on traditional understandings of state-federal responsibilities, the War Department on May 1, 1863, announced that the Provost Marshal General's Bureau would now be in charge of enlisting all volunteers. No longer would the states be involved in any way except to appoint regimental officers. Even so, the War Department could dismiss those officers that commanders deemed ineffective. With this change, the federal government would run the entire recruitment effort for the war. States would no longer have any responsibility for raising men for the Union war effort.[10]

[10]J. L. Bernstein, "Conscription and the Constitution: The Amazing Case of *Kneedler v. Lane*," *American Bar Association Journal* 53, no. 8 (1967):708–12; John W. Delehant, "Judicial Revisitation Finds *Needler v. Lane* Not So 'Amazing,'" *American Bar Association Journal* 53, no. 12 (1967):1132–35; James F. Simon, *Lincoln and Chief Justice Taney: Slavery, Secession, and the President's War Powers* (New York, 2006), p. 243; James B. Fry, *Final Report Made to the Secretary of War, by the Provost Marshal General, of the Operations of the Bureau of the Provost Marshal General of the United States*, 2 vols. (n.p., 1866), 2:109. The militia system after the war was "dead in spite of statutes to the contrary," according to John K. Mahon. Southern states were allowed to form militia companies in 1869 to support the army as it oversaw Reconstruction. Militia service became an obligation nationally in the late 1870s with the advent of labor riots. These militia were the nub of what would become the National Guard. John K. Mahon, *The History of the Militia and the National Guard* (New York, 1983), pp. 108–9; Martha Derthick, *The National Guard in Politics* (Cambridge, Mass., 1965), pp. 15–17.

Fig. 1. "Resumption of the Draft—Inside the Provost Marshal's Office, Sixth District—The Wheel Goes Round." An 1863 engraving depicts a blindfolded man drawing names for the draft in New York City. *(Library of Congress Prints and Photographs Division)*

The newly appointed provost marshal general, James B. Fry (fig. 2), was a West Pointer and career army man whom General Ulysses S. Grant had suggested for the job. Fry had made his name in the war not as a fighting man but as a highly competent administrator—or, as one historian wrote, "an efficient martinet." Little information about Fry is available. He did not leave personal papers behind, and few people in Washington seem to discuss him during the war years. In the postbellum era, he was engaged in several notable political fights and wrote a handful of books about them after his opponents died. Thorough to the point of being a stickler, Fry appears to have done little delegating. Almost every halfway important piece of correspondence to come into the Washington offices from the field has his initials on it. Under Fry, the bureau was as centralized and as top-down as a federal office could be in those days.[11]

In a law that induced many unhappy emotions, the most controversial element was the commutation fee. The commutation fee was not a new development in American military history. The authors of the Enrollment Act thought it would hold down the asking price for substitutes, which it did.

[11]Nevins, *The War for the Union*, 2:397.

Fig. 2. Provost Marshal James B. Fry. Appointed in 1863 with the rank of colonel, he was promoted to brigadier general in April 1864. *(Library of Congress Prints and Photographs Division)*

When commutation was all but eliminated in 1864, prices for substitutes shot up. Nevertheless, opponents of the fee said it turned the rebellion into "a rich man's war but a poor man's fight," even though options were available for men of lesser means. The most notable was draft insurance, which was available on both formal and ad hoc bases. The North American Life Insurance Company peddled coverage for the draft. For a premium of $100, the company would pay out $300 if the insured man's name was pulled out of the draft wheel. Draft insurance societies also popped up with every round of conscription. Sometimes these comprised friends, other times co-workers or people who lived in the same place. However they came together, members would sign a contract promising to pay a certain amount of money—ranging between one dollar and one hundred dollars—if any member was conscripted. The draftee could use the pooled money to pay a commutation fee, hire a substitute, or support his family if he decided to go into the army. No matter. The "rich man's war/poor man's fight" label stuck for the duration. *Yankee Notions* sent up "We Are Coming, Father Abraham" with a parody that made the point:

> We're coming, Ancient Abram, several hundred strong,
> We hadn't no $300, and so we come along;
> We hadn't no rich parents to pony up the tin,
> So we went unto the Provost, and there were mustered in.

Not surprisingly, Confederates had similar criticisms about their conscription, which had gone into effect a year earlier, but historian James M. McPherson has shown that the accusation was not true for either section.[12]

In the years after the Enrollment Act, Lincoln made four calls for additional men, and they resulted in nearly a quarter of a million Northerners being held to service. Thirty-five percent of those paid a commutation fee, which raised more than $26.3 million for the federal coffers—a sum that more than offset the cost of the draft effort. Forty-seven percent furnished substitutes. Nineteen percent actually served. Of the two million men who served in the Union army, only 6 percent by war's end had been drafted, and both contemporaries and historians considered them to be notoriously poor soldiers. Nevertheless, Provost Marshal General James B. Fry—along

[12]A Portland Conscript, "A Hymn," *Yankee Notions*, Nov. 1, 1863; Tables 20.1 and 20.2 in James M. McPherson, *Ordeal by Fire: The Civil War and Reconstruction*, 3d ed. (Boston, 2001), p. 387.

with later scholars—considered conscription to be a success because it prompted so many men to volunteer. This was true from the first round of conscription in the summer of 1863, Fry said. On its face, the Enrollment Act was "not directly fruitful in producing men," he admitted, but it helped spur enlistments.[13]

The law's success came at a cost, though. Conservative Democrats had long since established a pattern of claiming many of Lincoln's decisions were unconstitutional. Federalizing military recruitment and coercing men into the service against their will fit neatly into their existing narrative of a tyrannical administration. Chauncey Burr, a vociferous critic of Lincoln, wrote in *The Old Guard* that the new law "clothes the President with unlimited and unchecked military powers. It makes him, at one bound, as absolute a monarch as the Autocrat of all the Russias." The only one of President Lincoln's actions that Democrats objected to more strenuously than the draft was abolition, and even then not by much because enrollment and conscription were far more likely to touch many of Lincoln's foes personally. White people of any class could be called up. The draft did not care whether a conscript supported the war. Conscription's only obligation was to provide reasonably healthy men to fill the ranks. Claims to personal liberty fell on deaf ears where the law was concerned. For Republicans, at least, the idea that the federal government was sending at least some of these unwilling men to their deaths was a minor problem compared with the major existential crisis facing the country. On the other hand, the consequences of emancipation remained largely abstract to Northern civilians during the war. Contrabands may have been flocking to the Union army in the South, but they were not flooding the North and taking jobs.[14]

The Enrollment Act pushed many Democrats who had been warily supportive of Lincoln into the conservative, or "Copperhead," wing of their party. In a resolution to New York Governor Horatio Seymour, who had some Copperhead sympathies himself, a man named M. Benedict claimed to represent "350,000 working men" when he observed that conscription was a "monarchical principle & a sin in itself." Its burden fell on the poor twice over, Benedict wrote, first by drafting them, and then, if they were killed or

---

[13]E. B. Long and Barbara Long, *The Civil War Day by Day: An Almanac, 1861–1865* (Garden City, N.Y., 1971), pp. 707–8; Fry, *Final Report*, p. 34.

[14]Chauncey Burr, *The Old Guard* (March 1863):67.

maimed in battle, by forcing their families to beg. Writing as the draft riot in New York City was still raging, Benedict argued that no mob law could possibly be as "outrageous" as the draft law itself. Fry was unmoved by the complaints of the Copperheads. He boasted after the war that the law established "the power and determination of the government to proceed in the re-enforcement of its armies."[15]

Opponents of the draft were not without influential allies, especially within the judicial system. On November 9, 1863, the Pennsylvania Supreme Court ruled in *Kneedler v. Lane* that the draft law was unconstitutional because it infringed on the rights of the states to raise militias. Conscription in the commonwealth was therefore illegal. The 3–2 vote broke down on party lines, but the circumstances surrounding the case were highly political. One of the Democratic justices who voted with the majority, George Woodward, was running for governor when the case was heard September 23. He lost the October 13 election to incumbent Governor Andrew G. Curtin. The chief justice, Walter Lowrie, also lost his bid to remain on the court, but stayed on the bench long enough to write the majority opinion in *Kneedler.* Federal attorneys, who had refused to argue the case before the court, chose to ignore the ruling, and Fry told his men to conduct business as usual. When Lowrie left the court, Woodward, whose earlier opinions included one against soldiers voting in the field, rose to become chief justice. Woodward's promotion proved an empty victory, though, because the partisan majority of the court had flipped in favor of Republicans. On the very day Lowrie stepped down, the federal attorney moved to rescind the injunctions that the court had imposed on the draft effort. By a 3–2 vote the new court reversed *Kneedler* on January 16, 1864, and ruled conscription constitutional. For good measure, two justices also wrote opinions saying that Pennsylvania courts had no jurisdiction over federal provost marshals.[16]

The question of conscription did not go before the Supreme Court of the United States during the Civil War but during World War I. In the *Selective Draft Law Cases* of 1918, the court unanimously disagreed with the plaintiffs, who had argued that states were responsible for raising a militia and that a

---

[15]Jennifer L. Weber, *Copperheads: The Rise and Fall of Lincoln's Opponents in the North* (New York, 2006), chap. 1; M. Benedict to Horatio Seymour, July 16, 1863, Horatio Seymour Papers, Box 7, New York State Library, Albany; Fry, *Final Report*, pp. 352, 29.

[16]Richard A. Sauers and Peter Tomasak, *The Fishing Creek Confederacy: A Story of Civil War Draft Resistance* (Columbia, Mo., 2012), pp. 31–34.

draft violated their Thirteenth Amendment rights against involuntary servitude. Justices ruled that the government's right to conscript was "obvious upon the face of the Constitution," thereby cementing into law the unprecedented level of federal power that Republicans had created in 1863. Many legal scholars dispute the opinion to this day, but it still stands. The Founders were silent on the topic during the Constitutional Convention. Roger Taney, the chief justice of the United States for most of the Civil War, would surely object to the ruling. Although he never heard a case regarding the Enrollment Act, Taney went ahead and drafted an unofficial opinion about it, which he called "Thoughts on the Conscription Law of the U. States." The state and federal governments each had sovereign authority within their own spheres, he wrote; any undelegated powers remained in the hands of the states or the people. When the Framers gave the federal government the right to raise and support armies, they meant a national army fully under federal control. This was an entity separate from the militia, which was "always existing and needing no law to bring it into existence." While Congress could summon the militia under certain circumstances, the states remained responsible for training the militia and appointing its officers. Taney went on to interpret the Second Amendment as meaning that the militia was composed of "Citizens of the States, who retain all their rights and privileges as citizens who when called into service by the United States are not to be fused into one body—nor confounded with the Army of the United States." Regardless of the present circumstances, the federal government had no authority over the states or their militias, Taney concluded. To give the central government that power was to risk "purely unlimited military despotism."[17]

Coincidentally, Lincoln also wrote his own opinion on the matter. Like Taney's draft decision, this was never released or published in Lincoln's lifetime. It is undated, yet it echoes some of the points and rhetoric of his well-known letter to James Conkling, who read it September 3, 1863, at a rally in Springfield, Illinois. "You who do not wish to be soldiers, do not like this

[17]*Arver v. United States*, 245 U.S. 366 (1918); see, for instance, Jason Britt, "Unwilling Warriors: An Examination of the Power to Conscript in Peacetime," *Northwestern Journal of Law and Society* 4 (Fall 2009), http://scholarlycommons.law.northwestern.edu/njlsp/vol4/iss2/4, accessed June 30, 2016; Roger B. Taney, *A Great Justice on State and Federal Power: Being the Thoughts of Chief Justice Taney on the Federal Conscription Act*, ed. Philip G. Auchampaugh (n.p., 1936).

law," Lincoln wrote in his opinion. "This is natural; nor does it imply want of patriotism." What did suggest a want of patriotism was questioning the Enrollment Act. People who thought it unconstitutional were those "who desire the rebellion to succeed." In unusually peevish language, Lincoln argued that the law was wholly within the Congress's power to raise and support armies. Under the current state of affairs, the United States needed an army to maintain its territory and institutions, Lincoln said. Armies are raised either voluntarily or involuntarily, and the Union was no longer able to raise enough volunteers to fill the ranks. If enough critics joined voluntarily, he would happily get rid of the draft. A million of their "manly brethren" already had done so, Lincoln said. "Their toil and blood have been given as much for you as for themselves. Shall it all be lost rather than you too, will bear your part?"[18]

Many of the men already in the army could not have agreed with Lincoln more, and they greeted the Enrollment Act enthusiastically. The new law showed that the government was serious about putting down the rebellion, Isaac Jackson wrote from Milliken's Bend, Louisiana, and that the soldiers "are not to be left alone and forsaken." A draft was "the just and fair way of carrying on this war[.] It brings the burthen upon all evnally and not upon willing only. . . . I hope the people have become fulle aroused to their sense of duty and will attend to the double dyed trators at home while we attend to the open armed enemyes of the country down here." While many veterans shared such feelings, they were hardly universal. Some soldiers assessed their own experiences and then advised younger relatives to stay away from the army. A member of the 119th Illinois was relieved to learn that his younger brother had paid a commutation fee in the summer of 1864 and gotten out of the draft. "I do not want to see or know of any of my friends having to soldier in this war," he wrote his sister from Memphis, citing the hardships of being on the march "nearly all of the time" and having "a good deal of fighting" along the way. He hoped the end of the war was near, but he saw no sign of it.[19]

---

[18]Basler, *Collected Works*, 6:406–10, 6:444–49.

[19]Isaac Jackson to Ethan A. Jackson, Mar. 19, 1863, Isaac Jackson Letters, Schoff Civil War Collection, Clements Library, University of Michigan, Ann Arbor; William N. Winans to Sarah M. Winans Thornley, Sept. 2, 1864, Winans Family Correspondence, Huntington Library, San Marino, Calif.

In practice, the draft provoked opposition in multiple forms. In some parts of the country, hostility was so fierce that the government had a hard time hiring anyone to carry out even the enrollment. In others, resistors took violent action against draft agents, shooting at them, burning their crops or their homes, or exercising other forms of intimidation. By the end of the war, thirty-eight of Fry's men had lost their lives trying to carry out or enforce the draft, sixty had been wounded, and a dozen had suffered property damage. These figures do not include losses that regular troops or special forces supporting local provost marshals took. For months after the Enrollment Act passed, draft riots popped up in communities across the North. The most infamous of these took place in New York City just a few days after the Battle of Gettysburg ended. Gotham's weeklong uprising, which quickly morphed into a race riot, remains the deadliest civil disturbance in American history (figs. 3–5). That same week, riots broke out in five other Northern cities, and numerous others were on alert. By the end of the war, 200 cities, towns, or counties had asked the secretary of war for troops to help deal with resistance efforts.[20]

Most illegal resistance was not violent, nor did it take place in the context of a mob. More often it was a personal decision, and those individual choices mounted to put great pressure on an army that needed a steady flow of men to fill its maw. "Give us half the men called for by the draft, and there will be hardly any resistance made" by Confederates, Ulysses S. Grant wrote a longtime friend in August 1864. But that did not happen, and neither the conscripts who did show up nor the men who accepted bounties to enlist proved to be effective soldiers. One soldier said veterans like him were "indignant at the insult and degradation of their being made companions of Idiots, aliens and outlaws."[21]

Historians do not know how most of the men who avoided the draft did so, if they stayed in their communities or went somewhere else. We do know, however, that at times some places experienced something akin to an exodus. In February 1865, for instance, the *Chicago Tribune* reported that 300–400 people were leaving the city each day to avoid the draft. Some went west, to parts of the country that were still the United States but so thinly

---

[20]Fry, *Final Report*, 2:352; Wamsley, *Selective Service*, p. 28.

[21]Brooks D. Simpson, *Ulysses S. Grant: Triumph over Adversity, 1822–1865* (Boston, 2000), pp. 374–75; George Tobey Anthony to Benjamin Anthony, Sept. 4, 1864, George Tobey Anthony Letters, Schoff Civil War Collection, Clements Library.

FIG. 3. "Charge of the Police on the Rioters at the Tribune Office," *Harper's Weekly*, Aug. 1, 1863. *(Library of Congress Prints and Photographs Division)*

RUINS OF THE PROVOST-MARSHAL'S OFFICE.

FIG. 4. "Ruins of the Provost Marshal's Office," *Harper's Weekly*, Aug. 1, 1863. *(Courtesy Donald R. Kennon)*

Fig. 5. "The Riots at New York—The Rioters Burning and Sacking the Colored Orphan Asylum," *Harper's Weekly*, Aug. 1, 1863. *(Courtesy Donald R. Kennon)*

settled—and where the government had so little enforcement—that they could live with little fear of being caught. This seems to have been the case around Canton, Illinois, where the local newspaper reported in February 1864 that "gold fever" had broken out there "in great severity." Another option for draft dodgers was to leave the country. Senator Henry Wilson of Massachusetts estimated in March 1864 that 12,000–15,000 American deserters were outside U.S. borders. It is unclear whether this number included draft dodgers, who often were called deserters even if they had not been formally mustered into the army. Some of these emigrants went to Mexico, but Canada was the favored international destination for draft dodgers, especially if they lived in areas near the border. The assistant provost marshal in Elmyra, New York, estimated in the summer of 1863 that half the deserters from the state's volunteer companies were in Canada. Once in Canada, Americans avoiding military service could face a difficult existence. Jobs were hard to find because so many Americans had come across the border, and those jobs that were available often paid poorly. Again, the runaway Americans were responsible for this, there being so many of them that wages fell. Canadian laborers found their own solution by going to the United States, where the war had resulted in manpower shortages that raised wages, but this obviously was not an answer for draft dodgers and deserters. Men looking to avoid military service by leaving the country had a third, rather surprising option: the Confederacy. This would seem to be a surprising destination, but it was still out of the reach of the United States government, and 2,000–3,000 men fled there, historian Ella Lonn estimated.[22]

Other well-known methods of evading the draft illegally involved bribery and fraud. The local draft board was notoriously ripe for abuse, and its most influential member was inevitably the doctor who performed physicals. As with so much about draft evasion, the fraud levels are impossible to know, but the head of Illinois' draft operations said surgeons had "innumerable" opportunities to excuse conscripts for a fee. Fry was quick to strip his men of office if they were engaging in illegal activity. In September 1863, he fired the entire board of Connecticut's Fourth District for taking bribes. He ordered the physician to be court-martialed and the commissioner and local provost marshal to be drummed out of the service and prosecuted in civilian courts. Where fraud was more conspicuous, though, was on the other side of the table. As they had in the militia draft of 1862, men would hurt themselves, temporarily or permanently, in order to be declared unfit for service. "There are very few enrolled or drafted men who do not claim disability of some kind, and of course demand exemption," Dr. Benjamin P. Morgan of Rutland, Vermont, said. Some men would cut off fingers or toes or knock out their own teeth to avoid conscription. Others would put sand or cayenne pepper in their eyes or irritants such as lye on their skin to fake diseases. "We feel as if we were among the lame, blind, dumb, and halt," an Urbana, Illinois, medical examiner observed.[23]

---

[22]*Chicago Tribune*, Feb. 15, 1865; Dayton, "The Raising of Union Forces in Illinois during the Civil War," p. 434; *Congressional Globe*, Mar. 23, 1864, 38th Cong., 1st sess., p. 1250; *O.R.*, ser. 3, vol. 2, 425–26; John Boyko, *Blood and Daring: Canada and the American Civil War* (Toronto, 2013), p. 129; Elvira Aplin to George Aplin, Mar. 16, 1863, Aplin Family Papers, Clements Library; Ella Lonn, *Desertion during the Civil War* (Gloucester, Mass., 1928), p. 202.

[23]House Exec. Docs., 39th Cong., 1st sess., vol. 4, doc. 1, part 2, p. 35; James B. Fry to Edwin Stanton, Sept. 8, 1863, M621, RG 110: Title Reports and Decisions of the Provost Marshal General, 1863–1866, National Archives and Records Administration, Washington, D.C. (hereafter NARA); Peter T. Harstad, "Draft Dodgers and Bounty Jumpers," *Civil War Times Illustrated* 6 (1967):29–32.

One of the great concerns of Fry and the congressmen who voted for the Enrollment Act was civilian meddling in the mobilization process. The law provided a long list of offenses that could result in a fine of up to $200 and up to two years in jail. Offenses included enticing a soldier to desert, harboring a deserter, encouraging resistance to conscription, and assaulting or obstructing a draft official. The law instructed local provost marshals to arrest all deserters, find and detain enemy spies, and obey "such as may be prescribed by law, concerning the enrolment and calling into service of national forces." Fry's men quickly interpreted the law in its broadest possible way and began keeping tabs on anyone who might create trouble in either enlisting or drafting men. This marked a significant, though very quiet, change in the relationship between civilians and the federal government, because the Provost Marshal General's Bureau became, for all intents and purposes, the first nationwide domestic intelligence agency.[24]

Stephen E. Towne's excellent work on Confederate conspiracies in the Midwest shows that the Provost Marshal General's office was not the only agency to keep tabs on civilians during the war. When Stanton issued his order in August 1862 asking for nine-month men, he also directed local army commanders to arrest people "who may be engaged by act, speech, or writing, in discouraging volunteer enlistments, or in any way giving aid and comfort to the enemy." Cramped by insufficient budgets, neither federal marshals nor U.S. attorneys could adequately investigate the number of plots—real or alleged—they were hearing about. Frustrated state officials then turned to the deepest pockets then in the country—the army's—and asked for help. Sympathetic officers in some areas detailed their men to act as detectives to ferret out groups that either fanned unrest in the ranks, encouraged desertion, or discouraged enlistments. In Washington, D.C., Lafayette C. Baker had a small contingent of detectives working in the War Department who performed a variety of jobs, including policing the district, spying in the South, and investigating Confederate intelligence operations in the North and Canada. The Treasury Department used Baker and his men to investigate counterfeiters prior to the creation of the Secret Service in 1865. The government also employed private

[24]Enrollment Act, secs. 24 and 25.

detectives, most notably Allan Pinkerton, who spied for George B. McClellan in 1861 and 1862.[25]

These efforts all involved genuine intelligence gathering, but not in a holistic sense. Pinkerton mostly collected the kind of information that armies always wanted. Army officers such as Henry Carrington in Indiana and Ambrose Burnside in Ohio had agents investigating civilians, which was less common, but their efforts were limited to their own commands. The Provost Marshal General's office was different. Under the terms of the Enrollment Act, the bureau had at least one office, and often more, in every congressional district in the Union. The average district had three permanent clerks, five temporary clerks, four deputies, three special agents, one assistant surgeon, and one janitor. All of that was in addition to the draft board, which comprised the local provost marshal, a surgeon, and a commissioner. In all, Fry's bureau employed 4,716 people as of October 31, 1864. The information that Fry's people collected during the enrollment included a man's name, date of birth, occupation, workplace, height, weight, hair color, and eye color. This information made it easier to identify draft dodgers and deserters. The Provost Marshal General's Bureau was a federal agency with the power to pull a young man into the army, potentially putting him in a life-threatening position. Its representatives seemed to be everywhere. The bureau reached deep into the American countryside in a way that only the post office had before the war. But where the post office was a fairly benign institution, the Provost Marshal General's Bureau most decidedly was not.[26]

The agency zealously followed Congress's mandate to arrest anyone resisting conscription, encouraging others to do so, or obstructing the draft or the work of the provost marshal's men. In fulfilling this duty, agents kept close tabs on anyone they considered suspect. Reports poured in to Washington from across the North about conspiracies to overthrow local or state governments, plots to free Confederate prisoners and unleash them on the Northern public, people who were undermining recruitment efforts, people who were encouraging young men to desert, resistance to the enrolling effort, corrupt draft boards, and on and on. Some of these reports

---

[25] *O.R.*, ser. 3, vol. 2, pp. 280–82; Stephen E. Towne, *Surveillance and Spies in the Civil War: Exposing Confederate Conspiracies in the Heartland* (Athens, Ohio, 2015), pp. 32–37, 66–67.

[26] Fry, *Final Report*, p. 703.

turned out to be nothing but rumor; some turned out to be true. A typical communication was like that from the local provost marshal in Columbus, Indiana, who wrote Fry to tell him that trouble was brewing in Brown County, especially Hamlin Township. Locals there had arrested a pair of deserters, and since that time one Union man had been shot to death in his field and a number of other residents had been disarmed and had their property burned. Hundreds of reports of this kind arrived at Fry's office, amid the various reports on enrollments, enlistments, and bookkeeping. Major B. H. Hill, who oversaw all of the bureau's efforts in Michigan, was a heavy correspondent, regularly submitting reports about what Confederate agents and Copperheads were doing across the Detroit River in Canada. Amid the dry orders on how to carry out the draft, order stationery, or submit requests for reimbursement, Fry or his top assistants responded with instructions to virtually all of the letters bearing intelligence that they received.[27]

While the draft came under harsh criticism generally, the complaints about Fry's operation were mostly about the quotas he and his men set and, to a far lesser degree, questions about the quality of the local board. Conservative Democrats complained often about the government's "arbitrary arrests," but they never singled out the provost marshal's office. Most curiously from a distance of a century and a half, critics never discussed the intelligence role that the bureau carried out. It is hard to imagine that Copperheads were totally unaware of the surveillance that Fry's men were carrying out; they certainly were aware that the government had people spying on civilians, thanks to the highly publicized arrests of former Congressman Clement L. Vallandigham in Dayton, Ohio, in May 1863 and of editor and secret society founder Harrison H. Dodd in Indianapolis in August 1864. Perhaps opponents of the draft lumped the office's intelligence work into a more general category of official abuses. And yet the silence of even Lincoln's most strident enemies on the subject of domestic intelligence gathering by the Provost Marshal General's Bureau is deafening. Despite the

[27]Stansifer to Colonel James B. Fry, July 31, 1863, Provost Marshal General's Bureau, letters sent, Indiana District 3, 1863–1865, RG 110, entry no. 5176, NARA; for Hill's letters, see Provost Marshal General's Bureau, letters sent by the acting asst. provost marshal general, Michigan, 1863–1866, RG 110, entry nos. 5897 and 3349, NARA.

copious correspondence between Fry and his deputies, perhaps civilians were simply unaware that they were under scrutiny from that office.[28]

The Provost Marshal General's Bureau shut down in 1866 as part of the general demobilization of the army. The agency's legacy lasted far longer and helped shape the twentieth century. Most directly, the experience during the Civil War created a precedent that the federal government can coerce its citizens into military service. President Woodrow Wilson used Fry's postmortem on the department to create the Selective Service System, which administered the draft for World War I. (Congress never seriously considered conscription for the Spanish-American War.) Among the most important lessons that officials took from the Civil War experience was not to allow commutation or substitutes. The Selective Service System in turn was a model for the World War II draft. But the legacies of the Enrollment Act go well beyond conscription. States have never again been responsible for raising men for any of the federal service branches. The relationship between them and the federal government in that sense changed permanently, and with the blessing of the Supreme Court. The large and widespread bureaucracy of the Provost Marshal General's office presaged the vast government apparatus that would emerge in the twentieth century. Finally, subsequent presidents routinely cite Lincoln as a precedent for their incursions on civil liberties, not the least of which has been the government's surveillance of its own people. The Civil War changed the relationship between the states and the federal government and the federal government and its citizens in ways that remain very clear to us in the twenty-first century.

---

[28]Weber, *Copperheads*, pp. 95–99, 148–49.

Jenny Bourne

To Slip the Surly Bonds of States' Rights and Form a More Perfect (Financial) Union

One Legacy of the Thirty-Seventh Congress

> The policy of this country ought to be . . . to nationalize our country so that we shall love our country. If we are dependent upon the United States for a currency and a medium of exchange, we shall have a broader and more generous nationality.
>
> Senator John Sherman (R-Ohio), February 10, 1863[1]

As his brother William Tecumseh struggled at Vicksburg to make the father of waters again go unvexed to the sea, John Sherman sought support for a national currency on the floor of the United States Senate. What the Thirty-Seventh Congress did to pay for the Civil War not only transformed the nation's financial system, it also placed the federal government firmly in charge.[2] Just as Union troops prevailed over the rebels, so did federal-minded legislators triumph, in part because most of their states' rights counterparts sat in a different congress during these crucial years. Yet, by binding the fortunes of the bankers to the success of the federal government, the Thirty-Seventh Congress also put into motion a system that ensured the reverse for its descendants.

[1] *Congressional Globe*, Feb. 10, 1863, 37th Cong., 3d sess., p. 843, http://memory.loc.gov/ammem/amlaw/lwcg.html.

[2] Michael Les Benedict, "Abraham Lincoln and Federalism," *Journal of the Abraham Lincoln Association* 10 (1988/89):1–45, and David Currie, "The Civil War Congress," *University of Chicago Law Review* 73 (2006):1131–226, discuss the roles of Lincoln and Congress in elevating the role of the federal government.

What follows is a brief outline of the measures enacted by the Thirty-Seventh Congress, including information on votes by party for each major initiative. Because the usual source of funding for the antebellum federal government—import tariffs—was wholly inadequate, Congress resorted to innovative schemes, including the first-ever income tax, widespread use of fiat money issued via newly created national banks, massive amounts of government borrowing, and debt sold directly to the public. Although some of these schemes fell by the wayside for a few decades after war's end, they soon returned and, for better or for worse, have become part of the national landscape.

The Eve of the Civil War: The Federal Government Is Not a Big Player

On the eve of the Civil War, the federal government was not a large part of the American economy. The United States had no national banks or national currency, no federal income tax, and very little federal borrowing.[3] Federal spending and employment were minuscule compared with that of today, as figure 1 depicts.

Figure 1 also shows that state government in 1860 actually played a larger economic role than the federal government.[4] Many people, including various presidents, suggested that the predominance of states was necessary to preserve comity. In a typical instance, President James Polk sent a letter to the House of Representatives arguing against federal spending for internal improvements:

> It [bill to improve rivers and harbors] not only leads to a consolidation of power in the Federal Government at the expense of the rightful authority of the States, but its inevitable tendency is to . . . [benefit] the few at the

[3]Richard Sylla, John Legler, and John Wallis, "Banks and State Public Finance in the New Republic: The United States, 1790–1860," *Journal of Economic History* 47 (1987):391–403, offers a good discussion of antebellum state banking practices.

[4]Harry Scheiber, "Federalism and the American Economic Order, 1789–1910," *Law and Society Review* 10 (1975):57–188, and John Wallis, "American Government Finance in the Long Run: 1790–1990," *Journal of Economic Perspectives* 14 (2000):61–82, point out the dominance of state government during the antebellum period.

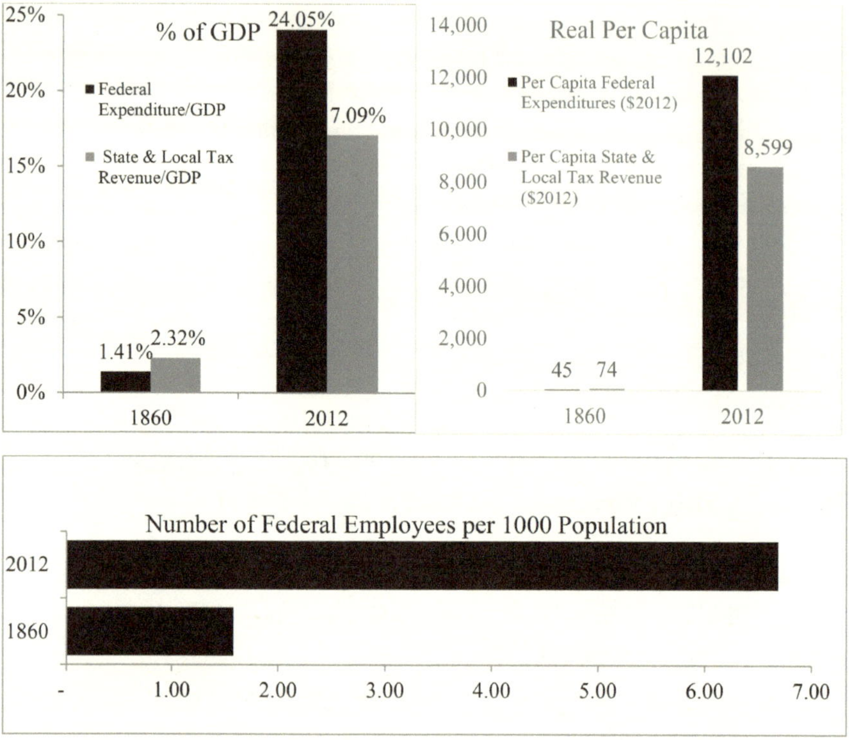

FIG. 1. Size of federal and state governments, 1860 and 2012. *(Sources: John Wallis, "American Government Finance in the Long Run: 1790–1990," Journal of Economic Perspectives 14 [2000]:-61–82; Susan B. Carter, Scott Sigmund Gartner, Michael R. Haines, Alan L. Olmstead, Richard Sutch, and Gavin Wright, eds., Historical Statistics of the United States, Millennial Edition [New York, 2006],* http://dx.doi.org/10.1017/ISBN-9780511132971.A.ESS.01 *[hereafter HSUS], Series Ca10, Ca16; Economic Report of the President, 112th Cong., 2d sess., H. Doc. 112–77 [2012])*

> expense . . . of the whole. It will engender sectional feelings and prejudices calculated to disturb the harmony of the Union.[5]

Import duties provided the main source of funds to the national government. Figure 2 shows that tariff revenue comprised between 50 and nearly 140 percent of federal expenditures in the score of years preceding the Civil

[5]*Congressional Globe*, Aug. 3, 1846, 29th Cong., 1st sess., p. 1182, http://memory.loc.gov/ammem/amlaw/lwcg.html.

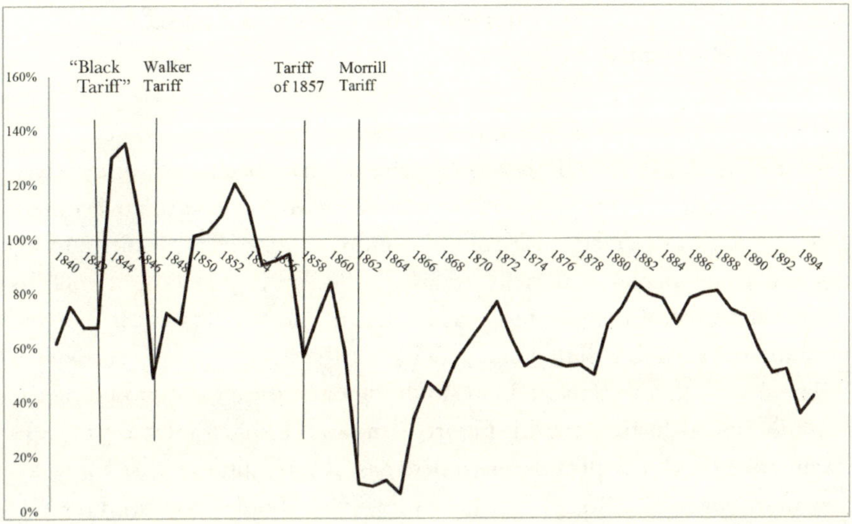

FIG. 2. Import duties as a percentage of federal expenditures, 1840–95. *(Source: HSUS, Series Ea585, Ee424)*

War.[6] But even these duties were small. Fifteen years before Abraham Lincoln took office, the U.S. Congress followed in Britain's footsteps to enact one of the lowest tariffs in American history to that point—the Walker Tariff.[7] Just over a decade later, Congress lowered rates even more with the Tariff of 1857.[8] In the House, the vote fell partly along party lines but also had a regional flavor, with the South, Indiana, and Illinois voting no, and the Northeast and the West (Wisconsin, Iowa, and Missouri) voting yes. Among those voting for the bill to reduce rates was Justin Morrill of Vermont. The Senate vote was more decisive, with thirty-three voting for the bill and only eight against.[9]

[6]As the figure indicates, the federal government ran a small surplus between 1844 and 1846, and between 1850 and 1855.

[7]The Walker Tariff (H.R. 384) was enacted by the Democrats to cut the high rates of the so-called Black Tariff of 1842, passed by the Whigs. The Walker Tariff coincided with Great Britain's repeal of the Corn Laws, which had protected domestic growers of cereal crops.

[8]For discussion, see Richard Hofstadter, "The Tariff Issue on the Eve of the Civil War," *American Historical Review* 14 (1938):50–55.

[9]*House Journal*, Feb. 20, 1857, 34th Cong., 2d sess., pp. 503–4; *Senate Journal*, Mar. 2, 1857, 34th Cong., 3d sess., pp. 307–8, http://memory.loc.gov/ammem/amlaw/lwcg.html.

Early Financing Measures: The Morrill Tariff and the Revenue Act of 1861

The nation's funding policies were ill suited to the enormous costs of war, as figure 3 makes clear.[10] This was particularly true because Southern customs officers simply stopped sending in revenue to the federal government after Lincoln was elected.[11] Lincoln himself recognized the problem: in his message to the special session of Congress called on July 4, 1861, he ruefully remarked, "One of the greatest perplexities of the government is to avoid receiving troops faster than it can provide for them."[12]

The frantic first step was a near doubling of tariff rates proposed by the aforementioned Justin Morrill. Figure 4 shows the sharp increase in rates as compared with the previous two decades. Representative Morrill was a busy man during the first years of the war—he not only sponsored the tariff bill but also authored the Land-Grant College Act and the Anti-Bigamy Act, both of which passed in 1862.

The House vote on the Morrill Tariff was largely regional in nature, as figure 5 illustrates. The gestation of the bill in the Senate took just over nine months; by then, most of the South had departed the halls of Congress, and the vote fell largely along party lines (fig. 6).[13] A logistical regression reveals that Democrats in the House were 42 times as likely to vote no on the Morrill Tariff as Republicans, whereas the Senate figure was 312.[14] The renegades in the Senate were Democrat William Bigler of Pennsylvania and Republican Benjamin Wade of Ohio.

Party-line votes were critical for funding the war, as figure 7 shows. Republicans held a majority in both houses of the Thirty-Seventh Congress (March 4, 1861–March 4, 1863), and this group of men was responsible for

---

[10]Robert Patterson, "Government Finance on the Eve of the Civil War," *Journal of Economic History* 12 (1952):35–44, makes this point as well.

[11]Bray Hammond, *Sovereignty and an Empty Purse: Banks and Politics in the Civil War* (Princeton, N.J., 1970), pp. 31–32.

[12]Roy P. Basler, ed., *The Collected Works of Abraham Lincoln*, 9 vols. (New Brunswick, N.J., 1953–55), 4:432.

[13]*Senate Journal*, Feb. 20, 1861, 36th Cong., 2d sess., p. 275, http://memory.loc.gov/ammem/amlaw/lwcg.html.

[14]Logistical regression is a statistical tool used to predict the likelihood of an outcome as a function of explanatory variables—here, the party of the representative or senator—when the dependent variable is dichotomous (that is, the vote is either yes or no).

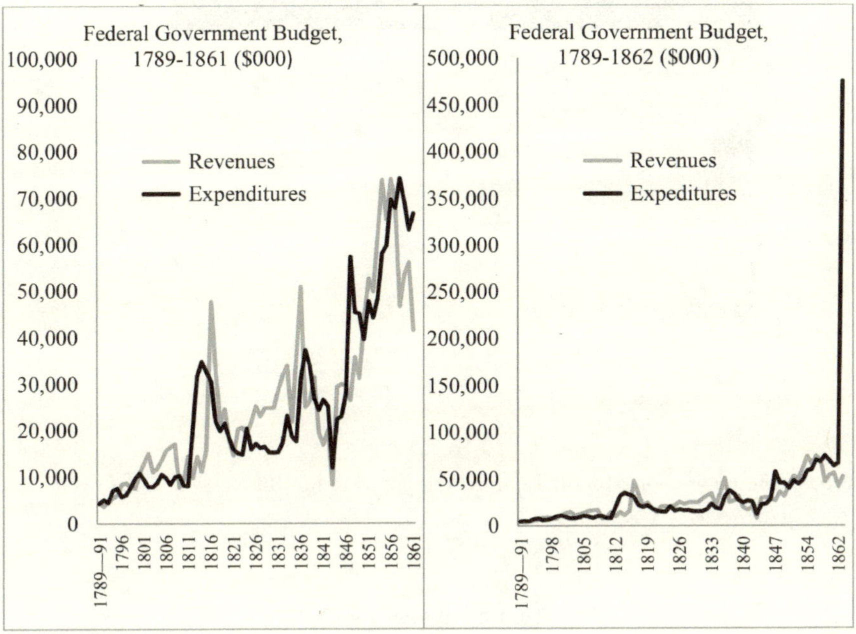

FIG. 3. U.S. government budget: what a difference a year makes! *(Source: HSUS, Series Ea584–5)*

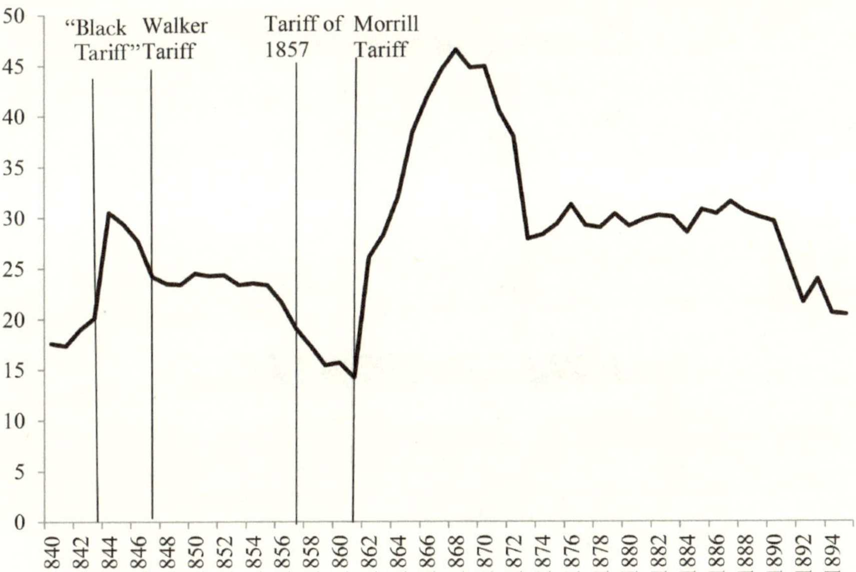

FIG. 4. Import duties as a percentage of import values, 1840–95. *(Source: HSUS, Series Ee429)*

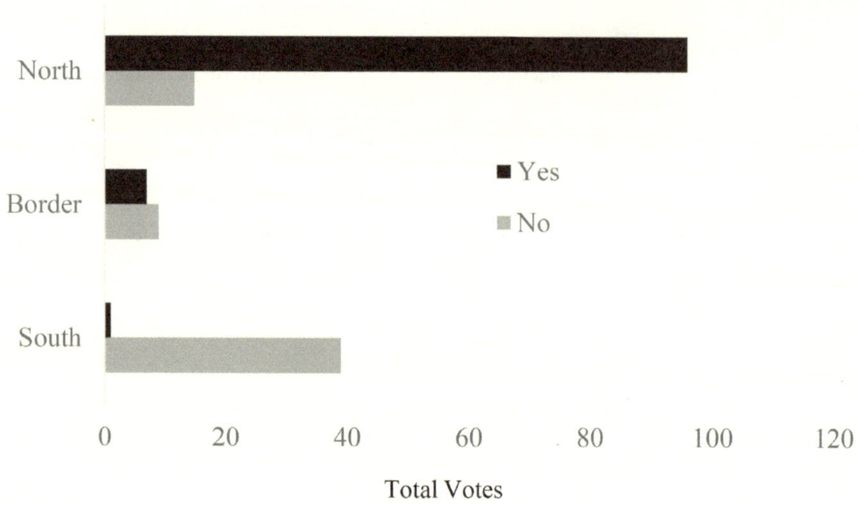

FIG. 5. House vote on Morrill Tariff by region, May 10, 1860. *(Source: http://memory.loc.gov/ammem/amlaw/lwcg.html)*

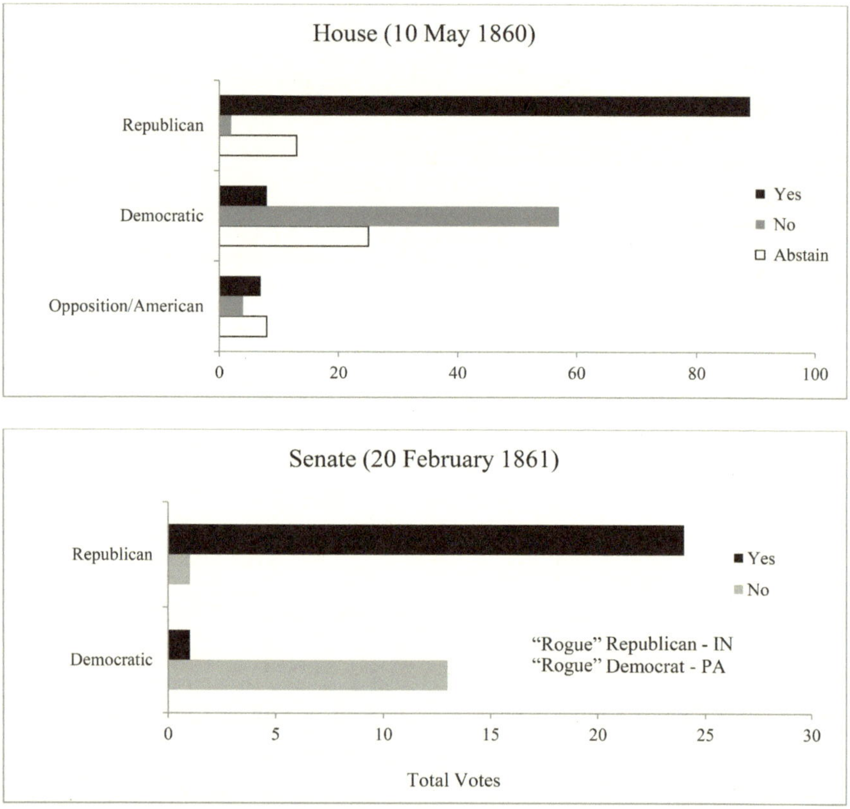

FIG. 6. Morrill Tariff vote by party. *(Source: http://memory.loc.gov/ammem/amlaw/lwcg.html)*

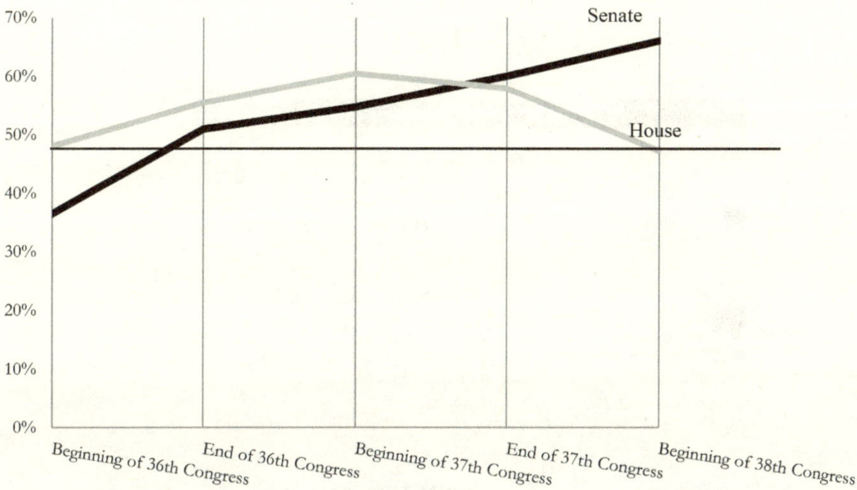

FIG. 7. Percent Republican, by House, Thirty-Sixth–Thirty-Eighth Congresses. *(Source: Congressional Globe, Thirty-Sixth–Thirty-Eighth Congresses, http://memory.loc.gov/ammem/amlaw/lwcg.html)*

shaping virtually all of the legislation concerning the nation's finances during the war.

But was Justin Morrill's tariff enough? Not by a long shot. As figure 2 illustrates, import duties went from covering about 80 percent of federal spending in 1860 to covering only 10 percent less than two years later. Tariff revenues did not come close to matching the federal government's enormous new expenditures.

So the Thirty-Seventh Congress had to resort to other measures. Shortly after the rout at Bull Run, the Revenue Act of 1861 increased customs duties still further, imposed taxes on real estate and other property, required direct taxes on each state, and, most shocking of all, included an individual income tax (which was beefed up a year later). House Democrats were 253 times as likely to vote no as House Republicans for this law. As figure 8 shows, however, I could not perform a logistical regression for the Senate, because not a single Republican senator voted no.[15]

How much did the various taxes bring in? Figure 9 breaks down federal receipts by category for the years 1861 to 1865. Just like today, "sin" taxes

[15]The vote appears in *House Journal*, Aug. 2, 1861, 37th Cong., 1st sess., pp. 226–27; *Senate Journal*, Aug. 2, 1861, 37th Cong., 1st sess., p. 167, http://memory.loc.gov/ammem/amlaw/lwcg.html.

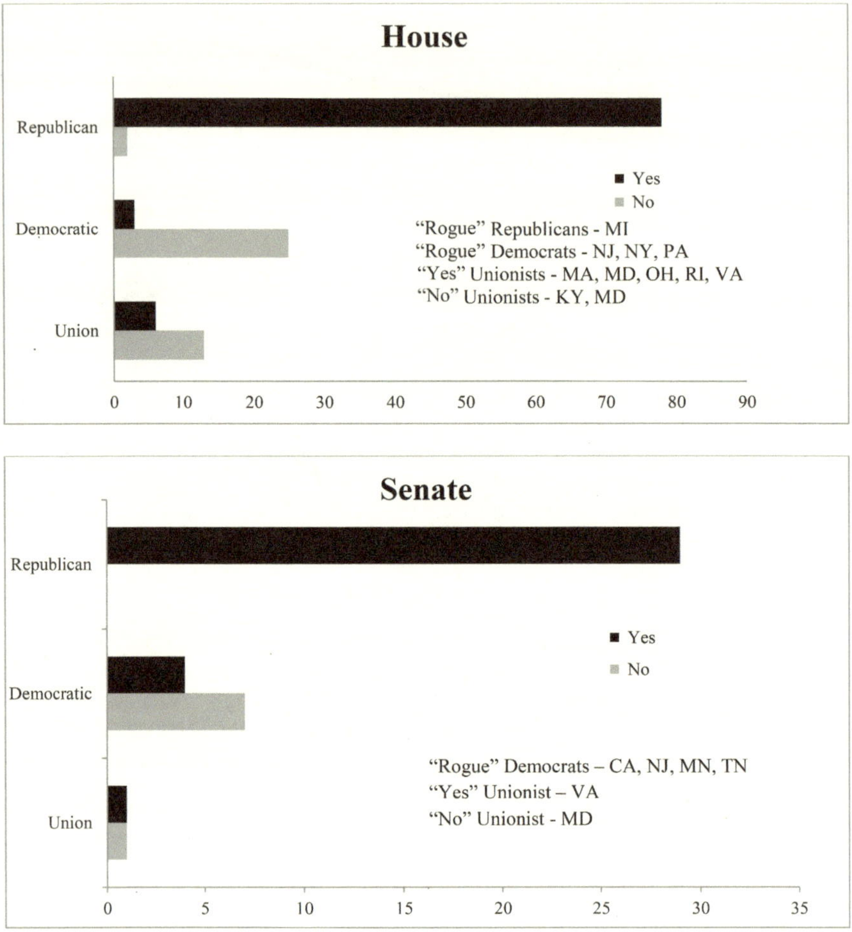

FIG. 8. Revenue Act of 1861 vote by party. *(Source: http://memory.loc.gov/ammem/amlaw/lwcg.html)*

on liquor and tobacco were part of the package. Liquor eventually bore a tax of almost ten times its cost, cigars up to 100 percent of cost. Of course, these high rates created incentives to avoid tax. The revenue from the liquor tax went from $28 million in fiscal year 1864 to only $15 million a year later—and I doubt that people became teetotalers.[16]

[16]Susan B. Carter, Scott Sigmund Gartner, Michael R. Haines, Alan L. Olmstead, Richard Sutch, and Gavin Wright, eds., *Historical Statistics of the United States, Millennial Edition* (New York, 2006), ser. EA588–592, pp. 600–602, http://dx.doi.org/10.1017/ISBN-9780511132971.A.ESS.01.

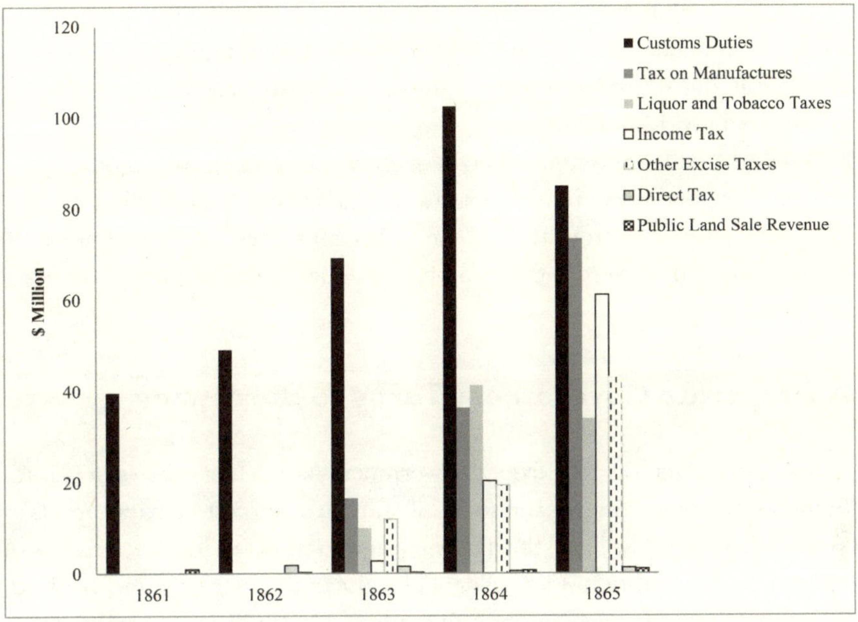

FIG. 9. Federal receipts by category, 1861–65. *(Source: HSUS, Series Ea588–92, 600–02)*

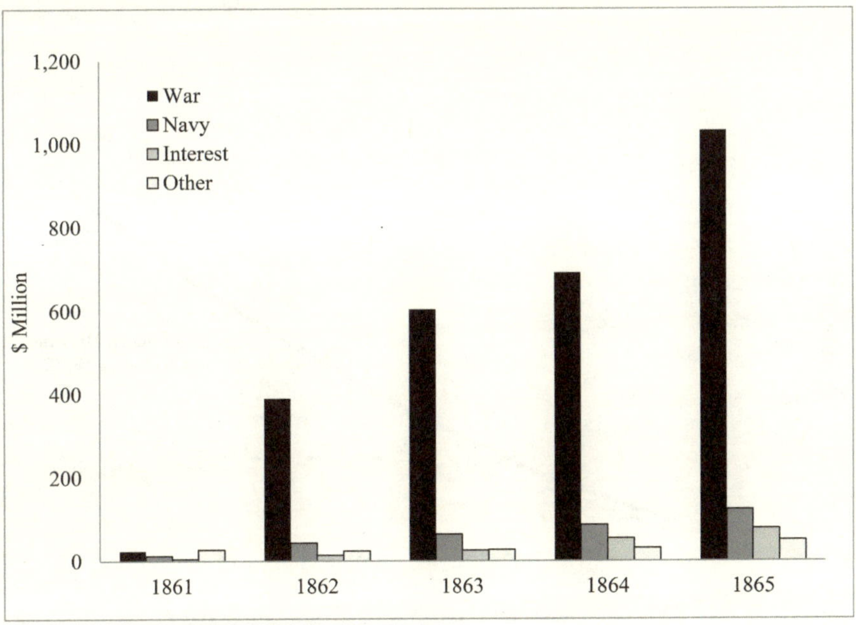

FIG. 10. Federal expenditures by category, 1861–65. *(Source: Wesley Mitchell, "Greenbacks and the Cost of the Civil War," Journal of Political Economy 5 [1897]:117–56)*

The income tax finally started generating funds by the end of 1864, and a tax on manufactured items played a role as well. One innovation was withholding at the source—by 1865, almost half of income tax revenue was collected via withholding.

Yet note that the maximum height of the columns in figure 9 is only about $100 million, and recall that expenditures had reached $500 million in 1862. Spending only grew from then on, as figure 10 shows. Taxes simply could not cover the massive bills piling up for the federal government.

A Desperate Government Turns to Borrowing

To meet its obligations, the federal government had to borrow—a lot (fig. 11). Some borrowing came in the form of standard interest-bearing bonds—although, as I discuss later, the Treasury had to resort to innovative ways of unloading this traditional sort of debt because of the sheer volume involved. The not-so-standard way of obtaining additional funds was to create them out of thin air.

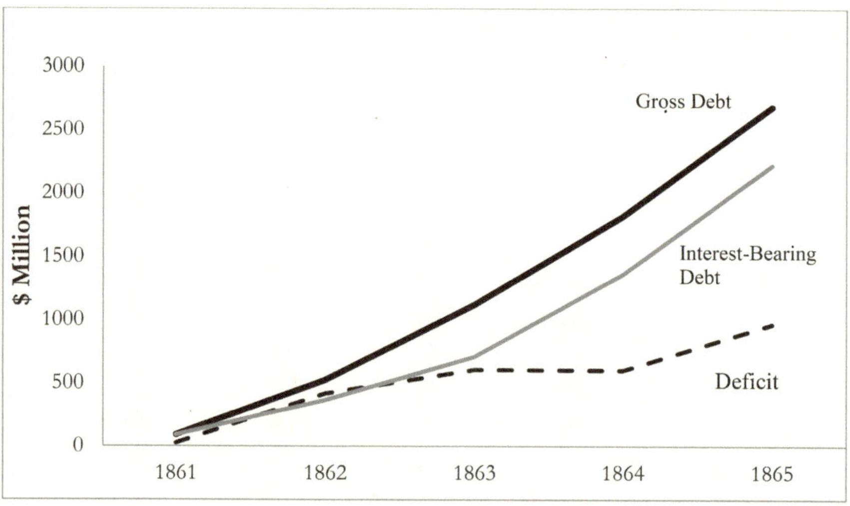

FIG. 11. Federal deficit and debt, 1861–65. *(Source: HSUS, Series Cj35, Ea586–7)*

Greenbacks and National Banks

How exactly did the federal government "create" funds? It simply printed up pieces of paper and required its suppliers, creditors, and employees to take them in lieu of any other form of payment. These pieces of paper were the (in)famous greenbacks depicted in figure 12, so named for the distinctive green ink on the reverse side.[17] Like the currency we have today, greenbacks were fiat money—they were not backed by gold or silver but rather drew their value from the government saying they had value.[18] The U.S. government thus made a radical decision: to finance the war, it departed from the specie standard to which it had adhered since colonial days and to which its major trading partners still subscribed.[19]

Note two features of the greenback: the unusual signature of U.S. Treasurer Francis E. Spinner and the portrait. Both deserve a short mention here.

Francis Spinner made history not only for his notorious signature but also for hiring the first female federal government employees. Although he endured merciless criticism for this act, he defended himself by saying that the women clerks were hardworking and efficient, and that they had excellent work habits and integrity. Best of all, many of them eventually could produce near-perfect copies of his signature—essential, given the number of greenbacks going out the door. Spinner left unmentioned the fact that females earned only half the pay of the male clerks.[20]

The face on the greenback is that of Salmon P. Chase, U.S. secretary of the Treasury at the time. Although his visage is commanding, not everyone held him in high esteem: as one scholar put it, "Mr. Chase is a man of

---

[17]State banknotes constituted the main form of paper currency after the demise of the Second Bank of the United States. State notes typically were blank on the reverse side. For discussion of the Second Bank, see Ralph Catterall, *The Second Bank of the United States* (Chicago, 1903).

[18]The value of fiat money implicitly comes from a government's ability to tax its citizens. The magnitude of its value depends on the trust people have in the government and the degree to which the government relies on fiat money to fund operations.

[19]The United States was officially on a bimetallic standard from the beginning of the republic until silver was demonetized in 1900, but it was effectively on a gold standard from 1834 to 1971, except for the period 1862–79. Michael Bordo and David Wheelock, "Monetary Policy," in Carter et al., *Historical Statistics of the United States.*

[20]Cindy Aron, *Ladies and Gentlemen of the Civil Service: Middle-Class Workers in Victorian America* (New York, 1987), and Margery Davies, *Woman's Place Is at the Typewriter: Office Work and Office Workers, 1870–1930* (Philadelphia, 1982), discuss the contributions of Francis Spinner.

FIG. 12. The (in)famous greenback. *(National Numismatic Collection, National Museum of American History, Smithsonian Institution)*

impressive appearance and of great capabilities other than financial."[21] Consistency was not among his capabilities. Chase enthusiastically supported the greenback when he sat in charge at the Treasury, but as chief justice of the Supreme Court, he flip-flopped, deciding in 1869 that Congress actually lacked the power to make paper money legal tender.[22]

Chief Justice Chase was responding to the Legal Tender Acts, which had provided the congressional approval necessary for this new form of money to be accepted by the general public. As figure 13 depicts, the vote on the First Legal Tender Act was largely, though not completely, along party lines.[23] In the House, Democrats were 250 times as likely to vote no as Republicans. The Senate was not quite as monolithic as it had been for the Morrill Tariff and the Revenue Act of 1861—Democrats were only eight times as likely to vote no as Republicans.

---

[21]Bray Hammond, "The North's Empty Purse, 1861–62," *American Historical Review* 67 (1961):1–18, quote on p. 9.

[22]*Hepburn v. Griswold*, 75 U.S. (8 Wall.) 603 (1869). *Hepburn* was soon reversed by the so-called Legal Tender Cases of *Knox v. Lee* and *Parker v. Davis*, 79 U.S. 457 (1871), and *Juilliard v. Greenman*, 110 U.S. 421 (1884). For discussion, see Kenneth Dam, "The Legal Tender Cases," *Supreme Court Review* (1981):367–412.

[23]The dates of the three Legal Tender Acts are February 25, 1862; July 11, 1862; and March 3, 1863 (12 *Statutes at Large* 345, 532, and 709). The details of the First Legal Tender Act vote appear in the *House Journal*, Feb. 6, 1862, 37th Cong., 2d sess., pp. 278–79, and the *Senate Journal*, Feb. 13, 1862, 37th Cong., 2d sess., pp. 206–7, http://memory.loc.gov/ammem/amlaw/lwcg.html.

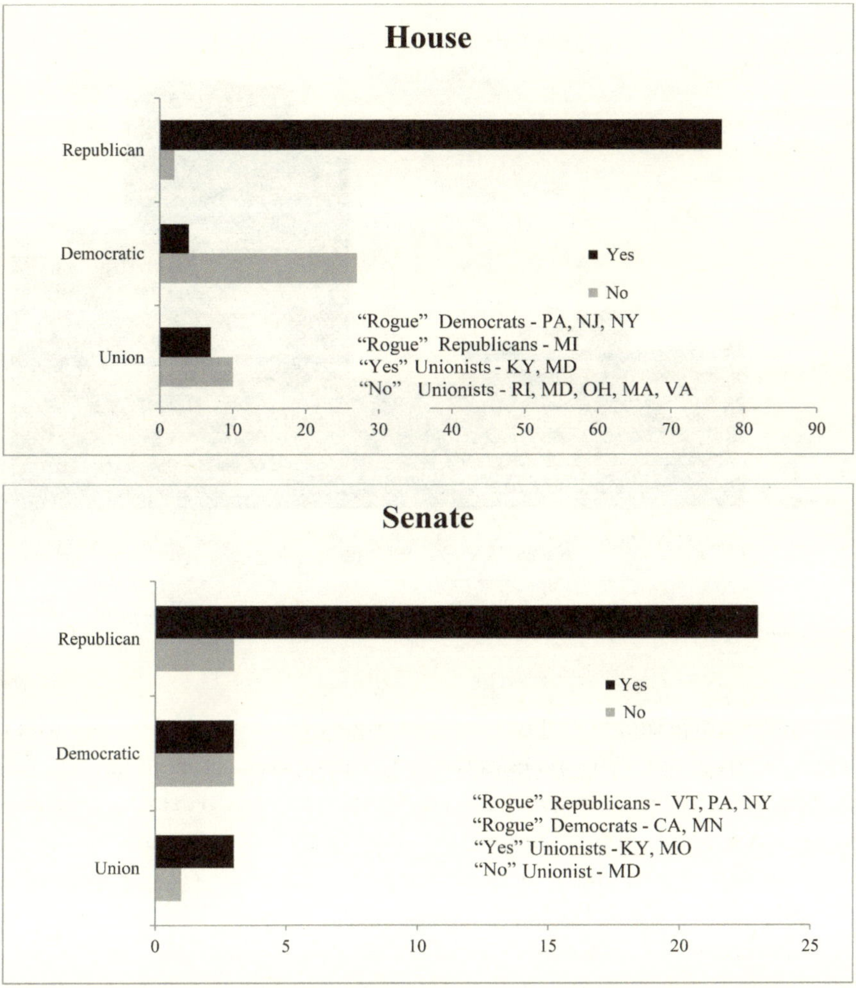

FIG. 13. First Legal Tender Act vote by party. *(Source: http://memory.loc.gov/ammem/amlaw/lwcg.html)*

Despite the new role of federal greenbacks in the monetary system, gold still mattered. Customs duties and, ironically, interest on government bonds had to be paid in gold.[24] Legal tender was not legal for everything.

---

[24]Wesley Mitchell, "Greenbacks and the Cost of the Civil War," *Journal of Political Economy* 5 (1897):117–56; Wesley Mitchell, "The Value of 'Greenbacks' during the Civil War," *Journal of Political Economy* 6 (1898):139–67.

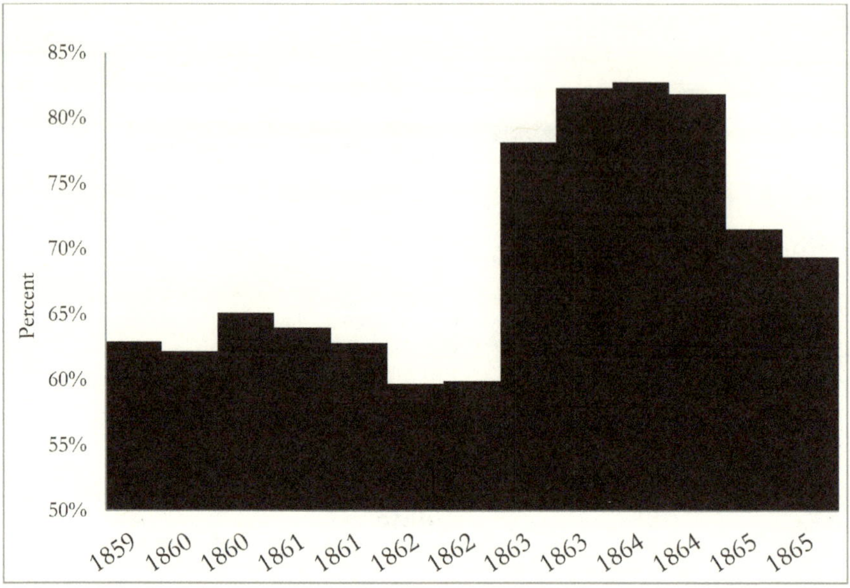

FIG. 14. Percentage of specie held by the public, 1859–65 (biannually). *(Source: HSUS, Series Cj29, 33)*

Not too surprisingly, ordinary citizens started hoarding gold, as figure 14 exhibits. By July 1, 1862, no coin larger than one cent remained in circulation. This only exacerbated the need for alternative currency and for federal control over financial markets. Although Congress made stamps acceptable as a form of payment, this approval created such a headache for the postal service that Postmaster General Montgomery Blair refused to issue additional stamps to be used as currency.[25]

Consequently, Congress took another bold step: it created a set of national banks, which could issue national banknotes. These notes were backed primarily by Treasury securities—that is, federal debt. To gain even more control over financial markets, Congress taxed state banknotes out of existence.[26] These measures thus formed a market for federal bonds while at the same time making the issuance of state banknotes too expensive to continue. Figure 15 shows what happened to the number of and

[25]Wesley Mitchell, "The Circulating Medium during the Civil War," *Journal of Political Economy* 10 (1902):537–74.

[26]Act of July 13, 1866, upheld in *Veazie Bank v. Fenno*, 75 U.S. 533 (1869).

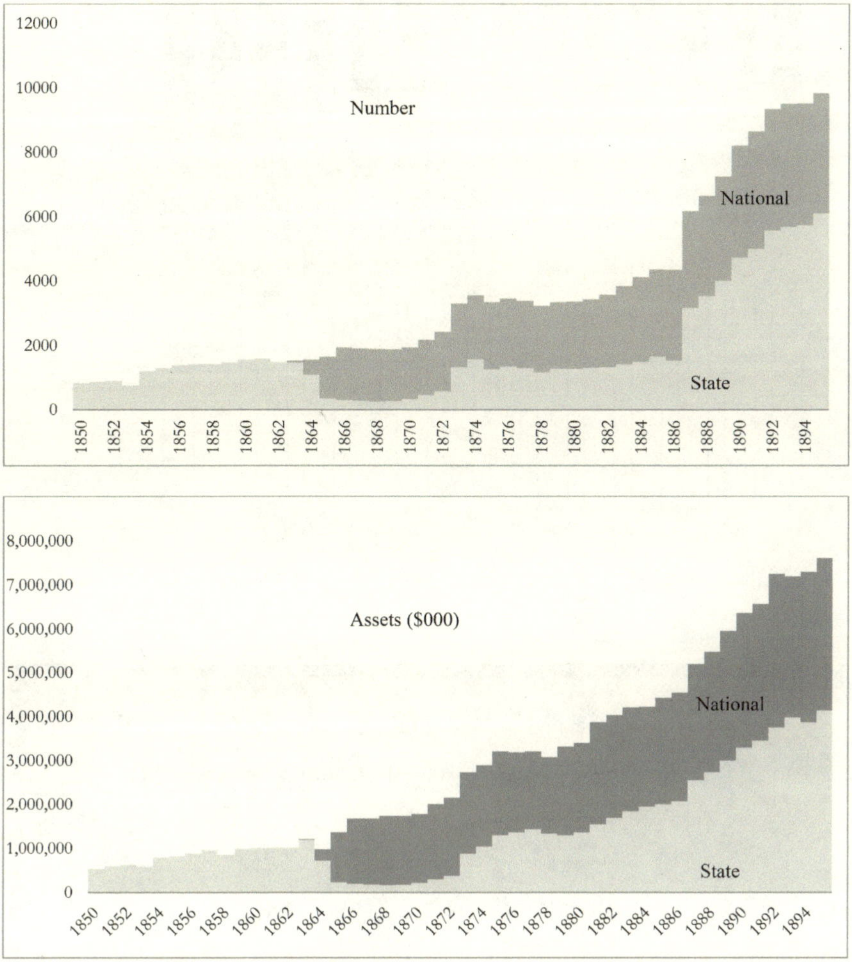

FIG. 15. Number of and assets in state and national banks, 1850–95. *(Source: HSUS, Series Cj149–50, 212–13)*

assets held by state and national banks between 1850 and 1895. During the Civil War and for about a decade thereafter, national banks dominated the financial arena.

Another way to visualize what happened during the war is to look at the composition of the money supply. As figure 16 depicts, the proportions of specie and state banknotes plummeted, whereas the proportions of greenbacks and federal debt skyrocketed.

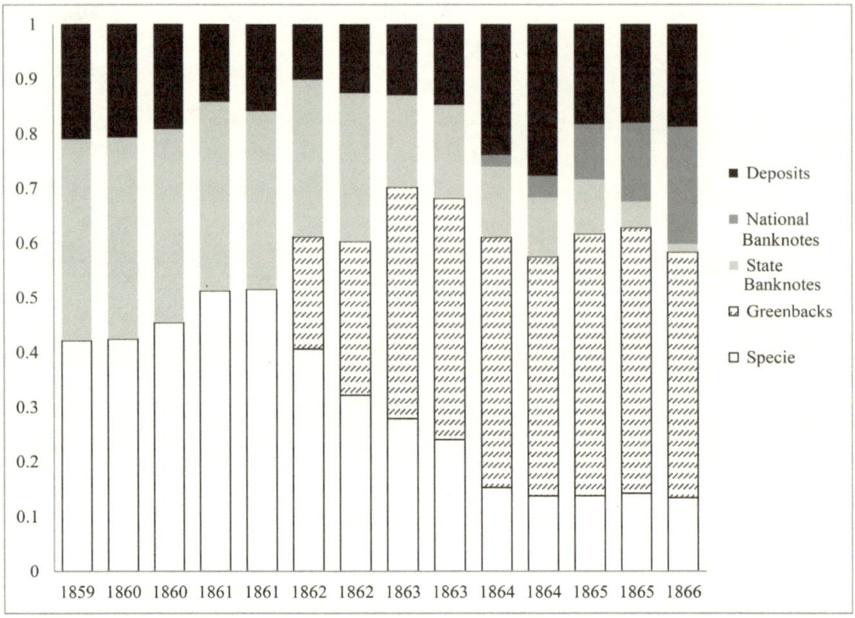

FIG. 16. Proportion of money supply by type, 1859–66. *(Source: HSUS, Series Cj29, 34–37, 41)*

FIG. 17. National banknotes. *(Source: Office of the Comptroller of the Treasury, Bureau of Printing and Engraving)*

Fig. 17. (Continued)

Although the United States now had a national currency (at least in the North), it was by no means the uniform set of bills we have today. Figure 17 shows a few examples of national banknotes: the prominent feature is not the phrase "national currency" but rather the name of the bank of issuance. The United States continued to have a number of different sorts of banknotes—although they were federal rather than state issued. This created its own set of problems, because to redeem them the holder had to take them back to the original bank of issuance.[27] Once issued, then, the notes circulated until they became so tattered and filthy that people considered them a public health hazard.[28] The original-issuance rule also meant difficulties in returning to the gold standard after the war, but that is history for another day.

Congress was not as eager to institute national banking as it had been to do other things to fund the Union war effort (fig. 18). In fact, the National Bank Act barely squeaked by in the Senate, where the vote was 22–21. Democrats were sixty-one times as likely to vote no as Republicans in the House; this figure was only nine in the Senate.[29]

As various graphs in this chapter have shown, tariffs and taxes were quite polarizing by political party. But the parties were closer together—particularly in the Senate—when it came to experiments with fiat money and national banks. It was not clear to politicians of the day that the country needed national banking, and some modern scholars agree. The New York Clearinghouse and the Suffolk Bank of Boston had done a decent low-cost job of evaluating state banknotes and lubricating financial transactions before the war.[30]

So why duplicate the banking system? Primarily because the national banks provided a ready outlet for the burgeoning government debt. The

---

[27]George Selgin and Lawrence White, "Monetary Reform and the Redemption of National Bank Notes, 1863–1913," *Business History Review* 68 (1994):205–43.

[28]Ibid., p. 209.

[29]*House Journal*, Feb. 20, 1863, 37th Cong., 3d sess., pp. 442–43; *Senate Journal*, Feb. 12, 1863, 37th Cong., 3d sess., pp. 240–41, http://memory.loc.gov/ammem/amlaw/lwcg.html.

[30]For discussion, see Hammond, *Sovereignty and an Empty Purse*, pp. 136–37; Charles Calomiris and Charles Kahn, "The Efficiency of Self-Regulated Payments Systems: Learning from the Suffolk System," *Journal of Money, Credit and Banking* 28 (1996):766–97; Arthur Rolnick and Warren Weber, "New Evidence on the Free Banking Era," *American Economic Review* 73 (1983):1080–91; and Gary Gorton, "Clearinghouses and the Origin of Central Banking in the United States," *Journal of Economic History* 45 (1985):277–83.

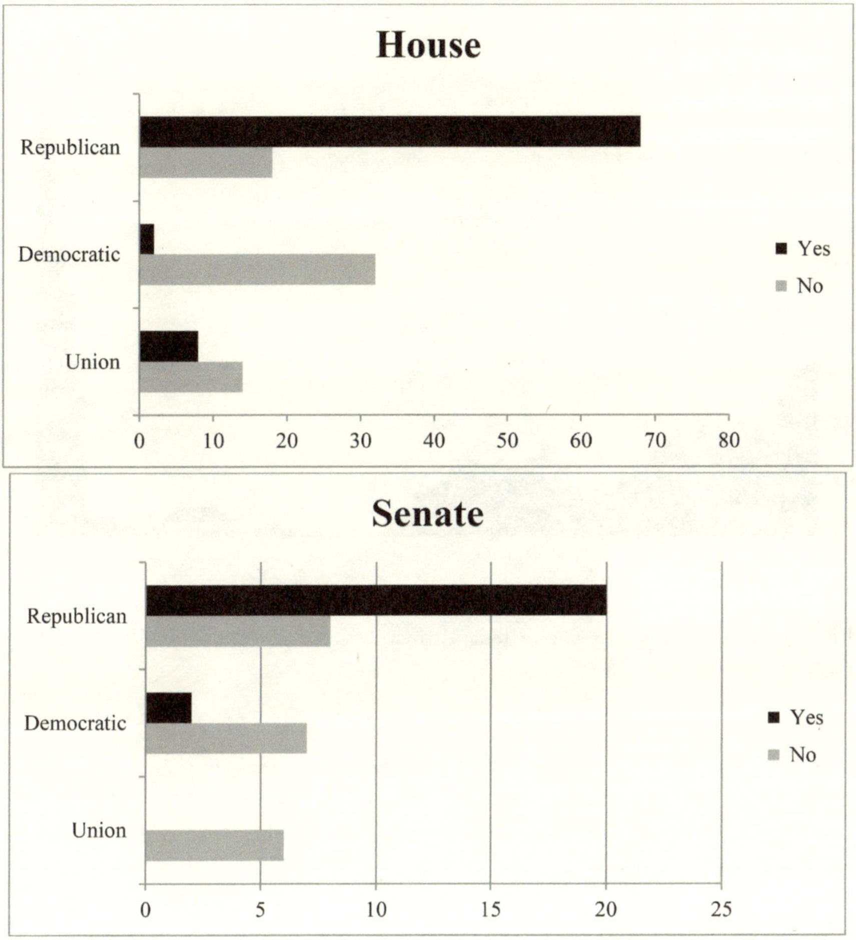

FIG. 18. National Bank Act vote by party. *(Source: http://memory.loc.gov/ammem/amlaw/lwcg.html)*

federal government needed a willing buyer for federal bonds, and the national banks provided it.

The sheer amount of debt gave people—and politicians—pause. Figure 19 shows the steep increase in real ($1860) per capita federal debt from the beginning of the republic. Part of the reluctance to sanction national banking stemmed from worries over the mounting obligations incurred by the federal government. The same fear colored the debate over greenbacks.

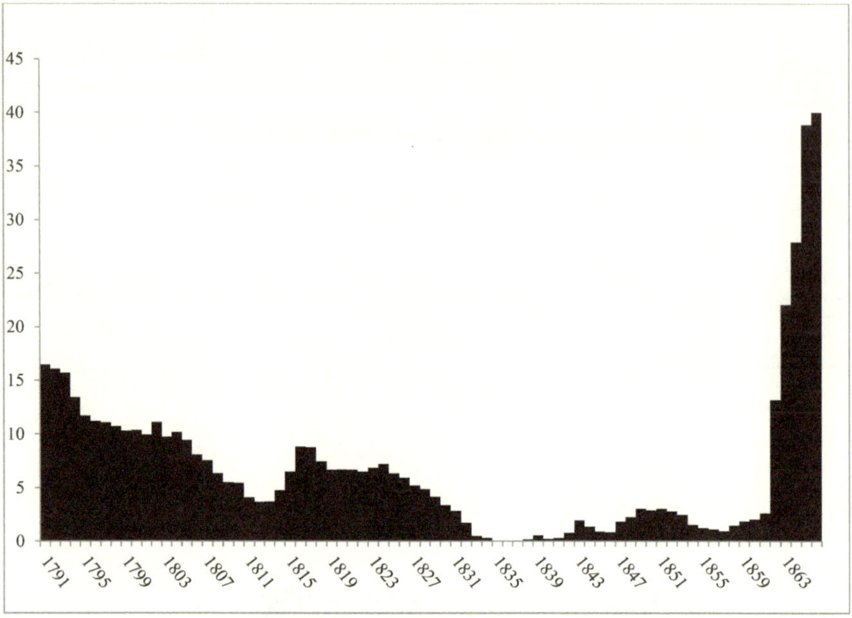

FIG. 19. Real ($1860) per capita federal debt, 1791–1866. *(Source: HSUS, Series Cc2; Ea587, 651)*

Because virtually everyone expected that the departure from the gold standard was a temporary wartime measure, greenbacks constituted a form of government borrowing as well.

Borrowing from the Private Sector

Swallowing the amount of borrowing necessary to pay its bills was no easy task for a country at war, even with the addition of the new national banks. Thus was born yet another financial innovation: the U.S. Treasury turned to a private financier, Jay Cooke, to get government bonds into the hands of the public.

Cooke advertised directly to the people, appealing to their patriotism. As an example, a notice placed in the *Philadelphia Inquirer* on November 12, 1861, said "Receipts . . . at the office of Mr. Jay Cooke were $38,079.16, much of which was from ladies. On Monday the office is kept open till nine o'clock, to enable those employed during the day to call and subscribe to this most patriotic and best of investments."

Two of the largest issues Cooke handled were the 5-20 loans of 1863—bearer bonds that paid 5 percent interest at maturity—and the 7-30s of 1861, 1864, and 1865, which paid 7.3 percent interest.[31] An opinion piece on the 5-20s appearing in the *Philadelphia Inquirer* on January 22, 1864, extolled Cooke's efforts and, again, appealed to patriotism: "Jay Cooke . . . and his sub-agents . . . sold $516 million . . . within nine months . . . all taken by the loyal people in our own country. . . . This loan . . . is a patriotic cord which unites the people and binds them to the welfare of the nation, and makes every man, and the women too, God bless them, feel an individual interest in the prosperity of the country."

When the later 7-30s came out, Cooke took out full-page ads in every Northern newspaper explaining that the federal bonds were not taxable by states and that holders could be sure that the federal government's taxing authority would guarantee bond redemption. Cooke even suggested that clergymen advocate the loan in their sermons.[32] His efforts succeeded: an article in the *New York Tribune* (March 30, 1865) reported the journey of a boy who traveled all the way to Philadelphia from western Indiana to buy 7-30s from Jay Cooke himself. The same article related the story of a German man who walked thirty miles to Dubuque, Iowa, in a protective cover of rags to invest his and his neighbors' money in the 7-30s.

Not only was Cooke's effort the first example of the use of marketing to encourage people to buy bonds, but it also familiarized the ordinary citizen with the notion of holding government debt. Before the war, less than 1 percent of Americans owned securities of any sort. By war's end, Jay Cooke alone had sold federal bonds to about 5 percent of the population of the North.

Whether this was a blessing or a curse is a matter of controversy. Jay Cooke himself wrote a front-page editorial in the *Philadelphia Inquirer* (June 17, 1865) declaring that our national debt was a blessing. But an opinion piece in the June 23, 1865, *New York Herald* said this:

---

[31]James Gherity, "Interest-Bearing Currency: Evidence from the Civil War Experience," *Journal of Money, Credit and Banking* 25 (1993):125–31.

[32]Ellis Oberholtzer, *Jay Cooke, Financier of the Civil War*, 2 vols. (Philadelphia, 1907).

> There is little dissimilarity between the national debt and the system of slavery. Under slavery three or four hundred thousand slaveholders lived upon the labor of 4 million blacks. Under the national debt 3 or 400 thousand bondholders are to live upon the labor of 30 millions of whites. . . . The holders of the national debt have a mortgage upon the bodies of all the working men in the land, just as the slaveowners had mortgages upon the bodies of their slaves.

This author expressed a valid point—what makes government bonds valuable to their owners is the promise of future taxation that will enable the government to pay up. So government bonds constitute an asset to their holders, but a liability to future taxpayers.

The "Inflation" Tax

The "worth" or "wealth" represented by government bonds clearly depends on viewpoint. But the situation is even more complicated than that: the asset value of government bonds can erode if the government does not maintain the value of the dollar. If antebellum bondholders paid for the obligations in currency worth one dollar in gold but redeemed them for currency worth far less, the government potentially extracted extra funds via an "inflation" tax.[33]

Inflation ran rampant during the Civil War, as figure 20 makes clear. Some prices increased as much as fourfold over the course of the conflict.[34]

As prices rose, the value of greenbacks fell. Figure 21 shows that greenback value depended on action on the battlefield as well as activity on the Hill. At the lowest point, one hundred dollars in greenbacks bought less than forty dollars' worth of gold.

But bondholders probably were not the ones who suffered most from inflation. Despite depreciation in the value of their portfolios, at least they had them. Many people did not, including most enlisted men. What

---

[33]The amount extracted depends on the interest rate for dollar-denominated assets relative to that for gold-denominated assets. If people anticipate inflation, for example, they would require a relatively higher interest rate on dollar-denominated assets to compensate for the loss in the value of the principal. Much of the inflation of the Civil War was unanticipated, however. Jeffrey Williamson, "Watersheds and Turning Points: Conjectures on the Long-Term Impact of Civil War Financing," *Journal of Economic History* 34 (1974):636–61.

[34]Mitchell, "Greenbacks and the Cost of the Civil War," p. 129.

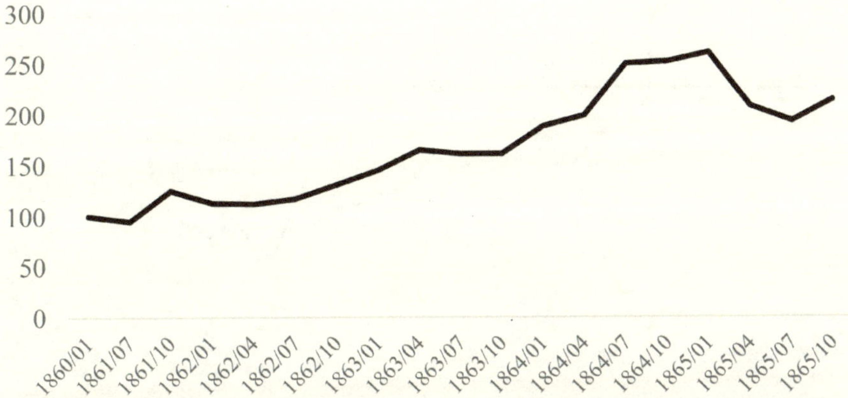

FIG. 20. Monthly commodity prices, 1860–65. *(Source: Wesley Mitchell, "Greenbacks and the Cost of the Civil War," Journal of Political Economy 5 [1897]:117–56)*

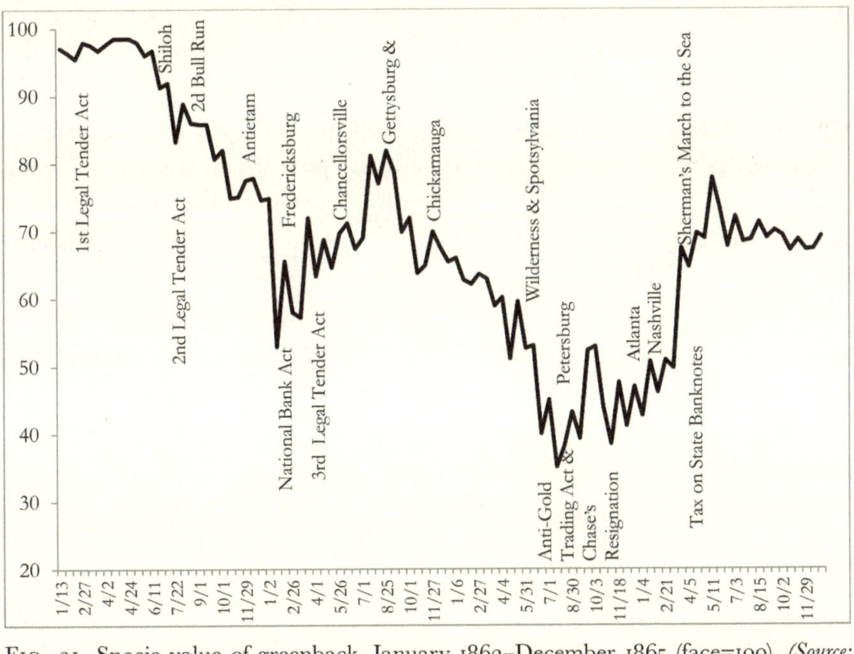

FIG. 21. Specie value of greenback, January 1862–December 1865 (face=100). *(Source: Wesley Mitchell, "The Value of the Greenback during the Civil War," Journal of Political Economy 6 [March 1898]:139–67)*

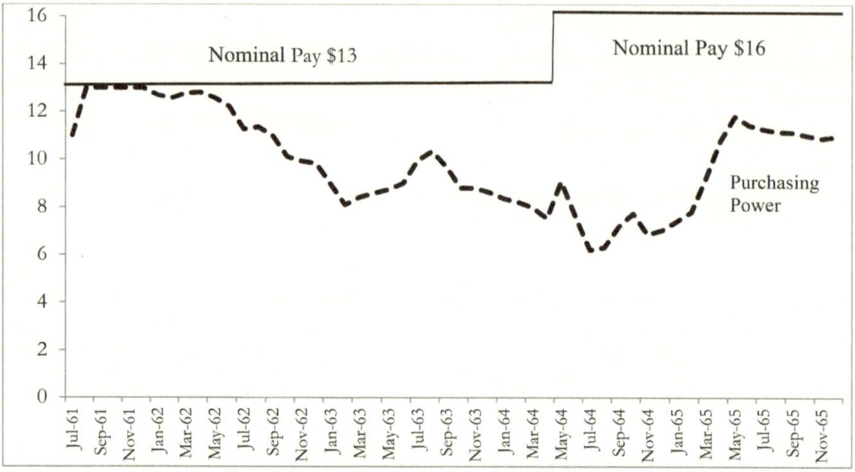

FIG. 22. Specie value (purchasing power) of monthly pay, white privates, July 1861–December 1865. *(Source: Wesley Mitchell, "Greenbacks and the Cost of the Civil War," Journal of Political Economy 5 [1897]:117–56)*

happened to their income during the war? One of the first war measures, enacted in August 1861, was to increase the pay of privates from eleven dollars a month to thirteen dollars a month—thirteen dollars in greenbacks, not in gold. There it stayed until May 1864, when it rose to a handsome sixteen dollars.[35] Figure 22 shows the erosion in purchasing power of the monthly pay of white privates. Things were even worse for African Americans, who until June 1864 earned a mere ten dollars a month, from which three dollars were taken for a clothing allowance.[36]

Soldiers were not the only ones to suffer a decline in the value of their paychecks. As just one example, teachers in 1865 earned about half of what they were paid at the beginning of the war in terms of gold.[37] In so many ways it was the ordinary citizen who paid for the Civil War.

[35]Ibid., pp. 134, 152.

[36]U.S. National Archives, http://www.archives.gov/education/lessons/blacks-civil-war/.

[37]Mitchell, "Greenbacks and the Cost of the Civil War," p. 140.

After the War: What Remained?

Several war measures disappeared after 1865, at least for a time. Tariff rates subsided and tariffs again loomed large in the revenue stream until the early 1890s, as figures 2 and 4 depict. The income tax vanished in 1872—at least for a few decades. Excise taxes went away too, except for the ones on alcohol and tobacco.

As figure 23 shows, federal spending subsided as well and the country returned to a more sustainable debt burden, although both state and federal governments settled down to a larger role than they had played before the war. The nation also went back to the gold standard in 1879; in so doing, it endured a deflationary process that was nearly as painful as the inflationary one.[38] In nominal terms, the debt burden per capita declined nearly continuously after the war, but the real debt burden did not begin to fall until after the country had fully restored the gold standard.

State banks regained their footing (see fig. 15), in part because of inefficient management of the national system.[39] But state banks never again issued their own notes.

Despite the apparent temporary nature of some war programs, the words of John Sherman ring true: by the end of the Civil War, Americans (at least in the North) had a "broader and more generous nationality" than they did at the beginning. This may have partly been due to widespread travels of young soldiers—my great-great-grandfathers had never left the confines of Baker Township in Morgan County, Indiana, until they traveled to Natchez, Mississippi, and Appomattox, Virginia. The world grew for them.

The financial experiments undertaken by the Thirty-Seventh Congress also planted seeds that grew strong roots and bore later fruit. The income tax returned via the Sixteenth Amendment in 1913 and remains an important

---

[38]For discussion, see James Kindahl, "Economic Factors in Specie Resumption in the United States, 1865–1879," *Journal of Political Economy* 69 (1961):30–48.

[39]Richard Sylla, "Monetary Innovation in America," *Journal of Economic History* 31 (1982):21–30.

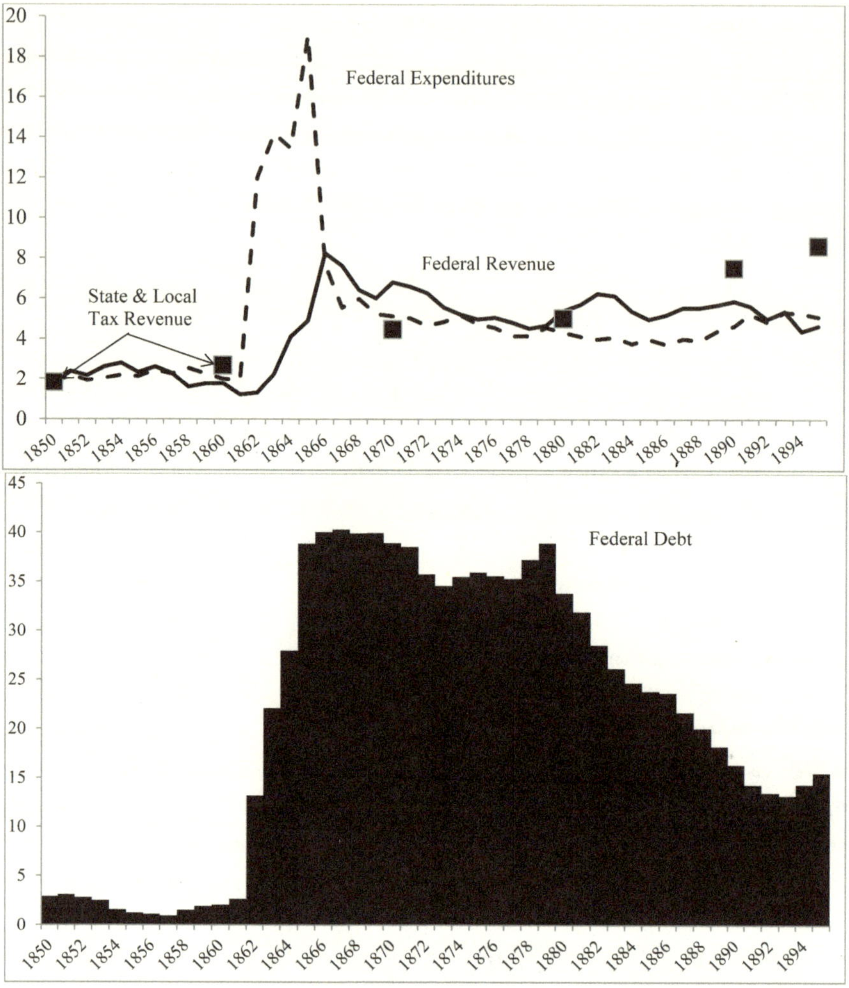

FIG. 23. Real ($1860) per capita federal revenue, federal expenditure, state and local tax revenue, federal debt, 1850–95. *(Sources: John Wallis, "American Government Finance in the Long Run: 1790–1990," Journal of Economic Perspectives 14 [2000]:61–82; HSUS, Series Cc2, Ea584–5, 587, 651)*

revenue raiser for the federal government today.[40] Wartime financing using massive government borrowing reappeared in both world wars and the

[40]The individual income tax raised 47 percent of revenue for the federal government in fiscal year 2012. Office of Management and Budget, Budget of the U.S. Government, Table 2.2.

Vietnam conflict, and it has now become routine even during times of relative peace—so much so that we have imposed "debt ceilings" on ourselves, which have in turn recently led the United States to the brink of default on its obligations.[41]

What is more, the impossibility of maintaining the gold standard in the face of monetary expansion and large federal expenditures on Vietnam and the Great Society programs meant a permanent shift to fiat money in 1971, which was undertaken by another (though quite different) Republican president. Not only does the United States operate on fiat money, but it now truly has a unified currency, which includes a portrait of Salmon Chase on the $10,000 bill.

The movement toward nationalization of banks and currency led to the creation of the Federal Reserve in 1913 and federal deposit insurance in 1933, which have ineluctably bound the federal government to the banking system. Banks and bank-like institutions are now considered "too big to fail," and the federal government has come to their rescue many times over the past thirty years. Actions include the bailouts of Continental Illinois in 1984, Long-Term Capital Management hedge fund in 1998, and AIG (American International Group) in 2008, as well as the Emergency Economic Stabilization Act of 2008, which authorized the Treasury Department to buy or insure up to $700 billion in troubled assets.

Perhaps most significantly, the Civil War made us grapple with fundamental questions about the role of government generally and the role of the federal government specifically. Importantly, monetary policies enacted by the Thirty-Seventh Congress later led to a broad interpretation of the necessary and proper clause of the Constitution[42] when the Supreme

[41]The website http://www.whitehouse.gov/omb/budget/Historicals offers numerous tables showing federal revenues and expenditures. Congress first imposed limits on the debt in 1917. In 1979, Representative Richard Gephardt (D-Mo.) proposed a parliamentary rule that effectively raised the debt ceiling when a budget was passed. Congress repealed the rule in 1995, which led to a budget controversy and a government shutdown. A delay in raising the debt ceiling in 2011 led to the first-ever downgrade in the federal government's credit rating. The United States struggled throughout 2013 after it reached the debt ceiling on December 31, 2012, with the government coming to the very brink of default in October 2013.

[42]U.S. Constitution, Art. I, Sec. 8, cl. 18: "The Congress shall have power to make all laws which shall be necessary and proper for carrying into execution the foregoing powers, and all other powers vested by this Constitution in the government of the United States, or in any department or officer thereof."

Court validated the use of paper money in the Legal Tender Cases.[43] As one scholar put it: "The authorization of the greenbacks was of greater significance in the evolution of federal powers than in monetary history and of greater importance to the student of government than to the economist."[44]

[43]Dam, "The Legal Tender Cases," p. 390, argues that the Legal Tender Cases are key to understanding current interpretations of the necessary and proper clause. Gerald Magliocca, "A New Approach to Congressional Power: Revisiting the Legal Tender Cases," *Georgetown Law Journal* 95 (2006):119–70, concluded that the operative standard in implied power cases comes from the Legal Tender Cases.

[44]Hammond, *Sovereignty and an Empty Purse*, p. 227.

Daniel W. Stowell

Abraham Lincoln and "Government Girls" in Wartime Washington

ALTHOUGH CLARA BARTON and a few other women had broken the gender barrier to employment in the federal government when they worked in the Patent Office in the early 1850s, by 1860 no women worked in federal government offices in Washington.[1] The wartime employment of female clerical workers in the federal government dates to the fall of 1861, when Francis E. Spinner (fig. 1), treasurer of the United States, began to employ women to cut and count Treasury notes. Abraham Lincoln had appointed Spinner, a former congressman from New York, as treasurer in March 1861. The mobilization for war drew tens of thousands of men from the workforce while simultaneously expanding the need for clerical laborers.

[1]Robert McClelland, secretary of the interior under Franklin Pierce from 1853 to 1857, wrote to Massachusetts Representative Alexander De Witt on September 27, 1855, regarding Clara Barton: "There is every disposition on my part, to do anything for the lady in question, except to retain her, or any of the other females at work in the rooms of the Patent Office. I have no objection to the employment of females by the Patent office, or any other of the Bureaus of the Department, in the performance of such duties as they are competent to discharge, and which may be executed by them at their private residences, but there is such an obvious impropriety in the mixing of the sexes within the walls of a public office, that I determined to arrest the practice, though not until after full consideration, on account of the probable effect on some, now enjoying the emoluments of such labor." Robert McClelland to Alexander De Witt, Sept. 27, 1855, vol. 1, 224, Record Group 48: Records of the Office of the Secretary of the Interior, Entry 186: Records of the Patents and Miscellaneous Letters Division, 1813–1943, General Records, 1813–1926, Miscellaneous Letters Sent, 1849–1906, National Archives and Records Administration, College Park, Md. (hereafter NARA).

FIG. 1. Francis Elias Spinner, treasurer of the United States (1861–75), photograph ca. 1860–65. *(Brady-Handy Photograph Collection, Prints and Photographs Division, Library of Congress)*

Fig. 2. "Lady Clerks Leaving the Treasury Department at Washington," by A. B. Waud, *Harper's Weekly*, Feb. 18, 1865. *(https://babel.hathitrust.org/cgi/pt?id=iau.31858029244328;view=1up;seq=106)*

When he arrived in Washington, Spinner found a "score or more of hale and hearty young men, armed with small shears, busy clipping the notes." Spinner went to Secretary of the Treasury Salmon P. Chase and declared that "these young men should have muskets instead of shears placed in their hands, and be sent to the front, and their places filled by women, who would do more and better work, at half the pay that was given to these 'men milliners.'" Spinner continued, "A woman can use scissors better than a man, and she will do it cheaper. I want to employ women to cut the Treasury notes." When Chase hesitated, Spinner suggested that they employ one woman as a test. Spinner's handpicked subject, Miss Jennie Douglass, did more work than any of the male clerks on the first day. "This decided the whole matter," Spinner recalled. An 1869 editorial in the *New York Times* explicitly declared that "it is . . . owing to Mr. Spinner, more than to any other man, that this department of labor is now open in any degree to women" (fig. 2).[2]

[2]Mary Elizabeth Massey, *Bonnet Brigades* (New York, 1966), 132; Mary Clemmer, *Ten Years in Washington: or, Inside Life and Scenes in Our National Capital as a Woman Sees Them*

Although the war created and relentlessly expanded the need for female clerical workers to perform various tasks in the burgeoning federal bureaucracy, it also created a supply of widows, orphans, and others desperate for work to support themselves and their families. The Treasury Department and other bureaus and offices in Washington became "a vast refuge for the unfortunate and the unsuccessful."[3] According to a woman familiar with the process, "in order to secure any Government position, the first thing a woman had to do was to go and tell her story to a man—in all probability a stranger—who possessed the appointing power." If the man took a personal interest in her story, he might recommend her appointment; if not, she had no chance of gaining the position, "unless she could succeed in winning over to her cause another man of equal political power."[4] Although most sought the aid of congressmen and senators, for a substantial number of women across the North, the only man to whom they felt they could apply for aid was President Abraham Lincoln.

As early as the fall of 1861, women began writing to and visiting Abraham Lincoln requesting assistance in obtaining jobs in the Treasury Department. On September 8, 1861, Mary V. Tennison wrote to the president, imploring him for assistance. Her husband had been dismissed from the United States Revenue Service for intoxication, and her mother and two little children depended on her for support. Having heard of Lincoln's "goodness and kindness," she "made bold to write and request" that she receive some copy-work from one of the departments or bureaus of the government. "I am quite hard of hearing," she continued, "which adds to my trouble, as that infirmity precludes my teaching or otherwise trying to support myself and family." She appealed to him as "most gracious President, believing that as the chief Magistrate and the Father of this great country, you will not hear my petition in vain." As with most of the surviving letters written to him,

(Hartford, Conn., 1873), pp. 371–73; Ross K. Baker, "Entry of Women into the Federal Job World—at a Price," *Smithsonian* 8 (July 1977):82–91; Nomination of Francis E. Spinner as Treasurer of the United States, Mar. 16, 1861, vol. 8, p. 220, Record Group 59, Entry 774: Appointment Records, Commissions, Miscellaneous Permanent and Temporary Presidential Commissions, 1789–1972, NARA; "General Spinner and the Women Clerks," *Woman's Journal* 16 (Jan. 10, 1891):1–2; *New York Times*, Feb. 18, 1869, p. 2. See also Cindy S. Aron, "'To Barter Their Souls for Gold': Female Clerks in the Federal Government Offices, 1862–1890," *Journal of American History* 67 (1981):835–53.

[3]Mrs. John A. Logan, *Thirty Years in Washington or Life and Scenes in our National Capital* (Hartford, Conn., 1901), p. 208.

[4]Clemmer, *Ten Years in Washington*, p. 374.

there is no endorsement by the president, so it remains uncertain whether he read the letter and forwarded it to the Treasury Department or whether his secretaries did so for him.[5]

Other women appealed in person to the president. On September 16, Lincoln wrote to Secretary Chase, "The bearer of this—Mrs. Ryder—has learned that there is some *'lady's work'* in your Department in connection with the Treasury notes, and wishes a chance for a share of it, if such be the fact." Lincoln closed his brief note, "Please give her a fair hearing."[6]

Another brief, ungrammatical letter arrived a few months later from Jane Munsell informing the president that "I have no imployment found yet" and requesting a place in the Treasury Department "cliping notes." This letter did receive a coveted endorsement from Lincoln. The president wrote simply, "Respectfully submitted to the Treasury Department. A. Lincoln, Nov. 13, 1861." There is no indication, however, that Jane Munsell obtained a job in the Treasury Department.[7]

Victorian codes of conduct discouraged women from writing to a man they had never met, even, or especially, the president of the United States. Most of Lincoln's female correspondents who sought jobs with the government asked his pardon for addressing a letter to him. "Pardon my presumption, in addressing you. Imperious necessity impels . . ." read one.[8] Charlotte S. Reed of Chambersburg, Pennsylvania, asked, "I must beg you to excuse my presumption in asking your interference in my behalf, I feel that it is a privilege, that every loyal citizen of the United States may address the highest authority known to our government."[9] Missouri G. W. Finley of New York City wrote, "I feel that it is presumptuous, for one so humble in position, to address a note, to one so high in power."[10] "You will I hope pardon the liberty I have taken," Helen V. White of Baltimore wrote

---

[5]Mary V. Tennison to Abraham Lincoln (hereafter AL), Sept. 8, 1861, Box 571, RG 56: General Records of the Department of the Treasury, Entry 210: Part II, Records of Various Divisions within the Office of the Secretary of the Treasury, Records of the Division of Appointments, Correspondence of the Division, Applications and Recommendations for positions in the Washington, D.C. Offices of the Treasury Department, 1830–1910, NARA.

[6]AL to Salmon P. Chase, Sept. 16, 1861, in Roy P. Basler et al., eds., *Collected Works of Abraham Lincoln, Second Supplement* (New Brunswick, N.J., 1990), p. 34.

[7]Jane Munsell to AL, Nov. 12, 1861, RG 56, Entry 210, NARA.

[8]Mrs. M. W. Perrine to AL, Dec. 12, 1861, ibid.

[9]Charlotte S. Reed to AL, May 27, 1863, ibid.

[10]Missouri G. W. Finley to AL, Nov. 30, 1863, ibid.

in December 1863, "by addressing you, considering the position you occupy, which is so far superior to my own, but owing to my circumstances I am compelled so to do."[11]

Young women sometimes wrote together to the president, perhaps encouraging each other to overcome the sense of impropriety they felt. Mollie Howard and Annie White of Friendship, New York, wrote to the president, "You will doubtless be surprised at receiving a letter from us, who are entire strangers, and may think we are presuming to much in thus familliarly addressing you. [W]e hope we are not transcending the bounds of propriety in so doing. But, sir it is from the most honorable motives we assume the liberty." They had learned from a young man in Rochester that "respectable young ladies could find employment in Washington in the Mint stamping Green Backs." As they were "fatherless, and dependent on our own resources for a livelihood," they thought they should apply for a position, "it being more lucriferous business than that which we are now engaged in; we are daily laboring for the small pittance of .25 *cts* which at the present time will hardly afford us the necessaries of life."[12]

Similarly, teachers Florence Watson and Delia Swain of Beaver Dam, Wisconsin, apologized for being "very bold and presumptious" in writing to the president, "for we know you have other and far more important matters claiming your attention." Together, the young women wrote, "we have formed this project of writing to *you*" because they had learned that in some departments, "lady-clerks are employed, and thinking such a situation would be far more agreeable and profitable than our present one, we came to the conclusion that there could be no harm in writing you a private letter." Surpassing Mollie and Annie's vocabulary display, Florence and Delia even included their photographs, "thinking you might wish to know how we look." The young women continued, "Now dear '*Uncle Abe*' we having taken one bold step, dare to take another, and say, that we want very much to hear from you—whether you can do us any good or not—and receive the assurance that you are not offended by our unusual conduct."[13]

Other applicants apologized for seeking his time because he had so many other pressing duties. "I deem it almost an intrusion at this time to ask you

[11]Helen V. White to AL, Dec. 13, 1863, ibid.

[12]Mollie Howard and Annie White to AL, Jan. 11, 1864, ibid.

[13]Florence Watson and Delia Swain to AL, Mar. 27, 186[5], ibid.

for one moments attention," wrote Carrie Roser of Philadelphia, "but the trouble which has befallen me within the past year almost forces me to so bold an act." Julia Richards of Schnectady, New York, assured the president that "I should not have thought of applying to you amid the multiplicity of your cares did I not hope you had something in your gift."[14]

Twenty-year-old Mary Ann Curry of Pottsville, Pennsylvania, was living in Washington, D.C., with her mother and siblings in the spring of 1862. On March 26, she wrote to President Lincoln asking for "some employment in any one of the Departments in any capacity where I should be competent." She asked for a job to "aid my mother in supporting a large and fatherless family." Two of her brothers were in the Union army, and she knew no one in Washington to aid her. President Lincoln endorsed the envelope on March 26, the same date as the letter, "Sec. of Treasury, please see Mrs Curry, and give her employment if possible. A. Lincoln." Perhaps this first endorsement on the envelope was ineffective, for three weeks later, Lincoln wrote a second endorsement on the back of the letter itself, "Sec. of Treasury, please see this poor woman, and give her employment if possible. A. Lincoln, April 15, 1862."[15]

The president's most recognizable petitioner was Grace Bedell of Albion, New York. In October 1860, eleven-year-old Grace Bedell wrote to candidate Abraham Lincoln to suggest that he grow a beard: "you will look a great deal better for your face is so thin." She told him that she had four brothers and "part of them will vote for you any way and if you will let your whiskers grow I will try and get the rest of them to vote for you. . . . My father is going to vote for you and if I was a man I would vote for you to but I will try and get every one to vote for you that I can." Four days later, Lincoln responded: "As to the whiskers, having never worn any, do you not think people will call it a piece of silly affection if I were to begin now?" and signed the letter "Your very sincere well-wisher." On his inaugural journey to Washington, President-elect Lincoln stopped in Westfield, New York, and asked a crowd

[14]Carrie Roser to AL, Mar. 3, 1862; Julia Richards to AL, Apr. 17, 1863, ibid.

[15]Mary Ann Curry to AL, Mar. 26, 1862, ibid.; U.S. Census Office, Eighth Census of the United States (1860), Schuylkill County, PA, Pottsville North East Ward, p. 425. According to the 1860 census, Mary Ann Curry was a milliner, and her father, Patrick Curry, was a sixty-year-old innkeeper born in Ireland. Her mother, Ellen Curry, was forty-four in 1860.

of admirers if Grace Bedell was present. When the crowd passed her forward, he showed her his new whiskers and gave her a kiss.[16]

On January 14, 1864, Bedell, now fifteen and "grown to the size of a woman" in her own estimation, again wrote to Abraham Lincoln. Having heard that "a large number of girls are employed constantly and with good wages at Washington cutting Treasury notes and other things pertaining to that Department," she asked the president to show that he was her "true friend and well-wisher," as he had signed his letter to her. Her father had lost nearly all of his property, and she wanted a job to support herself and perhaps help her parents, although they were "ignorant of this application to you for assistance." Apparently, she had written earlier but received no reply; she "chose rather to think you had failed to receive it. Not believing that your natural kindness of heart of which I have heard so much would prompt you to pass it by unanswered."[17] Unfortunately, we do not know if Lincoln ever saw either of the letters she sent. However, she did not get a job in the Treasury Department.

First Lady Mary Lincoln sometimes became involved in the recommendation of women for positions. In April 1862, Abraham Lincoln wrote a brief note to Secretary of the Treasury Chase on behalf of Matilda Ivers: "Mrs L. is acquainted with Mrs Ivers, bearer of this, and will be obliged if the Sec. of the Treasury can give her employment." Seventeen months later, Ivers wrote to Lincoln, "I ocupied a position in the note treming room in the Treasuary Department through yours and Mrs. L favor[.] when the worke ceased wee were all dismised and I have not yet bein reappointed." Ivers hoped that Lincoln would "bee kind enough to renew your faver for I am in the gretest need[.] Pleas give mee a note to Mr Chittenden and one to Mr Spinner[.]" In response, Lincoln wrote on the letter, "I have no recollection of Mrs Ivers, or of the card it seems I have given her; but as it is in my hand writing, I suppose Mrs L. told me that she knew the lady."[18]

The register of female clerks lists Mrs. Lincoln as one of those recommending Mrs. E. D. Baker of Illinois for a position. On May 18, 1864, Baker received an appointment as a copyist in the Treasury Department. She was the wife of Edward D. Baker Jr., son of Lincoln's Illinois friend and colleague

---

16Grace Bedell to AL, Oct. 15, 1860, Burton Historical Collection, Detroit Public Library, Detroit, Mich.; AL to Grace Bedell, Oct. 19, 1860, Private Collection.

17Grace G. Bedell to AL, Jan. 14, 1864, RG 56, Entry 210, NARA.

18AL to Salmon P. Chase, Apr. 4, 1862; Matilda Ivers to AL, ca. September 1863, ibid.

Edward D. Baker, after whom the Lincolns named their second son in 1846. After the elder Baker's death at the Battle of Ball's Bluff in October 1861, President Lincoln had helped Edward D. Baker Jr. in his ascent through the commissioned officer ranks from second lieutenant to captain and assistant quartermaster by March 1863.[19]

Other connections also prompted the president to act on behalf of particular candidates. In January 1864, M. A. Snead wrote to Lincoln, explaining that "Joshua F. Speed brought me to this city and obtained for me an appointment in the Office of Internal Revenue." She lost the position, and because both Speed and another supporter were out of town, she turned to Lincoln, "knowing your friendship for Mr Speed, in the hope that for his sake and because I was *one* of the only *two* Kentucky ladies employed in the Treasury, you will not refuse me your assistance." She closed, "Let my being a Kentuckian and the especial protégé of Mr Speed be my excuses for this appeal to yourself." Lincoln endorsed the letter by writing, "I do not personally know, or remember about, this lady; but would be glad for her to have a hearing."[20]

As some of his correspondents and petitioners hoped and believed, a recommendation from President Lincoln could be an important asset in seeking a job. Laetitia G. Plunkett wrote to the president on August 20, 1864. The wife of Major William H. Plunkett of the 17th Wisconsin Volunteers, twenty-three-year-old Laetitia Plunkett explained that her husband was discharged for "*disability* contracted in the line of duty," after serving from April 1861 to May 1863. "In his present state of health," she continued, "he is unable to earn enough for our support." She also reminded Lincoln that she was the daughter of Captain Charles Peshall, "an old and staunch friend of yours in Illinois," and told him that her brother died at Fort Donelson, "fighting for his country." Plunkett's letter also contained an endorsement from Leonard J. Farwell, former governor of Wisconsin and an examiner in the Patent Office, that the Plunketts were "highly respectable persons." On August 24, Lincoln added his own endorsement, "Commissioner of Internal Revenue, please see & hear this Lady." One

---

[19]AL to Andrew G. Curtin, May 26, 1862, Huntington Library, San Marino, Calif.; AL to Joseph P. Taylor, Jan. 31, 1863, Abraham Lincoln Presidential Library and Museum, Springfield, Ill.; AL to Montgomery C. Meigs, Feb. 27, 1863, in Roy P. Basler, ed., *Collected Works of Abraham Lincoln*, 9 vols. (New Brunswick, N.J., 1953–55), 6:119.

[20]Mary A. Snead to AL, ca. January 1864, RG 56, Entry 210, NARA.

week later, Laetitia Plunkett received an appointment as a counter in the Treasury Department.[21]

Seventeen-year-old Louisa Knowlton also relied on her father's relationship with Abraham Lincoln in her application for work. On October 20, 1864, Knowlton wrote to the president with some trepidation, "I wish to see you on business: but never having transacted any for myself before, I feared my courage might fail me, did I resort to a verbal communication, before so many strangers." She had introduced herself to Lincoln the previous day as the daughter of Lincoln B. Knowlton, a lawyer from Illinois. He and Lincoln had worked together or in opposition on several cases between 1840 and 1852, but Knowlton had died in the mid-1850s. Louisa Knowlton wrote to Lincoln that "I am a native of dear, old Illinois, as you are also." She preferred a job as a copyist, but if that was "difficult of obtaining, any situation, *respectable* and *remunerative*, will suffice." She came from Massachusetts "with the fond hope that you would assist me." Her widowed mother was struggling to educate her family of five children, and Louisa wanted to help by supporting herself and aiding her mother. "Mr. Lincoln," she continued, "I know you have a great many applications, which seem trivial and harrassing to you, but which are *everything* to the applicants. Please do not turn a deaf ear to my petition, but consult the feelings of your own warm, honest heart, and be assured, the blessing of the widow, and her orphaned children, shall rest upon you, for ever more, and God will show mercy even as you have done."[22]

Lincoln endorsed Knowlton's letter by writing, "I do not personally know this lady, but she is, I have no doubt, as she says within, the daughter of my old friend L. B. Knowlton. She writes a very good hand, and I shall be really glad, if she can get employment. Hon. Sec. of Treasury please see her." On December 12, 1864, Knowlton received an appointment in the Treasury Department. Fourteen years later, she was still working for the comptroller of the currency at an annual salary of $900.[23]

In many cases, female applicants mentioned the military service and sacrifices of fathers, sons, and brothers in support of their applications. In September 1864, New Yorker Julia R. Peck began her letter:

---

[21]Laetitia G. Plunkett to AL, Aug. 20, 1864, ibid., General Registry of Ladies, Treasury Department, RG 56, Entry 222: Register of Female Clerks, 1861–68, NARA.

[22]Louisa W. Knowlton to AL, Oct. 20, 1864, RG 56, Entry 210, NARA.

[23]*Annual Report of the Comptroller of the Currency*, 2:86, appendix for 1878.

Sir.

My brother Charles W. Peck A[*cting*]. A[*ssistant*]. Surgeon in the Navy, died while on duty at Pensacola, Florida; of Yellow Fever.

My brother Herbert, a Corporal in Duryea's Zouaves, in his *tenth* battle, the 2nd of Bull Run, lost one leg, had the bone of the other leg permanently injured, and lost a part of his left hand.

My brothers James B. and Edwin Peck, were both drafted. . . .

After reciting her brothers' service in the Union armed forces, she implored Lincoln's assistance. Although she had filed her application more than three months earlier with the endorsements of her representatives in Congress—Senators Ira Harris and Edwin D. Morgan and Representative Homer A. Nelson of New York—she had heard nothing more from the Treasury Department. Lincoln endorsed the letter on the same day, referring it to William P. Fessenden, the new secretary of the Treasury, with the additional comment, "If there is any such position vacant as that which this lady desires, I hope she may receive it." She did. Two months later, on December 23, 1864, Julia R. Peck received a position in the Treasury Department.[24]

D. W. Bliss, a surgeon at a hospital in Washington, wrote a testimonial for Mrs. Alice E. Rutdge. He explained that she had been a nurse for several months and had recently buried her son, who was a corporal in a New York artillery battery. Bliss declared that she was a "capable, devoted and valuable Nurse and a lady of estimable character." Upon reading this, Lincoln wrote, "Will Gen. Spinner please see and hear this lady, who, though a stranger to me, I believe is a worthy person, who has lost her son in our service." Not only the president but also many other officials in Washington believed that the government had an obligation to support women who had lost fathers, husbands, and sons in the Union armies and navy.[25]

The employment records in the Treasury Department also detail the military service of male relatives for some of the female clerks. Mrs. Fayetta C. Snead of Kentucky had two brothers in the army. Miss Juliet G. Shearer of Pennsylvania had two brothers who served for three months and two brothers who served for three years in the army. Miss Agnes C. Houston had one brother and seven cousins in the army, and the husband of Mrs. Harriet

[24]Julia R. Peck to AL, Sept. 28, 1864, RG 56, Entry 210, NARA.

[25]D. W. Bliss to unknown, Sept. 19, 1864, ibid.; Cindy S. Aron, *Ladies and Gentlemen of the Civil Service: Middle-Class Workers in Victorian America* (New York, 1987), p. 71.

McConnell of New York was also in the army. Mrs. Carrie S. Sheads of Pennsylvania lost four brothers in the army, and Miss F. S. Hoey of Ohio had a brother killed at Shiloh and another brother who served for three years. Mrs. Mary A. McCulloch's husband and her brother were killed in the military, and Mrs. Mary F. McCaffrey of Ohio lost her husband when he was killed at the Battle of Stone's River in Tennessee.[26]

Some of Lincoln's endorsements on these letters reflect his appreciation of the losses these women had suffered. On a letter from a provost marshal in New York City recommending Mrs. Mary L. Rusk, Lincoln wrote, "I shall be glad if any Department or Bureau, can & will give suitable employment to this lady who is widow of one who died in our Naval service."[27]

In one remarkable instance, a female applicant cited her own quasi-military actions on behalf of the Union cause in Baltimore. Informed that the president "possessed a kind and generous heart and that you were social and friendly with those around you," Helen M. Linscott wrote that "I am an orphan girl—dependent upon my own exertions for a livlihood." She continued, "I am a northerner, but at the commensement of this war I was living in the South." Because those with whom she was living were secessionists, she left them and traveled north, arriving in Baltimore in mid-March 1861. She stayed in Baltimore for several weeks and was personally acquainted with Marshal of Police George P. Kane, who had well-known Southern sympathies. Linscott asserted that on Sunday, April 21, 1861, two days after a mob attacked Massachusetts troops on their way to Washington, Marshal Kane was planning to attack federal troops encamped in a field a few miles from the city. Linscott went to the room where Kane's ammunition was stored and wet as many percussion caps and gunpowder as she could reach. Asking Lincoln's pardon for "taking some much liberty" in writing to him, she closed her letter, "If there is any prospects of my getting a situation in Washington, or if you think this scroll is worth your notice, you will please address Helen M. Linscott, South Boston, Mass."[28]

Several of Lincoln's female correspondents were teachers who had exhausted their health in teaching and were looking for a healthier and more lucrative alternative in clerical work. Maggie T. Millmore of Milwaukee,

---

[26]Alphabetical Index of Names, passim, RG 56, Entry 222, NARA.

[27]Moses G. Leonard to AL, Oct. 10, 1864, RG 56, Entry 210, NARA.

[28]Helen M. Linscott to AL, Nov. 14, 1864, Abraham Lincoln Papers, Library of Congress, Washington, D.C.

Wisconsin, had no brothers who were soldiers, but she had to support her elderly parents and had been teaching school for eight years. She had taught in Missouri, where she was "dismissed simply for being as they term it a *Union Lady*, a title in which I shall ever glory," even though it annoyed many of her pupils and their parents. Now twenty-seven, she wrote to the president, "being fully persuaded that among the distinguished Personages by whom You are surrounded I could apply to no one of them possessing a kinder or more paternal heart than the President Himself." She signed her letter, "I am with due reverence and esteem, Your Excellency's most obedient and docile subject" and added a postscript, which read, "A line from the President, even though it contain a refusal of my request; shall be treasured by me, as a golden thread, in the web of my existence."[29] President Lincoln was never able to respond with that "golden thread." Maggie Millmore wrote to him on April 13, 1865; the next day, he was fatally shot in the head at Ford's Theatre.

Together, this collection of letters from women seeking employment in the Treasury Department reveals much about public perceptions of Abraham Lincoln, at least among middle-class women in the North. Many letters mentioned Lincoln's "goodness," "honesty," and "kindness." While some of this rhetoric was the self-serving praise of the supplicant, much seems to be sincere expressions of admiration. Jennette E. Hamblin of Geneva, New York, wrote that "having heard much of the Presidents kindness of heart, I have presumed to lay my case before him well knowing that *one* word from *him*, in the right place, will do more for me than the united efforts of many congressman." Gertrude Dunn of Kenosha, Wisconsin, likewise declared that "I should not be this bold to solicit your aid did I not know that your kindness of heart always impells you to listen to appeals from the needy & helpless." Helen V. White of Baltimore had "heard of your being a true Christian, and I know if it is in your power to assist me, you will not turn a deaf ear to my petition." "[H]aving been assured that our present President reads all the communication addressed to him," Missouri G. W. Finley of New York City was hopeful that her "epistle may not be passed by without at least, a passing thought." Confident of the president's innate goodness,

---

[29]Maggie T. Millmore to AL, Apr. 13, 1865, RG 56, Entry 210, NARA.

kindness, and honesty, these women appealed to Lincoln directly, desperate to have him intervene on their behalf.[30]

Ultimately, the Treasury Department hired at least 351 female clerks between 1861 and Lincoln's assassination in April 1865. Of these clerks, 60 percent were single and 40 percent were married or widowed.[31] Ninety-four (27 percent) were appointed from the District of Columbia, but many of them had moved to the federal capital to follow husbands, fathers, or other family members who were in government service or the military. The remaining 246 clerks came from twenty-five states. They came from all of the states of the Union, including the four border slave states of Missouri (3), Kentucky (4), Maryland (21), and Delaware (1); the seceded states of Virginia (16) and Tennessee (4); and the twice-seceded state of West Virginia (1). New York was the home of the most female clerks with fifty-six, followed by Pennsylvania with twenty-eight, Maryland with twenty-one, and Massachusetts with twenty. The states of California and Oregon contributed two each.[32] The wartime female clerical employees of the Treasury Department ranged in age from fifteen to sixty at the time they were appointed. Their average age was thirty and their median age was twenty-eight. As might be expected, the married women were on average ten years older than the single women, but there were single women as old as fifty.[33]

The tasks outlined in the register of female clerks were predictably narrow. Although the first female clerks had been employed to cut Treasury notes, machinery soon began to perform that task. Nearly half (47 percent) of the clerks worked at counting notes, and 41 percent worked as copyists. The remaining 12 percent performed a variety of jobs, including bond

---

[30]Jennette E. Hamblin to AL, Oct. 1, 1864; Gertrude A. Dunn to AL, Mar. 17, 1865; Helen V. White to AL, Dec. 13, 1863, ibid.

[31]N=324. The records do not specify the marital status of twenty-seven of the female clerks (General Register of Ladies). The proportion of single female clerks increased to approximately two-thirds in the 1870s and to 73 percent by 1890. Aron, "'To Barter Their Souls for Gold,'" pp. 839–40.

[32]N=340. The records do not specify the state of origin of eleven of the female clerks (General Register of Ladies). See Aron, *Ladies and Gentlemen of the Civil Service*, pp. 43, 204n7.

[33]N=254. The records do not specify the ages of ninety-seven of the female clerks. Single clerks ranged in age from fifteen to fifty, and married clerks ranged in age from twenty to sixty (General Register of Ladies). Cindy S. Aron observes that "what is most striking about the age distribution of female federal clerks is how old they were compared to women workers generally and to female clerks in other cities and situations" (Aron, *Ladies and Gentlemen of the Civil Service*, p. 44).

examiner, cutter, trimmer, folder; paper clerk, and under the generic designation "For duty."[34]

Opportunities for women in the Treasury Department expanded in the fall of 1862, when Treasurer Spinner, supported by Assistant Secretary of the Treasury George H. Harrington, pressed Secretary Chase to employ women in clerkships to count both new notes that had been printed and old, damaged notes that had been submitted for exchange. On October 9, 1862, seven women became the first women to be appointed as clerks in any executive department of the federal government. "In the office of the Treasurer," Spinner later recalled, "it was soon found that in various services, and especially in counting money and in detecting counterfeits, women were altogether superior to men."[35]

Virtually all of the successful applicants received recommendations from someone, most from their congressman or senator. Of the 351 women listed in the "Register of Female Clerks," only two do not have a name listed in the column headed "Recommended by." Twelve list President Lincoln as a recommender, and others received recommendations from the secretary of the Treasury or a governor. Eight received a recommendation from the wife of the president, the wife of a cabinet secretary, or the wife of a senator. Without some prominent person to recommend them, it appears that very few, if any, applicants secured a position in the Treasury Department.[36]

The Treasury Department was the largest, but not the sole, government agency to employ women as clerks during the Civil War. The newly formed but tiny Department of Agriculture employed at least one female clerk, after its formation in 1862. The new department assumed responsibilities formerly handled by the Patent Office.[37] By 1863, the Patent Office employed a baker's dozen of female clerks, and thirty female clerks worked in the quartermaster general's office. Postmaster General Montgomery Blair hired ten

---

[34]N = 320. The records do not specify the jobs of thirty-one of the female clerks (General Registry of Ladies). *New York Times*, Feb. 18, 1869, p. 2.

[35]"General Spinner and the Women Clerks," pp. 1–2. The first seven female clerks were Mrs. Abbie C. Harris of Maine, Miss Libbie Stoner of Pennsylvania, Miss Mary Burke of Washington, D.C., Miss Fannie L. Halsted of New Jersey, Miss Belle S. Tracy of New Jersey, Miss Jennie L. Wall of Maine, and Miss Annie York of Maryland. Halsted, Tracy, Wall, and York received transfers from the note-clipping room, but Harris, Stoner, and Burke were all new employees.

[36]General Registry of Ladies.

[37]Lois Bryan Adams, *Letter from Washington, 1863–1865*, ed. Evelyn Leasher (Detroit, 1999), p. 20.

women in 1862 to work as clerks in the Dead Letter Office, and by 1863, sixteen of the thirty-two clerks in that office were women.[38]

The War Department also employed female clerks as copyists. In October 1864, Mary A. Watson wrote to President Lincoln from western New York. She was "informed the War Department has in its employ Ladies to do writing." "Consequently," she continued, "I ask, is there a situation I could get . . . to do writing for some of the different branches of the Department." She had a widowed mother dependent on her for support, and she wrote to Lincoln because "I am not informed of the proper persons I should address in business like this." She signed her letter, "Yours very Respectfly, The sister of a Soldier, Mary A. Watson."[39]

The opportunity for women to work in clerical positions in the Treasury and other departments during the Civil War continued to provide women with employment opportunities after the war. Although some women left these clerical positions with the return of peace, more women were ready to take their places, and the number of women working in federal government offices continued to grow through the remainder of the nineteenth century. Income disparities were severe at first, with female clerks earning between one-third and one-half the salary of male clerks. Female clerks in the Treasury Department were initially paid an annual salary of $600, which eventually rose to $720 for most by war's end. By 1870, federal legislation authorized departments to appoint female clerks to the same positions as male clerks and pay them accordingly, but enforcement remained uneven.[40]

The entry of women into federal offices raised fears among the general public about the "corrupting" influence of women in the workplace (fig. 3). Critics believed that the presence of women workers would distract male employees, undermining their productivity. They also feared for the virtue of female employees when the sexes mixed "promiscuously" in government

[38]"Government Girls," in Judith E. Harper, ed., *Women during the Civil War: An Encyclopedia* (New York, 2004), p. 174; Historian, United States Postal Service, "Women of Postal Headquarters," August 2008.

[39]Mary A. Watson to AL, Oct. 27, 1864, box 91, Record Group 107: Records of the Office of the Secretary of War, 1791–1947, Entry 259: Records of the Chief Clerk and the Administrative Assistant, Records Relating to Personnel, General Records, 1816–1899, Applications for Civilian Appointments and Regular Army Commissions, 1847–1887, NARA.

[40]Massey, *Bonnet Brigades*, pp. 340–41.

Fig. 3. "The Treasury Department—the New Secretary Looking Around," *Harper's Bazaar,* Apr. 3, 1869. The suspicions of the corrupting influence and improprieties in the employment of women in government jobs continued after the Civil War, as this 1869 engraving demonstrates. *(http://hearth.library.cornell.edu/cgi/t/text/text-idx?c=hearth;idno=4732809_1443_014)*

offices. Even Secretary Chase was concerned that female clerks would "demoralize" the department in the literal sense that the workplace would become less "moral."[41] These concerns eventually bred scandalous rumors of "orgies and bacchanals" that reached even the floor of Congress.

Several months before Congress took notice, however, Secretary Chase asked Secretary of War Edwin M. Stanton in December 1863 to loan him the services of Colonel Lafayette C. Baker. Baker was the leader of a secret detective service organized by Stanton to identify and imprison traitors, spies, and deserters. Chase asked Baker to investigate the charges of corruption and immorality in his department and to arrest those responsible for any wrongdoing. In the course of his investigation, Baker arrested a few people and obtained confessions from three female employees of immoral activities with Treasury officials.[42]

---

[41] Aron, *Ladies and Gentlemen of the Civil Service,* p. 71.

[42] Jacob Mogelever, *Death to Traitors: The Story of General Lafayette C. Baker, Lincoln's Forgotten Secret Service Chief* (Garden City, N.Y., 1960), pp. 248–78.

Late in April 1864, Representative James Brooks, a War Democrat from New York, charged on the floor of the House of Representatives that the printing bureau of the Treasury Department was the scene of both the theft of public money and sexual immorality, involving female clerks employed by the department. In response, freshman representative and future President James A. Garfield of Ohio introduced a resolution on April 30 that the Speaker of the House appoint a select committee to investigate the charges.[43] The Speaker appointed nine congressmen to the select committee and named Representative Garfield as the chair.[44]

The committee began its investigations the following week and focused on two issues—the printing of public money in the Treasury Department in Washington and the alleged immoralities of employees in the Treasury Department. At the center of the controversy was Spencer M. Clark (fig. 4), the superintendent of the National Currency Bureau (which became the Bureau of Printing and Engraving), who was responsible for the printing of federal currency at the Treasury building in Washington and who employed many of the female clerks at work in the Treasury Department. In its investigation, the congressional committee confined its attention to whether Clark had allowed or participated in any "disreputable or immoral conduct" in the Treasury building and whether Clark had made any arrangements with female employees for "immoralities" outside the Treasury Department. Although the Democratic minority of the committee objected to the narrowness of the investigation, the majority allowed Representative Brooks to introduce "very voluminous" testimony, much of it having "only a remote bearing on the subject-matter of the investigation." Brooks used Colonel Baker's investigations to make six primary allegations, outlined in the report the committee filed on June 30, 1864.[45]

---

[43] *Congressional Globe*, Apr. 29, 1864, 38th Cong., 1st sess., p. 1968; *House Journal*, Apr. 30, 1864, 38th Cong, 1st sess., p. 597.

[44] Committee members included Republicans James A. Garfield of Ohio (chair), James F. Wilson of Iowa, Reuben E. Fenton of New York, and Thomas A. Jenckes of Rhode Island; Unconditional Unionist Henry Winter Davis of Maryland; and Democrats James Brooks of New York, John T. Stuart of Illinois, John L. Dawson of Pennsylvania, and William G. Steele of New Jersey. *House Journal*, Apr. 30, 1864, 38th Cong, 1st sess., p. 598.

[45] House Select Committee to Investigate Charges against the Treasury Department, *Report*, 1864, 38th Cong., 1st sess., Report No. 140, pp. 1, 13–15.

FIG. 4. Spencer M. Clark, supervisor of the National Currency Bureau (1862–68), was the subject of a congressional investigation into suspected improprieties involving women employees at the Treasury Department. He placed his own likeness on the five-cent U.S. fractional currency note seen here. *(National Numismatic Collection at the Smithsonian Institution)*

First, Brooks and Baker insisted that Clark had offered a bribe to one of his female employees for "dishonorable purposes." In testimony before the committee, however, the woman who served as the alleged messenger of this offer denied that she had delivered any message and declared the entire story false. Second, they alleged that "a piece of gross immorality" had taken place between Clark's principal assistant and a female employee in the bonnet room in the basement of the Treasury building. Fourteen-year-old former employee Clara Donalson testified that she saw the man leave the room by another door just as she entered and that the woman was in the room. A thorough cross-examination by the committee failed to yield any more details of "gross immorality." Third, the accusers declared that the superintendent of the bronzing room offered a female employee double wages if she would "submit to his wishes" and work evenings as well as during the day. Her father later told her that his expression could have a dishonorable meaning. She also said that the same man winked at her on another occasion.[46]

Fourth, Brooks and Baker alleged that Clark and G. A. Henderson, a male clerk in the department, met with two female employees at the Central Hotel and spent the night with them there under assumed names. The witness who allegedly saw the two men with the two women changed the month in which he saw them three times in three different testimonies, and his sister had worked at the Treasury Department twice after the alleged tryst but had been dismissed. The testimony of three members of this same family was, in the judgment of the majority of the committee, a "tissue of contradictions." Fifth, they charged that Clark and Henderson had the same female employees dress in "male attire" and "accompany them to a disreputable place of amusement" in Washington. The evidence was an anonymous note signed "H," assumed to have been written by Henderson. Sixth, Baker presented "very contradictory statements" of a similar meeting in Philadelphia, but he admitted he had no personal knowledge of the charge. The committee questioned Superintendent Clark extensively on all of the charges, and he denied each of them.[47]

Baker was so zealous in proving the immoral actions of men and women in the Treasury Department that he even stopped a funeral procession and insisted on an autopsy to prove that the woman had died while attempting to have an abortion. The autopsy not only revealed that she was not pregnant but also "afforded incontestible evidence of the unsullied virtue of the deceased." In moral outrage, the majority of the committee condemned the charges and characterized them as, "in part, the result of an effort on the part of some to break up the plan of printing in the Treasury Department, and partly the result of a conspiracy on the part of Colonel Baker and the female prostitutes associated with him, by the aid of coerced testimony, to destroy the reputation of Mr. Clark, and, by the odium thus raised against the Treasury Department, shield himself and justify his unauthorized arrest of one of the officers in the Printing bureau." The majority report continued, "The charges are exceedingly unjust and cruel, from the fact that they have to some extent compromised the reputation of the three hundred females employed in the printing division. A majority of them are wives or sisters of

---

[46]Ibid., p. 15.
[47]Ibid., pp. 15–16.

soldiers who have fallen in the field." Finally, it concluded, "in no community in the country will there be found a larger proportion of noble and respectable women than those employed in the Treasury Department."[48]

The four Democratic congressmen on the committee submitted a minority report, written by Representative James Brooks, that insisted that the allegations of immorality were true. "These affidavits disclose a mass of immorality and profligacy, the more atrocious as these women were employés of Clark, hired and paid by him with the public money." Clark seemed to select female employees for their "youth and personal attractions," and "neither the laws of God nor of man, the institution of the Sabbath, nor the common decencies of life, seem to have been respected by Clark in his conduct with these women." Clark and his accomplices converted the Treasury Department into a "place for debauchery and drinking, the very recital of which is impossible without violating decency."[49]

Both the partisan division of the congressional committee's report and the charges of immorality that may have been motivated by a larger attempt to discredit Spencer M. Clark reveal more about Civil War America than they do about the actual behavior of female employees of the Treasury Department. That the committee divided along strict party lines, with Unconditional Unionist Henry Winter Davis siding with the Republicans, suggests that politics may have played a stronger role in the committee's deliberations than a desire to find the facts to prove or disprove the allegations. Republicans on the committee found the witness testimony contradictory, coerced, and self-interested. Democrats believed that Clark had violated the public trust for his own personal gain in printing the public money and were disposed to find his morals as repulsive as his ethics or perhaps his politics. If any of the charges were motivated by a desire to discredit the printing of public money in a central location under one man's authority rather than by multiple printers in multiple locations, as the Republican majority believed, it is perhaps unsurprising that the accusers chose to focus on sexual

[48]Ibid., pp. 16–17.

[49]Ibid., pp. 18–21. Lafayette C. Baker made the investigation of the Treasury Department an important part of his *History of the United States Secret Service*, published in 1867. After recounting and defending his investigation and reprinting the minority report of the congressional committee, Baker closed the chapter, "I doubt not, the people will be surprised to learn that a conspicuous object of this inquiry, S. M. Clark, still holds (June, 1866) his position in the United States Treasury Department." Lafayette C. Baker, *History of the United States Secret Service* (Philadelphia, 1867), pp. 261–328, quote on p. 328.

immorality. Drawing on the nation's ambivalence toward the mixing of the sexes in the workplace, critics could use public fears and fascinations to construct a plausible portrait of a publicly funded harem, presided over by a man in his mid-fifties, surrounded by hundreds of young women who owed their jobs to him.[50]

Some critics condemned female clerks as a class, insisting that they had stepped out of the proper sphere of women into compromising situations where their virtue and their reputation were at risk. From this perspective, jobs in government offices were likely to attract women whose morals were questionable. For virtuous women who took such employment, critics insisted, the working conditions were likely to encourage unacceptable sexual behavior and expose them to the seductions of immoral male supervisors and promiscuous coworkers.[51]

Others followed the majority of the congressional committee in defending the virtuous and respectable character of most female clerks. When John Ellis wrote a description of the capital city in 1869, he described hearing a young man outside the National Theatre exclaim to a companion, "We've seen all the ladies! The rest of these women are only Treasury Clerks!" Ellis decried the "melancholy fact" that many of the female employees of the Treasury Department were "either suspected of immoral practices, or looked down upon by the Washingtonians as beings of a lower order." The pure women were in a large majority, Ellis insisted, and "the suspicion which rests upon these clerks, as a class, is most unjust and unfounded." Despite his defense of the virtue of the majority of female clerks in federal service, however, Ellis concluded that "their positions are not to be envied, and ought to be shunned by women who can obtain honest employment elsewhere."[52]

In her memoir *Ten Years in Washington*, Mary Clemmer in 1881 concluded of female employees in the Treasury Department that, "the truth is, there is not another company of women-workers in the land which numbers so many ladies of high character, intelligence, culture, and social position." Admitting that some women were forced to trade their virtue for an appointment, Clemmer insisted that it was the "unjust mode of appointment" of leaving female applicants at the mercy of powerful men that created the problem.

---

[50]Nina Silber, *Daughters of the Union: Northern Women Fight the Civil War* (Cambridge, Mass., 2005), pp. 117–19.

[51]Aron, *Ladies and Gentlemen of the Civil Service*, pp. 165–67.

[52]John B. Ellis, *The Sights and Secrets of the National Capital* (New York, 1870), pp. 383–86.

The hardships of war and the intense competition for employment "placed side by side, with pure and noble women, the women-adventurers and sinners, whose presence cast so much undeserved reproach on the innocent, and who caused the only shadow of disrepute which has ever fallen upon woman's Treasury-service."[53]

Women who sought federal employment during the Civil War risked much in social status and reputation. Often desperate to support themselves or dependents, they stepped outside the socially prescribed boundaries of women's work into an area of labor previously dominated by men. Applying to men in power for assistance in obtaining these jobs, female clerical workers needed the approval of male supervisors to retain their positions. Although the demands for sexual favors were unlikely to have been as widespread as the minority of the select committee believed, the threat and incidence of such demands were probably more prevalent than the majority wished to believe. Certainly, many people in the North believed that the scandalous charges leveled in 1864 merely confirmed their belief that introducing women into the offices of the Treasury Department was a grievous mistake.

Abraham Lincoln accepted the need for female clerks to fill clerical roles in the offices of an expanding federal government. His personal intervention aided many women in getting an interview and some in securing a job in the Treasury Department. Female applicants appealed to the president from across the North, many feeling that he alone could help them. Their letters shed light on Lincoln's reputation among women in the North, and his endorsements on some of the letters illustrate his willingness to assist dozens of women in dire straits. Occupied with leading a nation, defending it against a domestic rebellion, and experimenting with the status of four million of its most downtrodden inhabitants, President Lincoln still found time to aid individual women who turned to him for help.

---

[53]Clemmer, *Ten Years in Washington*, pp. 357–58, 375.

Peter Wallenstein

The Morrill Land-Grant College Act of 1862

Seedbed of the American System of Public Universities

MANY OF THE past essays published in this series of books on the history of Congress have pointed toward the future, more specifically to the Civil War, and have therefore kept their attention focused on events *before* the 1860s. With the current volume, we find ourselves *in* the war; and therefore pointing toward the future suggests a very different shape, one that can readily, as this chapter does, take the story all the way down to the recent past. At the same time, a chapter on the 1862 Morrill Land-Grant College Act offers an opportunity to assess what becomes of congressional intentions, what degree of discretion gets put in the hands of those actors who implement the outlines contained in congressional legislation, and how Congress itself returns to the original issues and reconsiders how best to carry out changing intentions going forward.

A few years ago, at a conference at the University of Illinois, the 200th anniversary of the birth of Abraham Lincoln kicked off with an examination of Lincoln's connection to the Land-Grant College Act of 1862, which itself was soon to turn 150. More than one participant took exception to a high-profile television series at the time directed by Ken Burns, coupled with a coffee-table book, on "America's best idea": the system of national parks. Not to take anything away from the national parks—Yosemite, Grand Canyon, Mount Rainier, and all the rest—but these speakers proposed a rival for the title "America's best idea." Maybe they were willing to consider sharing top billing, maybe not, but regardless, they wished to nominate the nation's land-grant system of higher education as "America's best idea." This alternative nomination supplies a place to begin examining how America's other "best idea" took legislative shape and—beyond that, central to its *becoming* a "best idea"—what was made of it over time.[1]

During the decade 1862–72, under the 1862 Morrill Land-Grant College Act, American states collectively embarked on the establishment of a constellation of new institutions of higher education. Another transformation, or collection of transformations, over the course of the next hundred years built on these nineteenth-century beginnings such that a new kind of institution emerged. What typically began as colleges to train farmers and engineers (in many cases both white and male and nobody else) grew into a whole new complex: coeducational, multiracial research institutions offering a near universe of programs to a near universe of constituencies. According to one leading thesis of this chapter, the "colleges of 1862" led the way in these innovations.

Rather than use the phrase "the American *constellation* of public universities," I prefer to say "the American *system* of public universities." The Morrill Act offers a fitting example of what Henry Clay and other Whig leaders had in mind during an earlier period, generally referred to by historians as "the American system": federal power motoring change in policy and in the development of society, but in cooperation with state governments, and assembling private as well as public resources and decision making in producing the end results.[2] The tariff is often seen as the main source of revenue fueling the Whigs' American system, but the national government's *other* main source of funds, receipts from the sale of public lands, served as well, as exemplified in the land-grant colleges.

One way to highlight the extraordinary origins of the Land-Grant College Act is to position that breakthrough measure against what was happening to education in the Confederacy at the very time that Congress passed

---

[1]Dayton Duncan, *The National Parks: America's Best Idea—an Illustrated History* (New York, 2009); Rededication of the Morrill Act Conference, University of Illinois, Urbana-Champaign, Ill., October 2009. The term is often ascribed to Wallace Stegner, in "The Best Idea We Ever Had," *Wilderness* 46 (Spring 1983):4–13, a quotation from which is often featured at national park visitor centers. But see Alan MacEachern's blog, "Who Had 'America's Best Idea'?" *Network in Canadian History and Environment*, Oct. 23, 2011, http://niche-canada.org/2011/10/23/who-had-americas-best-idea/.

[2]Robert A. Lively, "The American System: A Review Article," *Business History Review* 29 (1955):81–96.

the bill and Lincoln signed it. In every Confederate state, and at every level, school after school suspended operations for any or all among a complex of reasons related to the wartime emergency. Funds grew even less available, and both teachers and male students of military age went off to fight. Campus buildings were repurposed to serve as headquarters for army officers or hospitals for wounded soldiers, whether for the Confederacy or the Union or first one and then the other.[3]

This chapter is necessarily selective. Among the dimensions emphasized here are race and gender—that is, which "people" in a given state could attend that state's so-called public land-grant school. The period covered here ends around 1972, after a decade for the system to get up and running and then a century for it to evolve, although there have certainly been new developments since then.

Congressional legislation supplied the programs and policies that framed the origins and development of the land-grant college system, but other forces contributed to the varied institutional transitions that emerged over the generations after 1862. State policy, in particular, did much to shape every land-grant school. Private funds, too, have always played important roles—as any parent writing a check to cover tuition at a land-grant school these days might readily observe. Within each institution, moreover, presidents influenced the development of the school they served as custodian and leader. Also initiating new departures were black applicants, for example, to institutions that opposed their enrollment, applicants who persisted in their efforts, sometimes with some success.

Origins, 1857–62

In 1854, Justin S. Morrill of Vermont (fig. 1) gained a seat in the U.S. House of Representatives, where Abraham Lincoln too had, for a single term in the 1840s, once represented *his* constituents. Morrill, born the year after

---

[3]Peter Wallenstein, "The Struggle to Learn: Higher Education in Civil War Virginia," in William C. Davis and James I. Robertson Jr., eds., *Virginia at War, 1864* (Lexington, Ky., 2009), pp. 99–119, for a case study of the South; Michael David Cohen, *Reconstructing the Campus: Higher Education and the American Civil War* (Charlottesville, Va., 2012), pp. 19–50, on a small sample of institutions in the Union as well as the Confederacy. See also Wayne Flynt, "Southern Higher Education and the Civil War," *Civil War History* 14 (1968):211–25.

FIG. 1. Congressman Justin S. Morrill of Vermont (1810–98) was chiefly responsible for the 1862 Land-Grant College Act. *(Library of Congress Prints and Photographs Division)*

Lincoln, shared a background with the future president that included persistent poverty, scant schooling, social and political ambition, and a strong sense of what the nation could and should become. Elected to his first term as a Whig, Morrill was elected to subsequent terms as a Republican; in 1867, during Reconstruction, he began a lengthy tenure in the Senate, where he served until his death in 1898.[4]

Increasingly in the 1840s and 1850s, an idea had been circulating that new colleges to train farmers were in order. By the end of the 1850s, a number of states, among them Maryland and Michigan, had established such schools, and there were increasing calls for federal assistance to help develop these institutions. Several state legislatures instructed their U.S. senators and advised their U.S. representatives to support the 1861–62 bill. The Ohio legislature, for example, instructed Senator Benjamin F. Wade (fig. 2) to support it, which he did so effectively that the measure can be, and sometimes is, referred to as the Morrill-Wade Act.[5]

As a member of Congress, Morrill, in particular, promoted an idea that might put to great good the vast expanse of public land in the West, to improve the lives of citizens throughout the nation, including in Lincoln's Illinois and Morrill's Vermont. Back in the 1830s, in earlier parts of the adult lives of both Lincoln and Morrill, the nation's Treasury had suffered the embarrassment of a chronic fiscal surplus, a result of land sales in what at that point was a less westerly West. Unable to agree on whether or how to spend the resulting surplus directly, Congress had arranged for this budgetary "surplus" to be "distributed" to the states, on the basis of their representation in the electoral college—that is, each state's combined representation in both houses of Congress—and the recipient states would then

[4]William Belmont Parker, *The Life and Public Services of Justin Smith Morrill* (1924; reprint ed., New York, 1971), pp. 1–62; Coy F. Cross II, *Justin Smith Morrill, Father of the Land-Grant Colleges* (East Lansing, Mich., 1999).

[5]George N. Rainsford, *Congress and Higher Education in the Nineteenth Century* (Knoxville, Tenn., 1972), pp. 72–83; John Y. Simon, "The Politics of the Morrill Act," *Agricultural History* 37 (1963):103–11; Earle D. Ross, *Democracy's College: The Land-Grant Movement in the Formative Stage* (Ames, Iowa, 1942), pp. 14–45; Roger L. Williams, *The Origins of Federal Support for Higher Education: George W. Atherton and the Land-Grant College Movement* (University Park, Pa., 1991), pp. 11–39; William Edwin Sawyer, "The Evolution of the Morrill Act of 1862," Ph.D. dissertation, Boston University, 1948, pp. 25–94; Hans L. Trefousse, *Benjamin Franklin Wade, Radical Republican from Ohio* (New York, 1963), p. 188.

FIG. 2. Senator Benjamin F. Wade of Ohio (1800–1878) proved instrumental in securing passage of the 1862 Land-Grant College Act. *(Library of Congress Prints and Photographs Division)*

determine how best to put such new funds to work for the benefit of their people.[6]

Morrill's bill fine-tuned that idea, to give it more particular direction, yet still leave it up to the states to manage the funds he intended to go their way. The direct object of this largesse was to be institutions, most of them new, that would transform the traditional approach of higher education. Rather than seek to enhance the opportunities of the social elite—the sons of prosperous families, who might train to be lawyers and doctors—Morrill championed providing formal training for the nation's next generation of farmers and engineers, of agriculturalists and mechanics. And those lands in the West could supply a means to support this new system.

Congressman Morrill introduced a land-grant college bill for the first time in December 1857, during the first session of the Thirty-Fifth Congress. The House passed it in April 1858, but it ran into too much opposition in the Senate to make it through that chamber. The struggle resumed after the second session convened, in December. After a few amendments, to which the House agreed, the measure went to the White House in February 1859.[7]

President James Buchanan vetoed it. In the House, the vote had been 105–100, and in the Senate, 25–22, so there was no chance of a legislative override. Much of the opposition came from the West, whose representatives saw no compelling reason for lands in their region to subsidize education in the East. President Buchanan's menu of reasons given for the veto, however, better reflected the adamant opposition of most congressional members from the South, committed to strict construction and finding nowhere in the Constitution any authorization for such a measure giving public land to states for educational purposes.[8]

---

[6]Edward G. Bourne, *The History of the Surplus Revenue of 1837* (New York, 1885); Peter Wallenstein, "Reintegrating the American Past: Revisiting the West, Frederick Jackson Turner, and the Early Republic," *Virginia Social Science Journal* 47 (2012):86–102.

[7]Rainsford, *Congress and Higher Education*, pp. 85–88; Williamjames Hull Hoffer, *To Enlarge the Machinery of Government: Congressional Debates and the Growth of the American State, 1858–1891* (Baltimore, 2007), pp. 17–34.

[8]Rainsford, *Congress and Higher Education*, pp. 87–91; Sarah T. Phillips, "Antebellum Agricultural Reform, Republican Ideology, and Sectional Tension," *Agricultural History* 74 (2000):799–822; Hoffer, *To Enlarge the Machinery of Government*, pp. 35–36.

Morrill tried again in February 1860, in the first session of the Thirty-Sixth Congress. With the West leading the charge in the House Committee on Public Lands, the bill died there.[9]

In December 1861, early in the Thirty-Seventh Congress, Morrill introduced a new version of his earlier efforts. One substantive change increased the original figure of 20,000 acres of public land for each member of Congress to 30,000. Another, reflecting the Civil War (by then raging), specified the inclusion of studies in military tactics.

On Morrill's third attempt, conditions had changed such that when Congress approved the 1862 measure, it was by wide margins: 32–9 in the Senate and 90–25 in the House. Those margins reflected, to a degree, the absence of so many men who had earlier represented the eleven states by then in the Confederacy. A bigger difference, though, was in the White House. A new president held office, and Abraham Lincoln signed the measure on July 2, 1862.[10]

The Land-Grant College Act came in a package that included two other measures enacted in 1862. The Pacific Railroad Act laid the groundwork for the transcontinental railroad, a massive line that would be completed in 1869. The Homestead Act supplied agricultural lots that farmers claimed over the decades that followed. All three laws fostered benefits requiring no actual transfer of money out of the federal treasury. Each figured in the politics of enacting the others, as the East and the West could find some common ground in signing on to assist in passage of measures that would variably affect their own direct well-being. A new American system emerged, one that promoted both education and transportation, and offering land to farmers as well as the encouragement of scientific farming.[11]

In the midst of a huge war, the federal government embarked on an immense new endeavor in the realm of higher education. The land in question,

---

[9]Rainsford, *Congress and Higher Education*, p. 91.

[10]Ibid., pp. 91–97; Parker, *Morrill*, pp. 259–84; Heather Cox Richardson, *The Greatest Nation of the Earth: Republican Economic Policies during the Civil War* (Cambridge, Mass., 1997), pp. 154–60; Hoffer, *To Enlarge the Machinery of Government*, pp. 37–60; Randal Leigh Hoyer, "The Gentleman from Vermont: The Career of Justin S. Morrill in the United States House of Representatives," Ph.D. dissertation, Michigan State University, 1974, pp. 68–72; Sawyer, "The Evolution of the Morrill Act of 1862," pp. 103–258.

[11]Simon, "The Politics of the Morrill Act"; Harold M. Hyman, *American Singularity: The 1787 Northwest Ordinance, the 1862 Homestead and Morrill Acts, and the 1944 G.I. Bill* (Athens, Ga., 1986); Roger D. Billings, "The Homestead Act, Pacific Railroad Act and Morrill Act," *Northern Kentucky Law Review* 39 (2012):699–736.

held by the U.S. government in the West—or, rather, scrip representing a certain amount of acreage—was apportioned to states on the basis of their congressional representation, at 30,000 acres per member of the House and the Senate. Each state arranged for the sale of its allocation of land, created an annuity, and began contributing to the support of a school (or in some cases more than one school) with programs of study consistent with flexible specifications as outlined in the 1862 law.

People are often unclear as to the origins of land-grant institutions. According to one typical notion, for Virginia, for example, the state long ago owned some land in Blacksburg, the state granted the land to a school, and a university emerged on that land. The notion is wrong on three counts. One, the land was granted by the federal government to the state of Virginia, not from the state to the college. Two, the land that fostered the growth of a school came in the form of land scrip—paper representing a certain acreage—to be sold for an endowment, and the endowment provided an annuity, not a location. And three, by the 1850s and 1860s, most remaining public land was in the West, not the East. The land scrip conveyed control of land in the Great Plains, beyond the Mississippi River. President Thomas Jefferson had bought the land for the nation from France in the Louisiana Purchase of 1803. In later years the United States obtained that land again—by conquest, by treaty, by hook or by crook—this time from its aboriginal occupants, the Indian peoples of the American West. Like Virginia, most states were granted land far outside their own boundaries, so they could hardly situate a college on that land. Moreover, since the land could be widely scattered, one might envision students making their way across campus between classes from Nebraska to North Dakota.

How might "America's best idea" work out? One Lincoln scholar has said about the president, always distracted as he was by extremely pressing military matters, that he "apparently played no role" in the act's passage and then "forgot to mention it" later that year in a list of his administration's accomplishments. Another notes that the press paid scant attention to it either, though once it had become law one leading journalist suggested that it could bring "wide and lasting good."[12]

[12]Olivier Fryssé, *Lincoln, Land, and Labor, 1809–60*, trans. Sylvia Neely (Urbana, Ill., 1994), p. 179 (first two quotes); Ross, *Democracy's College*, p. 65; Richardson, *The Greatest Nation of the Earth*, p. 160 (final quote).

Indeed, the congressman's handiwork proved—in the twentieth century—to have a stunning impact on the course of American social and economic history in general and the history of higher education in particular. Yet, throughout the system's first quarter century, the evidence to support such a prospect was hardly compelling. Launching the new system proved daunting, but after Congress enacted two new measures in 1887 and 1890, genuine progress proved widespread.

Implementation, 1862–87

As one historian of the origins of the land-grant system observed, the Morrill Act "offered to the states a grant insufficient to establish agricultural colleges, but too large to refuse."[13] States moved along various timetables toward resolving whether to accept, or at least what to do with, the limited largess that could soon be heading their way. They had to accept the bounty, then convert it to cash, then invest the cash in a fund whose proceeds could provide some operational support for one or more institutions of higher education. They had to settle on a location, typically selecting among a number of hopeful claimants. Much of this was contentious, and all of it took time. Nonetheless, every state launched its share of the new system.

As with the original American system, the land-grant system proved something of a patchwork of private and public institutions, and with financial support as well as policy guidelines from the states and the federal government. Most of the states sent their land-grant funds to public institutions, whether new ones or old ones, and whether these were flagship universities or separate institutions.

The Morrill Act permitted limited use of the land-grant funds to purchase land for a school farm, but it did not permit expenditure of Morrill Act money for buildings. So legislatures tended to favor localities that could offer appropriate real estate. Often, therefore, the new funding and programs were attached to already-existing institutions, in some cases private colleges.

In New England, the Connecticut legislature first attached the program and funds to Yale; Rhode Island, to Brown; and New Hampshire, to

[13]Simon, "The Politics of the Morrill Act," p. 111.

Dartmouth. Massachusetts considered doing so at Harvard, before splitting the money between a recently established private institution, the Massachusetts Institute of Technology, where engineering education would be promoted, and a new facility to be established at Amherst, the Massachusetts Agricultural College. Proponents of a new institution in Vermont proved unable to come up with the funds necessary for such a separate venture, so the money went to the University of Vermont.[14]

Farmers in Maine had been calling for some time for an agricultural college, and the state finally created one under the Morrill Act. At first, several private colleges sought the money: Bowdoin, Bates, and Waterville (soon renamed Colby). Eventually the town of Orono offered both a central location and financial support—$14,000 and a farm—and the legislature settled on that choice in 1866 and supplied $10,000 toward the construction of a dormitory and a laboratory. Classes began at the new school in 1868, and the first cohort to graduate, six young men in 1872, took their degrees the same year that the school admitted its first young women. Maine State College—a land-grant school, a coeducational institution, a start on a new state university—was under way.[15]

A similar range of responses soon emerged, mostly in the 1860s, in all the states outside the Confederacy. Already in 1863, Bluemont Central College, a private institution at Manhattan, became the Kansas State Agricultural College. That same year, what had started out in 1857 as the Agricultural College of the State of Michigan, a public institution, became a land-grant school, now Michigan State University. By 1867, after the usual bruising competition among various schools and communities, Illinois established a new institution, now the University of Illinois at Urbana–Champaign. California accepted an offer in 1868 made by the debt-ridden College of California, a private school in Berkeley, of its buildings and 160 acres of land in return for a pledge to establish "a University of California" in its place.[16]

---

[14]Nathan M. Sorber, "Creating Colleges of Science, Industry, and National Advancement: The Origins of the New England Land-Grant Colleges," in *The Land-Grant Colleges and the Reshaping of American Higher Education*, ed. Roger L. Geiger and Nathan M. Sorber, *Perspectives on the History of Higher Education* 30 (2013):41–71.

[15]David C. Smith, *The First Century: A History of the University of Maine, 1865–1965* (Orono, Maine, 1979), pp. 1–40.

[16]James C. Carey, *Kansas State University: The Quest for Identity* (Lawrence, Kans., 1977), pp. 3–37; Madison Kuhn, *Michigan State: The First Hundred Years, 1855–1955* (East Lansing, Mich., 1955), pp. 1–81; Winton U. Solberg, *The University of Illinois, 1867–1894: An Intellectual*

As in Maine, gender swiftly emerged as an issue. Were women eligible to attend these schools? Could public land-grant schools legitimately exclude them? Year by year, state by state, the question elicited an answer, and then maybe a different answer. When classes began in 1874 at Purdue University, a new land-grant institution in Indiana, thirty-nine students were enrolled, a number that would have been larger except that the eight female applicants had all been rejected; but the following year, the school reversed its policy of exclusion and admitted women.[17]

Matters of race, too, inevitably came up. Cornell University, both a private institution and New York's land-grant school, opened its doors in 1868 without regard to race or gender. Legislation establishing the University of Illinois would have specified "white" had it passed in 1863, but by 1867 such restrictive language had vanished. More generally, schools across the Northeast and Midwest slowly demonstrated their willingness to accept black applicants. In degree, the schools' slowness was an artifact of the trickle of black applications to these small new schools from state populations with typically small black proportions; regardless, the schools grew in size, and so did their states' black populations. In 1877, to take an overwhelmingly white state, the University of Vermont graduated Virginia native and former slave George Washington Henderson, who was also elected to Phi Beta Kappa. Andrew Hilyer, born a slave in Georgia, graduated from the University of Minnesota in 1882. Probably the first black graduate of Ohio State University was Sherman Hamlin Guss, in 1892. Michigan Agricultural College's first known male and female black graduates were William O. Thompson in 1904 and Myrtle Craig in 1907.[18] Each was a pioneer, and each represented a

---

and Cultural History (Urbana, Ill., 1968), pp. 59–83; Verne A. Stadtman, *The University of California, 1868–1968* (New York, 1970), pp. 1–83, quote p. 31. See also Peter L. Moran and Roger W. Williams, "Saving the Land Grant for the Agricultural College of Pennsylvania," in Geiger and Sorber, *Land-Grant Colleges*, pp. 105–29.

17. Robert W. Topping, *A Century and Beyond: The History of Purdue University* (West Lafayette, Ind., 1989).

18. Morris Bishop, *A History of Cornell* (Ithaca, N.Y., 1962), pp. 1–179; Solberg, *University of Illinois*, p. 81; http://vermontcivilwar.org/units/8/henderson.php; Richard Melvin Breaux, "'We Must Fight Prejudice Even More Vigorously in the North': Black Higher Education in America's Heartland, 1900–1940," Ph.D. dissertation, University of Iowa, 2003, pp. 102–3; Pamela Pritchard, "The Negro Experience at the Ohio State University in the First Sixty-Five Years, 1873–1938: With Special Emphasis on Negroes in the College of Education," Ph.D. dissertation, Ohio State University, 1982, pp. 32–34; "The African American Presence at MSU, 1900–1970," http://www.archives.msu.edu/collections/african_presence.php.

beginning, a possibility to build on, though no straight-line measure of progress toward full racial inclusion actually emerged. The South displayed a different approach.

Eleven states were warring against the United States when the Morrill Act became law. Not until after Confederate defeat and political restoration could they qualify for land-grant funds, but by 1872 all of them had. Southern land-grant schools typically featured a greater emphasis on a military dimension of campus life than those elsewhere.[19] On gender and, especially, race, the South contrasted even more with the non-South. Yet in the challenges of settling on a location and launching the new institutions, the southern states more closely resembled the range of patterns displayed by states of the North and the West.

Tennessee, alone among the eleven states of the former Confederacy, ratified the Fourteenth Amendment without delay or compulsion. As a consequence, its members of Congress quickly gained readmission, and in early 1867 Congress approved Tennessee's obtaining its share of the land-grant funds. The same Republican leanings that permitted ratification and early readmission led to a legislative decision to put the land-grant funds to work in East Tennessee, the area of the state that had displayed strong Unionist attitudes and behavior among whites during the Civil War. By 1869, the Tennessee legislature had settled on an established school in Knoxville, East Tennessee University, as the state's sole land-grant institution. After Democrats returned to power in 1870, they tried but failed to undo that settlement, and in 1879 the school became the University of Tennessee. The Volunteer State subsequently fumbled through various resolutions to the question of where, if at all, black Tennesseans might benefit from the Morrill Act money.[20]

The Alabama legislature might have created a new land-grant unit as a wing of the University of Alabama, in Tuscaloosa, an outcome supported by both the board of education and the state university. But rivals called for it to go either to Auburn, in the southeast, where a struggling Methodist school, the East Alabama Male College, could supply appropriate real estate,

---

[19]Rod Andrew Jr., *Long Gray Lines: The Southern Military School Tradition, 1839–1915* (Chapel Hill, N.C., 2001).

[20]James Riley Montgomery, Stanley J. Folmsbee, and Lee Seifert Greene, *To Foster Knowledge: A History of the University of Tennessee, 1794–1970* (Knoxville, Tenn., 1984), pp. 65–86, 96, 101–5.

or to Florence, a North Alabama town that could offer another Methodist school, Florence Wesleyan University. Then a new town, Birmingham, stepped forward, with a generous promise of cash, a drill field, acreage for experimental farming, barracks for the cadets, and other buildings as well. Moreover, a black legislator, Holland Thompson, called for either space for black as well as white students wherever the new institution might end up or a division of the funds to support a black school too. In the end, the entire land-grant endowment went to Auburn, with nothing for black citizens. Florence, bridesmaid in the land-grant sweepstakes, received a new state teachers' institute for whites.[21]

In Virginia, loyal supporters of each of the two state-supported institutions of higher education, the University of Virginia and the Virginia Military Institute, canceled each other out, nor—in what one newspaper termed the "war of the colleges"—could any contender among a collection of private institutions secure sufficient legislative support. Instead, a former Methodist boys' academy, the Preston and Olin Institute, in the process at the time of seeking to emerge as a small college, gave up its single building on five acres as well as its name, and Montgomery County voters offered $20,000, so an improbable candidate from the western reaches of the state emerged with the land-grant designation for young white men, Virginia Agricultural and Mechanical College.[22]

Unlike Alabama and Tennessee, some former Confederate states arranged for black citizens to benefit in some fashion from the land-grant money. In Virginia, the same statute that gave two-thirds of the Morrill money to a new public white male school gave the other third to a coeducational private black institution, Hampton Normal and Agricultural Institute. In Georgia, the entire amount of money available under the Morrill Act, some $17,000, went to the University of Georgia. Into the 1880s, nonetheless, the legislature appropriated to Atlanta University the same amount, $8,000, that it gave the University of Georgia in state funds. That arrangement did not go uncontested through the vagaries of post–Civil War politics, but

[21]William Warren Rogers, "The Founding of Alabama's Land-Grant College at Auburn," *Alabama Review* 40 (1987):14–37.

[22]Duncan Lyle Kinnear, *The First 100 Years: A History of Virginia Polytechnic Institute and State University* (Blacksburg, Va., 1972), pp. 19–65, quote on p. 32; Clara B. Cox, "Olin and Preston Institute and Preston and Olin Institute: The Early Years of Virginia Polytechnic Institute and State University, Part II," *Smithfield Review* 20 (2016):1–26.

at one point early on whites conceded that there might be a "negro interest in the land scrip fund"; there was a perceived threat that one way for black Georgians to realize those benefits might be for the state university to "admit all students, regardless of color"; and white legislators could see real merit in finding a way to "finally settle this complicated trouble."[23]

The view from Mississippi—majority black and cash poor, but relatively free of physical destruction from the war—offers another perspective. In 1871 the Republican-controlled Mississippi legislature designated two land-grant schools—one for black students and one for whites. An established public school, the University of Mississippi—Ole Miss—received two-fifths of the state's land-grant funds. A new public school, the nation's first black land-grant college, Alcorn University, received the other three-fifths. At Ole Miss, no students showed up for the agricultural and mechanical program in 1872, a grand total of five students came in 1873, and then three the next year. The program disintegrated, and by 1876 the state was down to one land-grant site, the one for black Mississippians. In 1878 the legislature tried again, and the Agricultural and Mechanical College of the State of Mississippi, today's Mississippi State University, began classes in 1880.[24]

Having accepted the terms of the Morrill Act, every state embarked on an experiment to bring into being a college for which there often appeared limited demand and insufficient resources, but a college that served as a precursor, at least, to an institution that—especially after 1887—gained ever greater traction, resources, and significance.[25]

Elaborations, 1887–1938

In the years between 1887 and the New Deal, shifts in the nation's policy environment brought a series of transitions in the mission and operations of

[23]Robert F. Engs, *Freedom's First Generation: Black Hampton, Virginia, 1861–1890* (Philadelphia, 1979), pp. 139–60; Peter Wallenstein, *From Slave South to New South: Public Policy in Nineteenth-Century Georgia* (Chapel Hill, N.C., 1987), pp. 160–65, 167–68, quotes on p. 164.

[24]John K. Bettersworth, *People's University: The Centennial History of Mississippi State* (Jackson, Miss., 1980), pp. 1–30; David G. Sansing, *Making Haste Slowly: The Troubled History of Higher Education in Mississippi* (Jackson, Miss., 1990), pp. 55–68.

[25]See Eldon L. Johnson, "Misconceptions about Early Land-Grant Colleges," *Journal of Higher Education* 52 (1981):333–51.

the land-grant schools.[26] The Hatch Act of 1887, followed by the Second Morrill Act three years later, put the entire land-grant system on far sturdier financial footing than had been the case during its first quarter century. Assured of far more generous funding, a number of states redirected their efforts, and the land-grant colleges undertook a host of new initiatives. That the new funds were conditional on states' providing access to prospective black students, moreover, led to the emergence of a new group of institutions, the "colleges of 1890," in the segregated South. With each new step, as with the 1862 Morrill Act, Congress took up ideas already floating about and built on institutional beginnings in various states to promote an enhanced system throughout the nation.

A Changing Policy Environment

The land-grant institutions clearly had a teaching mission, but in many cases little to no research wing. For this deficiency, as it soon came to be viewed, a new leadership of the land-grant movement shepherded a remedy through congressional enactment. Chief among this new generation of leaders was George W. Atherton, president in the 1880s and 1890s of Pennsylvania State College. The Hatch Act of 1887 authorized experiment stations for every state and supplied substantial new funds to support their work in agricultural research.[27]

Three years later, Congress turned its attention to the land-grant colleges themselves. Enacted a generation after the initial 1862 legislation, the 1890 Morrill Act substantially increased the colleges' annual funds—by $15,000 per state for the first year, an amount to be increased by $1,000 each year for the next decade—and also their discretion as to how to deploy that money. Everyone won in the Second Morrill Act. It offered considerably higher funding for all states' land-grant institutions—but on the condition that black students, too, benefit from the money. In legislation that prefigured the "separate but equal" formula constitutionalized six years later in the Supreme Court's ruling in *Plessy v. Ferguson*, the two groups need not

[26]For a survey of these changes, see Willis Rudy, *Building America's Schools and Colleges: The Federal Contribution* (Cranbury, N.J., 2003).

[27]Rainsford, *Congress and Higher Education*, pp. 115–23; Williams, *Origins of Federal Support*, pp. 84–122; Henry C. Dethloff, *A Centennial History of Texas A&M University, 1876–1976* (College Station, Tex., 1975), pp. 218–26.

attend the same institution, provided the funds were "equitably divided" between "a college for white students" and an "institution for colored students."[28]

Southern white educators and politicians alike could support the measure because it conferred much greater financial support for their institutions while safeguarding those schools from any calls for desegregation, in fact clearly indicating that Congress had accepted black exclusion from those schools. Black southerners could support the measure because it would reinforce their claims on black access to higher education and in several states would supply institutions that had not previously existed. State legislators could determine that little or no additional money, drawn from state budgets, would supplement the federal money going to black schools. From a black perspective, "not much" was a lot more than "none at all." Across the twentieth century, seventeen states each supported a "college of 1890" (historically black land-grant institution) as well as a "college of 1862" (historically white land-grant school): the eleven states of the former Confederacy, plus the Border South states of Delaware, Maryland, West Virginia, Kentucky, Missouri, and Oklahoma.

Some of the colleges of 1890 were outright new institutions. Others were repurposed from earlier—as a rule, not much earlier—schools the state had set up. Georgia revived public support for black access to land-grant benefits; the Georgia State Industrial College, opened in 1891 to only black students taught by only black faculty, would receive both the $8,000 that Atlanta University had received for many years (in lieu of funds from the 1862 act) and one-third of the 1890 funds. Kentucky's State Normal School for Colored Persons, established shortly before the 1890 Morrill Act, suddenly received an infusion of new funds—14.5 percent of both the 1862 and the 1890 money. The white school did not lose any money when some of the 1862 fund was redirected to the black school, because the new money from the 1890 act far surpassed the loss of a portion of the old and, moreover, kept climbing every year through the following decade.[29]

---

[28]Rainsford, *Congress and Higher Education*, pp. 103–14; Williams, *Origins of Federal Support*, pp. 141–56; Joel Schor, *Agriculture in the Black Land-Grant System to 1930* (Tallahassee, Fla., 1982), pp. 165–71.

[29]Wallenstein, *From Slave South to New South*, pp. 168–69; Schor, *Agriculture in the Black Land-Grant System*, pp. 47–149; Leedell W. Neyland, *Historically Black Land-Grant Institutions and the Development of Agriculture and Home Economics, 1890–1990* (Tallahassee, Fla., 1990). See also Lester C. Lamon, "The Tennessee Agricultural and Industrial Normal School: Public

In North Carolina, black citizens had called for years, with little or no support from any whites, for a state-supported institution of higher education. Some argued to let black students attend with whites. Within weeks of enactment of the 1890 Morrill bill, Interior Secretary John W. Noble wrote North Carolina Governor Daniel G. Fowle inquiring about black access to an agricultural college in that state. Fowle conceded the current situation, declared his intention to request establishment of a black institution at the next legislative session, in early 1891, and put out his hand for the first year's $15,000 of the 1890 Morrill Act money. Fowle did make the promised recommendation, "for only this," he explained to legislators, "will entitle our State to her portion of the appropriation." The legislature did authorize the requisite black college, the Agricultural and Mechanical College for the Colored Race. The city of Greensboro soon secured the location with an offer of twenty-five acres and $15,000, and the new school opened in 1893. The carrot-and-stick of the 1890 Morrill Act made all the difference between black access to a public institution in that state and continuing to have none.[30]

By no means were new land-grant institutions for black students the only schools that the 1890 Morrill Act helped launch. The surge of new money spurred a number of states to redirect the land-grant designation and funds to new institutions. This was true in the Northeast with the establishment of state universities in Connecticut, Rhode Island, and New Hampshire, so the land-grant mission was moved from private institutions to incipient flagship universities. And it was true in the Southeast with the establishment of new colleges of 1862 in both North Carolina and South Carolina, where the land-grant operations were moved from flagship institutions to stand-alone land-grant schools, much as Mississippi had done earlier. Regardless, new funds meant new possibilities.[31]

Education for Black Tennesseans," *Tennessee Historical Quarterly* 32 (1973):42–58; William C. Hine, "South Carolina State College: A Legacy of Education and Public Service," *Agricultural History* 65 (1991):149–67; Larry Eugene Rivers and Canter Brown Jr., "'A Monument to the Progress of the Race': The Intellectual and Political Origins of the Florida Agricultural and Mechanical University, 1865–1887," *Florida Historical Quarterly* 85 (2006):1–41; John R. Wennersten and Ruth Ellen Wennersten, "Separate and Unequal: The Evolution of a Black Land Grant College in Maryland, 1890–1930," *Maryland Historical Magazine* 72 (1977):110–17.

[30]Frenise A. Logan, "The Movement in North Carolina to Establish a State Supported College for Negroes," *North Carolina Historical Review* 35 (1958):167–80.

[31]Nathan M. Sorber, "Farmers, Scientists, and Officers of Industry: The Formation and Reformation of Land-Grant Colleges in the Northeastern United States, 1862–1906,"

In a single year in the mid-1890s, the land-grant institutions absorbed totals of $505,630 from the 1862 act, $652,576 from the Hatch Act, and $891,389 from the 1890 act.[32] These figures indicate how crucial the new legislation was for enabling the land-grant institutions to perform their expanding functions—and why there was a return to jousting over where those funds should be directed.

Yet it soon became clear that the agricultural experiment stations needed additional resources. The intellectual capacity to conduct research was growing, as ever more frequently the typical station scientist had done graduate work at a land-grant college; yet into the twentieth century, the Hatch Act stipend remained constant at $15,000 per state. At the behest of some agricultural station leaders, Congressman Henry C. Adams of Wisconsin introduced a bill to double the annual stipend over the next five years. In return, each station was directed to propose specific research projects to the Department of Agriculture for approval, each with a research design and a cost estimate. The Adams Act of 1906 further entrenched the principle of federal funding, channeled through the experiment stations, for scientific research in general and agriculture in particular. The concept of a national science policy along these decentralized lines, building on this approach, eventually took on a more general and robust configuration. Later enhancements included the Purnell Act of 1925 and the Bankhead-Jones Act of 1935.[33]

In the 1910s, Congress fostered further enhancement of land-grant institutions, both black and white, by enacting additional laws, new mandates, new opportunities, and new missions. With the Smith-Lever Act of 1914, Congress created the cooperative extension service, according to which land-grant schools had a big new responsibility of seeing to it that the knowledge being taught—or even generated—at the home campus be extended

---

Ph.D. dissertation, Pennsylvania State University, 2011, pp. 192–250; Everett B. Sackett, *New Hampshire's University: The Story of a New England Land-Grant College* (Somersworth, N.H., 1974); David A. Lockmiller, *History of the North Carolina State College of Agriculture and Engineering of the University of North Carolina, 1889–1939* (Raleigh, 1939), pp. 19–42; Helene M. Riley, *Clemson University* (Charleston, S.C., 2002), pp. 2, 7–13. Scott M. Gelber, *The University and the People: Envisioning American Higher Education in an Era of Populist Revolt* (Madison, Wis., 2011), emphasizes developments during these years in Kansas, Nebraska, and North Carolina.

32 Williams, *Origins of Federal Support*, p. 155.

33 Ibid., pp. 174–78; Rainsford, *Congress and Higher Education*, pp. 123–27; Norwood Allen Kerr, *The Legacy: A Centennial History of the State Agricultural Experiment Stations, 1887–1987* (Columbia, Mo., 1987).

throughout society. People should benefit from the land-grant system regardless of whether they had ever set foot on a college campus, or whether they even knew such a school existed. The president of Virginia Polytechnic Institute (VPI) declared his wish "to make the state of Virginia the campus" for his school. The historian of Texas A&M observes that the Smith-Lever Act "had an even more profound effect" on land-grant schools than did the Hatch Act with its experiment stations.[34]

Three years later, the Smith-Hughes Act of 1917 promoted the training of teachers for vocational education in the emerging high schools: teachers of home economics for girls and agriculture for boys. Land-grant colleges contributed mightily to schooling the teachers who would undertake that teaching.[35]

During the New Deal years, the land-grant schools picked up a collection of new responsibilities and opportunities. The Agricultural Adjustment Administration depended on the extension agents scattered throughout most counties in the nation to implement the production controls and other features of New Deal agricultural policy. Massive funding from the Works Progress Administration and successor entities assisted with the construction of countless new administration and classroom buildings as well as residence halls and other structures at land-grant schools (as well as other campuses), from VPI to Louisiana State University. The National Youth Administration, created under an executive order by President Franklin D. Roosevelt, offered work-study opportunities that assisted many tens of thousands of students at land-grant institutions.[36]

Race and Gender in the Land-Grant Schools

The land-grant system in the South long featured distinctive regional variations on the national pattern, starting with the distinction between the

---

[34]Rainsford, *Congress and Higher Education*, pp. 127–29; Kinnear, *The First 100 Years*, p. 229; Dethloff, *Texas A&M University*, pp. 260 (quote), 382–403.

[35]Dethloff, *Texas A&M University*, pp. 131, 218; John Gadell, "Charles Allen Prosser: His Work in Vocational and General Education," Ph.D. dissertation, Washington University, 1972.

[36]Christopher P. Loss, *Between Citizens and the State: The Politics of American Higher Education in the 20th Century* (Princeton, N.J., 2012), pp. 53–87; Richard A. Reiman, *The New Deal and American Youth: Ideas and Ideals in a Depression Decade* (Athens, Ga., 1992). See also Hine, "South Carolina State College," pp. 157–58.

colleges of 1862 and the colleges of 1890. The South's historically white land-grant schools tended to combine three characteristics in a configuration that proved not only typically long-lasting in that region but ever more anomalous elsewhere: a greater emphasis than outside the South on a military regimen, a legislated mandate for racial segregation, and a rejection of coeducation.

White women found places in the land-grant system early on at most institutions outside the South. Even in institutions that inaugurated female enrollment at about the same time, experiences could vary widely. In 1890, in establishing the Oklahoma Agricultural and Mechanical College, the first Oklahoma territorial legislature provided for coeducation from the very beginning. Both "males and females shall be admitted to all the privileges" of the new school, the law declared, and at the institution's first session, in 1891, the twenty-three young women slightly outnumbered the twenty-two young men. Women's experiences at Oklahoma A&M often differed from men's—for example, whether they might represent their school in intercollegiate athletics—but the differences proved less stark than at many other schools, and a few women as well as men were hired for faculty positions.[37]

One scholar, having explored the early history of some Great Plains land-grant schools, has observed that, where men and women together entered newly founded institutions, women were perceived by their male classmates and teachers far less as intruders, far more as partners in a shared enterprise, with more or less equal proprietary claims on their school. The general adoption of coeducation moved apace, at least outside the white institutions of the South.[38]

With respect to gender, Oklahoma acted in a manner more consistent with its neighbors in the West than with its fellow segregated states. In Alabama, after two decades of operation, Auburn began admitting women as degree candidates in 1892. But the numbers remained very small—at least before the Smith-Lever Act in 1914 and especially the Smith-Hughes Act

---

[37]Pauline W. Kopecky, *A History of Equal Opportunity at Oklahoma State University* (Stillwater, Okla., 1990), pp. 21–31.

[38]Andrea G. Radke-Moss, *Bright Epoch: Women and Coeducation in the American West* (Lincoln, Neb., 2008), a study that emphasizes the land-grant institutions of Iowa, Nebraska, Utah, and Oregon between about 1870 and 1920. For another school open to women from the beginning, see Pouneh Moghadam Alcott, "Women at The Ohio State University in the First Four Decades, 1873–1912," Ph.D. dissertation, Ohio State University, 1979.

in 1917 inaugurated a home economics program, as well as possible career tracks for women graduates, and a women's dormitory came onstream in 1921.[39]

West Virginia University, located in Morgantown, in response to a package of resources that included the Woodburn Female Seminary, refused admission to graduates of that predecessor institution. Having opened its doors to male students in 1867, West Virginia University at last opened a door, at least a bit, for women as degree candidates in 1889. The first female graduate, Harriet Eliza Lyon, class of 1891, wrote years later that she had felt like "an alien and an intruder."[40]

Despite significant divergences, the South and the non-South were not all that different. Race is the best indicator of how these regions, the South and the rest of the nation, were not polar opposites. The South, however, was categorical in its exclusion of black students from white campuses, and not very good at supplying the second adjective in the phrase "separate but equal"; thus, black citizens often found themselves simply excluded from a range of opportunities.

Among African Americans associated with the land-grant system in the late nineteenth and early twentieth centuries, perhaps the most famous is George Washington Carver. He was born in Missouri in 1864 or 1865, his mother either still a slave or just recently having been emancipated. After growing up on farms or attending school in Missouri, Kansas, and Iowa, Carver began what turned out to be his life's work in the land-grant constellation when he enrolled in 1891 as Iowa Agricultural College's first black student. When he graduated three years later, he immediately became the school's first black graduate student and also its first black instructor of white students. Unlike most black graduates of land-grant schools outside the South, he could have stayed on at his alma mater. But before he earned his master's degree in 1896, Mississippi's black land-grant school offered him a faculty position, and then so did Tuskegee Institute's Booker T. Washington, newly famous after his 1895 Atlanta Speech. Alabama of

---

[39]Leah Rawls Atkins, *Blossoms amid the Deep Verdure: A Century of Women at Auburn* (Auburn, Ala., 1992).

[40]William T. Doherty Jr. and Festus P. Summers, *West Virginia University: Symbol of Unity in a Sectionalized State* (Morgantown, W.Va., 1982); Lillian J. Waugh and Judith G. Stitzel, "'Anything but Cordial': Coeducation and West Virginia University's Early Women," *West Virginia History* 49 (1990):68–80.

course had a black land-grant school too, the State Agricultural and Mechanical College for Negroes; but Washington managed to wrest the new black branch experiment station for Tuskegee Institute, at just about the time Carver chose to work at Tuskegee.[41]

Carver's relatively smooth acceptance at a predominantly white land-grant school should not be taken as representative, even outside the South, especially a generation after he attended Iowa State. In 1932, Doris Weaver sought equal admission into a capstone course in the home economics program at Ohio State University. The program required students to complete a laboratory course, Home Economics 627, which gave students "the responsibility of home-making under conditions approximating those of a modern home." In a special structure, students lived two to a room. Weaver, the only black senior in the program, had not named a roommate, and the school pointed out that it could not require someone of a different race to room with her. When her college arranged an alternative place for her to live during the same period, where she could satisfy all course requirements, she resorted to the Ohio judicial system as she sought admission on equal terms.

In the South, black citizens were simply barred from admission into white schools. Elsewhere, enrollment generally proved no particular obstacle, but discrimination within the institution did. Ohio State University officials used a local version of separate but equal to accommodate a black senior looking to complete the requirements for her degree. Drawing in large part on the separate-but-equal language of *Plessy v. Ferguson*, the Ohio Supreme Court saw no conflict with the Fourteenth Amendment.[42]

Nor was Ohio State by any means unique among northern land-grant institutions in setting barriers to full black participation in school operations and activities. Rather, Doris Weaver's experience was recapitulated across

[41]Mark D. Hersey, *My Work Is That of Conservation: An Environmental Biography of George Washington Carver* (Athens, Ga., 2011), pp. 17–48. If Carver had an opportunity to stay on at a predominantly white institution, more typical of the experiences of black graduates of northern land-grant schools during the half century after 1890 is George Washington Owens, Kansas State class of 1899. Owens went to work with Carver at Tuskegee and then, in 1908, moved to Virginia Normal and Industrial Institute to direct the agriculture program at what, in 1920, became Virginia's black land-grant school.

[42]*State ex. rel. Weaver v. Board of Trustees of Ohio State University*, 126 Ohio St. 290 (1933); Pritchard, "The Negro Experience at the Ohio State University," pp. 119–34; Tyran Kai Steward, "Time Not Ripe: Black Women's Quest for Citizenship and the Battle for Full Inclusion at Ohio State University," *Ohio History* 121 (2014):4–34.

the land-grant system (much as it was at flagship schools that were not also land-grant colleges). At some institutions, such impediments were long standing; at others, they proved innovations. At the University of Nebraska, on-campus residence facilities were closed to black students until around the end of World War II. At Cornell, where black women had long been allowed to live in the dorms, for some years beginning in the 1920s such was no longer the case.[43]

The legal scholar A. Leon Higginbotham Jr., in a magisterial book published in 1978 on race and the law, recounted an experience at Purdue in 1944. As a sixteen-year-old freshman, he, together with the eleven other black students, had to live off campus in the unheated attic of a house. One frigid winter morning he had had enough and made an appointment to speak to Purdue president Edward C. Elliott. He requested rooms for the twelve in a heated on-campus dormitory, even a segregated wing. The reply, as he recalled it all those years later: "Higginbotham, the law doesn't require us to let colored students in the dorm, and you either accept things as they are or leave the University immediately." The young man left Purdue for a more welcoming collegiate environment—and changed his career choice from engineering to law.[44]

At the University of Minnesota, black students found themselves excluded from both home economics and nursing, in part because both had residential requirements, and dormitories were unavailable to black students. In fact, at the University of Minnesota, Frances McHie and her supporters were preparing a court challenge to her exclusion from the nursing program until the institution relented, and she graduated in 1932. Yet it took a huge effort to line up political backers before Martha Murphy, daughter of the publisher of the *Baltimore Afro-American*, could gain entrance into the university's residence halls in 1938. Exclusion from housing—and therefore sometimes from programs of study—was widespread, discrimination blatant, albeit not quite as categorical or interminable as at white southern schools.[45]

---

[43]Breaux, "'We Must Fight Prejudice Even More Vigorously in the North,'" p. 181; "Early Black Women at Cornell: Part and Apart, 1890s–1930s," http://rmc.library.cornell.edu/earlyblackwomen/introduction/index.html.

[44]A. Leon Higginbotham Jr., *In the Matter of Color: Race and the American Legal Process—The Colonial Period* (New York, 1978), pp. vii–ix; http: //www.discoverlbj.org/item/oh-higginbothama-19761007-1-84-47.

[45]Breaux, "'We Must Fight Prejudice Even More Vigorously in the North,'" pp. 181–89.

Intercollegiate athletics provided another significant marker for calibrating black inclusion in the predominantly white land-grant schools of the North. Jesse Owens's time at Ohio State supplies a glimpse of black inclusion from the 1930s. Yet in basketball and football, to take two notable examples, though there were instances of black participation from the late nineteenth century on, the modern era of increasing black inclusion dates in general from the post–World War II years.[46]

Race and ethnicity appeared in various configurations across the land-grant system. Patterns of race in a black-white context were complex enough, but then there was the matter of people who, though typically classified as nonwhite, were also not black, and therefore might have access to institutions of higher education from which African Americans were barred. Oklahoma law expressly classified Native Americans as "white" unless they had some African ancestry, so, from early on, Oklahoma Indians attended Oklahoma State. Many land-grant institutions, whether in the South or not, including VPI, admitted Asians or Asian Americans in the 1920s or 1930s, although Chinese Mississippians did not begin enrolling at Mississippi State until the close of World War II.[47]

By the end of World War I, the two "best ideas" had each emerged in a form that went far beyond its origins in the 1860s. The national parks originated with the Yosemite Grant, forerunner of Yosemite National Park, in mid-1864—or during the Civil War albeit two years after the Land-Grant College Act—and of Yellowstone National Park, established in 1872. Many parks later, Congress created the National Park Service in 1916, or in between the two major new initiatives—the 1914 Smith-Lever Act and the 1917 Smith-Hughes Act—that propelled the growth of the land-grant system during the Progressive Era.[48]

---

[46]Ibid., pp. 271–316; William J. Baker, *Jesse Owens, An American Life* (1986; reprint ed., Urbana, Ill., 2006), pp. 33–53; Charles H. Martin, "The Color Line in Midwestern College Sports, 1890–1960," *Indiana Magazine of History* 98 (2002):85–112.

[47]Kopecky, *Equal Opportunity at Oklahoma State*, pp. 233–45; China Institute in America, *A Survey of Chinese Students in American Universities and Colleges in the Past One Hundred Years* (New York, 1954), esp. pp. 26–32, 40–50, 63; Peter Wallenstein, *Higher Education and the Civil Rights Movement: White Supremacy, Black Southerners, and College Campuses* (Gainesville, Fla., 2008), pp. 6–8, 16 n.13.

[48]Alfred Runte, *National Parks: The American Experience*, 4th ed. (Lanham, Md., 2010), pp. 95–96.

By the 1920s and 1930s, the land-grant institutions had long featured significant research functions, mostly of an applied kind related to mining and engineering and agriculture. And they had, for some years, set out to enhance rural life, to upgrade the reliable availability of inexpensive and nutritious food for urban as well as rural dwellers, and to promote the development of high school curricular offerings, whether as preparation for collegiate studies or as preparation to go out into the world as farmers and mechanics in the absence of a post–high school education.

By that time, the land-grant system had grown up. Although people might be categorically excluded from some institutions on account of their race or gender, all states had made some kind of provision for people of every race and both genders. The funds went much further than the nineteenth-century legislation had gone, whether dating from 1862, 1887, or 1890. And the modern triple mission of teaching, research, and service had clearly emerged.

Congressional initiatives, as they unfolded from one generation to the next, profoundly shaped the course of higher education in every state, from the foundational Morrill Act of 1862 on. When the United States entered World War II, the land-grant system had been evolving for nearly eight decades. The system's first quarter century, from 1862 to 1887, had brought some implementation of the Morrill Act, with mixed results: vibrant beginnings at some institutions, faltering at others, and restrictions often placed on white women or on any African Americans. Between the beginnings of the next phase in the system's development—the Hatch Act of 1887 and the Morrill Act of 1890—and the expansion of the New Deal years, the land-grant colleges had realized far greater growth in size of student populations, in curricular offerings, in constituencies accommodated, in research, and in outreach.

Yet the system in the 1920s or even the 1930s had reached only something of a halfway mark on the road to what it would become by the 1970s, especially in the South but also elsewhere. The quarter century after World War II brought tremendous additional change.

Convergences, 1938–72

During the quarter century after World War II, all of American higher education underwent various transformations, and the stand-alone land-grant schools in particular had relatively far to go to reach university status. Transitions took place in the varied sorts of land-grant institutions, as well as at the flagship universities that were not land-grant schools, such that by the 1970s they had very much converged.

Policy changes at the federal level were central to change on such varied fronts as race, gender, and research. At midcentury, the U.S. Supreme Court ruled in ways that made it ever more difficult for state segregation laws and practices to pass constitutional muster, at least with regard to higher education. In particular, black exclusion from graduate and professional programs came under fire when otherwise qualified black applicants were turned away on racial grounds and then filed suit, usually in federal court, to plead their case.[49] Moreover, the Court's 1954 and 1955 rulings in *Brown v. Board of Education* each spurred change, mostly in the Border South.[50] Race was only one of several main fronts on which change had to come before land-grant institutions could reach university status in terms of both a breadth of curricular offerings and an end to categorical exclusion from enrollment in those programs.

Time and again, Congress intervened to shape the course of higher education in general and of the land-grant schools in particular. Such interventions included the GI Bill of 1944, the National Defense Education Acts of 1958 and 1964, the Higher Education Facilities Act of 1963, the Civil Rights Act of 1964, the Higher Education Act of 1965, and Title IX in 1972. Federal dollars for research in the interests of national defense came during World War II and then all through the Cold War years, embodied most clearly in the National Science Foundation Act of 1950 and the 1958 National Defense Education Act.[51] The land-grant institutions played very

---

[49]Mark V. Tushnet, *Making Civil Rights Law: Thurgood Marshall and the Supreme Court, 1936–1961* (New York, 1994), pp. 126–49; Cheryl Elizabeth Brown Wattley, *A Step toward* Brown v. Board of Education: *Ada Lois Sipuel Fisher and Her Fight to End Segregation* (Norman, Okla., 2014); Gary M. LaVergne, *Before* Brown: *Heman Marion Sweatt, Thurgood Marshall, and the Long Road to Justice* (Austin, Tex., 2010).

[50]Wallenstein, *Higher Education and the Civil Rights Movement*, pp. 33–34.

[51]Edward Humes, *Over Here: How the G.I. Bill Transformed the American Dream* (Orlando, Fla., 2006); Wayne J. Urban, *More Than Science and Sputnik: The National Defense Education Act of 1958* (Tuscaloosa, Ala., 2010); Erinn McComb, "Taking Off: National Security, Identity, and Aerospace Engineering at Land-Grant Universities, 1957–1972," in Alan I. Marcus, ed., *Service as Mandate: How American Land-Grant Universities Shaped the Modern World, 1920–2015* (Tuscaloosa, Ala., 2015), pp. 192–215; Clay Risen, *The Bill of the Century: The Epic Battle for the Civil Rights Act* (New York, 2014); Andrew Fishel and Janice Pottker, *National Politics and Sex Discrimination in Education* (Lexington, Mass., 1977). For a comparison of the research

important roles in that research, and by the same token those research funds propelled the land-grant schools toward an even greater emphasis on research, whether pure or applied.

Other impulses for change, outside of the policy framework, came in the postwar baby boom, which reached higher education in the 1960s; in the postwar prosperity that directed ever-greater proportions of young people, young women as well as young men, toward college; and in the social and cultural shifts in the 1960s on both race and gender.

It serves here to distinguish once again several variants among the constellation of institutions of higher education discussed in this chapter. One model is the stand-alone colleges of 1862, such as Purdue University, Kansas State, Michigan State, Iowa State, and Utah State or—in the officially segregated states—the institutions that grew into Virginia Tech, Texas A&M, North Carolina State, Oklahoma State, Mississippi State, Auburn, and Clemson. Another is the category of institution that served both as land-grant institution and as the state's flagship public university, such as the Universities of Vermont, Maine, Illinois, Wisconsin, Minnesota, Nebraska, Idaho, and California—or Louisiana State University and the Universities of Delaware, Maryland, Kentucky, Missouri, Tennessee, Georgia, Florida, and Arkansas. Yet a third is the colleges of 1890 group, the historically black land-grant schools of the seventeen historically segregated states, including Langston University in Oklahoma, Lincoln University in Missouri, and the institutions that became Virginia State, South Carolina State, and Florida A&M.

The stand-alone state universities between the 1860s and the 1960s provided a model of a fairly broad curriculum, often including programs in law or medicine, though with highly variable entrance criteria as to race or gender. The University of Virginia, for example, long made no space available for students who were not both white and male. Absolute exclusion on the basis of gender began to recede in the 1920s, though complete access for female enrollment did not come until the 1970s. Categorical exclusion of African Americans from any curriculum whatever persisted into the 1950s—when it eased in law, medicine, and engineering—and still longer

---

profiles of "nonflagship land-grant" and other universities in the quarter century after World War II, see Hugh Davis Graham and Nancy Diamond, *The Rise of American Research Universities: Elites and Challengers in the Postwar Era* (Baltimore, 1997), pp. 1–12, 26–50, 79–83, 144–59.

for most programs. Yet by the 1970s the University of Virginia qualified for membership in the club of public research institutions that were, at the same time, comprehensive, coeducational, and nonsegregated. So the very institutions that exemplified the model in the 1970s—the model toward which all the different types of land-grant institutions were evolving—went through tremendous change themselves along every dimension during the century following the 1862 passage of the Morrill Act.[52]

The emergence of the 1970s model of American higher education can be vividly seen at Texas A&M University. Before the 1960s, none of the Aggies were African American, very few were female, and all entering male undergraduates had to participate in the Corps of Cadets. The curriculum itself continued to reflect the school's historical name, Texas Agricultural and Mechanical College. But in the single year 1963, the institution abandoned the hallmarks of both its restricted constituency and its narrow curriculum. Under the leadership of President James Earl Rudder, the school accepted its first black students that year and adopted a new model of coeducation as well, thus beginning the process of moving away from both types of exclusion. More than that—despite fervent resistance against what one opponent termed the "curriculum-broadeners"—Texas A&M attained university status that year. In one final big move away from the traditional model, in 1965 the newly designated Texas A&M University ended mandatory participation by male freshmen in the Corps of Cadets.[53]

So this stand-alone land-grant from the far western end of the former Confederacy depicted the dominant pattern in the South's quite-sudden and virtually simultaneous transition on race and gender as well as military organization at its colleges of 1862, not to mention the development of a comprehensive research university out of an agricultural and mechanical college. The institution's governing board declared the school in 1971 to be "a coeducational university admitting all qualified men and women to all academic studies on the same basis without regard to race, creed, color or national origin."[54] Thus it implied the school's extended range of "academic

---

[52]Peter Wallenstein, *Cradle of America: A History of Virginia*, 2nd ed., rev. (Lawrence, Kans., 2014), pp. 301–2, 307, 365–66, 402–3.

[53]Dethloff, *Texas A&M University*, pp. 555–79, quote p. 571; Wallenstein, *Higher Education and the Civil Rights Movement*, p. 45.

[54]Dethloff, *Texas A&M University*, p. 570.

studies" even as it expressly stated the newly inclusive criteria for joining those programs' constituencies.

At the stand-alone land-grant institutions outside the South, curricular changes of the sort that Texas A&M exhibited had to come about before those schools could begin to approximate what the flagship campuses, including those that shared a designation as their state's land-grant school, had long been developing. Kansas State University is a good example of such an institution. In the quarter century between 1950 and 1975, during the presidency of James A. McCain, Kansas State went a great distance toward shedding its traditional identity, or at least acquiring key characteristics of its flagship counterpart, the University of Kansas. The proportion of faculty with doctorates rose significantly, and the institution gained authority in 1956 to grant the bachelor of arts degree in the humanities and social sciences. In 1959, Kansas State College of Agriculture and Applied Science took on a new public identity as Kansas State University.[55]

Changes came along various paths. Curricular offerings at land-grant institutions in the segregated South could either spur or retard the beginnings of black enrollment at historically white schools, but either way black applicants for admission to white schools propelled the emergence of some portion of the new paradigm.

In 1935, when Lloyd Gaines graduated from Lincoln University, Missouri's black land-grant school, he applied for admission to the state's only law school, which was at the University of Missouri, an institution that combined the roles of flagship university and historically white land-grant school. Gaines was rejected on racial grounds. After the U.S. Supreme Court ruled in 1938 that Missouri had to provide him access to a law school curriculum, the legislature established a new law program at Lincoln, rather than permit his enrollment at the state university. A similar set of developments, spurred by black applicant Lucile Bluford, led to Lincoln University's establishment of a graduate program in journalism. But in 1950, three additional black applicants to the University of Missouri, among them prospective graduate student Gus T. Ridgel, went to court to gain entrance to

[55]Already, or finally, in 1949, football player Harold Robinson became the first African American to represent Kansas State in intercollegiate athletics. Carey, *Kansas State University*, pp. 181–85, 198–216, 259–62.

one program or another not available at Lincoln, and the judge in their case directed the university to admit them.[56]

Five black applicants in this one state had collectively changed both the curricular offerings at the black land-grant school and then the racial profile of students at the white school. Efforts in the late 1930s and the early 1950s had different outcomes, but each set brought some change. *Brown v. Board of Education* later in the 1950s spurred further change at the University of Missouri, as did congressional action in the 1960s.

In most states in the Deep South, no change whatever took place on the racial front at the colleges of 1862 before the 1960s, but even there the official response in Missouri to Lloyd Gaines had its counterparts at some colleges of 1890. A new law school at South Carolina State, established after S.C. State graduate John Howard Wrighten III applied in 1946 to the University of South Carolina to study law, supplies one example.[57]

A more comprehensive example unfolded in Florida, where five black citizens applied in 1949 to the University of Florida, each to a different program. Rather than open the state's college of 1862 to black enrollment, the legislature authorized new programs at Florida's college of 1890 and in fact upgraded and reincarnated the school as Florida Agricultural and Mechanical University. A particularly persistent candidate for admission, Virgil Hawkins, eventually won a court order that opened the law school at the University of Florida to its first black student in 1958. But the university still refused to enroll him (it raised the minimum test score to just above his) and instead admitted a few other black students into a variety of graduate or professional programs that year and the next.[58]

Missouri in 1938 and Florida after 1949 supplied one model for change—that is, change at the black land-grant school rather than the white one.

---

[56]Wallenstein, *Higher Education and the Civil Rights Movement*, pp. 22, 201–2, 266–69; James W. Endersby and William T. Horner, *Lloyd Gaines and the Fight to End Segregation* (Columbia, Mo., 2016).

[57]Another example was the creation of a new graduate program at S.C. State in education, similarly a response to Cleveland M. McQueen's application to the state university for such a program. Peter Wallenstein, "Higher Education and Civil Rights: South Carolina, 1860s–1960s," *History of Higher Education Annual* 23 (2003–4):1–22.

[58]Wallenstein, *Higher Education and the Civil Rights Movement*, pp. 41–43; Samuel Proctor and Wright Langley, *Gator History: A Pictorial History of the University of Florida* (Gainesville, Fla., 1986), pp. 47–48. Supplying an internal explanation for the change is Leedel W. Neyland and John W. Riley, *The History of Florida Agricultural and Mechanical University* (Gainesville, Fla., 1963), pp. 237–53.

But change might come at a state's white institution, in the way that Lloyd Gaines had sought, albeit without success, and that Gus Ridgel had actually achieved.

The "mechanical" component of the A&M curriculum provided an entering wedge for breaking up the categorical exclusion of black students from some of the segregated states' colleges of 1862. The first black undergraduates at the Border South's Universities of Maryland (Hiram Whittle), Delaware (Elbert C. Whisner), Kentucky (Holloway Fields), and Missouri (Elmer Bell Jr. and George Everett Horne), as well as at Oklahoma State (Dolphin Al Wharton Jr. and Glenn Bernarr Wharton), had applied for the engineering curriculum.[59]

So did the pioneer black students throughout the 1950s at Virginia Tech, never more than four at one time, beginning with Irving L. Peddrew III, whose admittance in 1953 reflected the unavailability of an engineering program at Virginia State. The story at VPI illustrates how simple change might compound. Peddrew never would have applied to VPI except that one of his high school teachers in Hampton told him she had heard that some white schools in Virginia (the University of Virginia and the College of William and Mary) had begun admitting black students. Hearing of Peddrew's enrollment, John Perry, a physics teacher at Booker T. Washington High School "across the water" in Norfolk, recruited three black seniors—Lindsay Cherry, Floyd Wilson, and Charlie Yates—to join Peddrew in the VPI engineering program.[60] Peddrew would be more likely to survive, Perry no doubt thought, if he had the companionship of fellow black students, and regardless of whether he left, the experiment must continue. And it did.

In view of the lack of a similar opportunity at their state's black land-grant school, in each of these states these pioneers had been admitted to the historically white institution in a manner consistent with the newly emerging constitutional understanding at midcentury of the old separate-but-equal formula. Segregation persisted, but at school after school one or more black students took their limited place on a campus that previously would have excluded them. On every such campus, under the new graduate and professional program exception, apartheid had been compromised, even for an occasional undergraduate.

[59]Wallenstein, *Higher Education and the Civil Rights Movement*, pp. 26, 28–30, 33, 266–68.
[60]Ibid., pp. 36–41.

Meanwhile, like the colleges of 1862, the colleges of 1890 moved toward university status. Florida A&M's trajectory from college to university was matched in degree in the other southern states. To take one example, Virginia Normal and Industrial Institute grew into the Virginia State College for Negroes, then Virginia State College, and eventually (in 1979) Virginia State University.

Despite the resistance to racial change in the historically white land-grant institutions of the South, without exception they were admitting black undergraduates by 1965.[61] Black persistence, court action, and congressional legislation had combined to push the process along. From the outer edges of the former Confederacy, both Texas A&M and VPI illustrated the partial yet significant transformation.

One man's pilgrimage through the land-grant circuit embodies the ways the system operated and how it was changing in fundamental ways in the third quarter of the twentieth century, both within the South and outside it, as—or soon after—the system turned one hundred years old. T. Marshall Hahn Jr. grew up in Lexington, Kentucky, where his father taught physics at the University of Kentucky. The junior Hahn raced through his undergraduate work there before heading off for a tour in the U.S. Navy at the end of World War II, after which he quickly completed his doctorate at another land-grant school, MIT. He returned to the University of Kentucky and taught physics there, looking, however, for a place where he might quickly advance. He found such a position in 1954 as department head in physics at yet another land-grant school, VPI. But seeking still a bigger pond to oversee, he moved in 1959 to Kansas, where that state's land-grant school was just that year becoming Kansas State University. Hahn served as dean of the College of Arts and Sciences.[62]

Recruited in 1962 to return to VPI, he served as president there for a dozen years. His tenure began just as the new College of Arts and Sciences was coming onstream—with bachelor's degrees and, soon, master's programs as well, in the social sciences and the humanities—and on the very cusp of congressional enactment of major legislation on both civil rights and

---

[61]For accounts of Clemson, Auburn, and Mississippi State, see ibid., pp. 17–20, 35–36, 209.

[62]Warren H. Strother and Peter Wallenstein, *From VPI to State University: President T. Marshall Hahn Jr. and the Transformation of Virginia Tech, 1962–1974* (Macon, Ga., 2004), pp. 5–14.

higher education. He cultivated state political leaders and the VPI board of visitors, appointed new deans, and lined up the other stakeholders whose cooperation he had to have. In addition to leading the way in redirecting the institution toward a greater emphasis on faculty research and a tremendous growth in graduate studies, his administration's major policy initiatives included adopting full coeducation (1964), making optional the participation by all male undergraduates in the Corps of Cadets (also 1964), and actually recruiting black undergraduates (young women as well as young men), with the promise of financial assistance, into any program of study (1966). In 1970 the school's name was changed to Virginia Polytechnic Institute and State University.[63]

From its new birth in 1872, VPI, the state's historically white land-grant institution, embodied a transformation that reached across the South and indeed the nation. And by 1966 it had been transformed into the state of Virginia's first institution to showcase all of these features, not just some: an arts-and-sciences curriculum, a commitment to research, and a wide range of graduate programs, *together with* active recruitment of undergraduates across lines of both race and gender.

The evolution, even transformation, of the land-grant schools—as well as the convergence of structures, functions, and identities—can be seen in the organizational changes in national associations representing the different types of schools. In the late nineteenth century, institutional leaders of higher education formed various associations to promote their common interests. In 1919, two such organizations—the Land-Grant College Engineering Association and the Association of American Agricultural Colleges and Experiment Stations—merged to form the American Association of Land-Grant Colleges, which itself underwent a name change in 1928 to the Association of Land-Grant Colleges and Universities. In 1954 (a few weeks before *Brown v. Board of Education*), the association's executive committee approved inviting the colleges of 1890 to become members (all but Lincoln University promptly accepted the invitation). That same year, looking toward an eventual merger with a counterpart association for non-land-grant universities, the group changed its name to the American Association of Land-Grant Colleges and State Universities. The merger itself took place in 1963 with the formation of the National Association of State Universities and

[63]Ibid., pp. 14–15, 45–92, 111–19, 151–70, 289–96, 310–11, 376–86.

Land-Grant Colleges. In 2009, the group took a new name, the Association of Public and Land-Grant Universities.[64]

A Democracy at Work in Higher Education

In the middle of a gigantic, consuming war, Congress passed, and the president signed, a peacetime kind of law that promised—or at least promoted—the establishment of a new kind of college in every state. America's "best idea" continued to develop across the next century and beyond. State politics and policies shaped local developments, as did institutional leadership and other groups and individuals, but the federal government—mostly Congress—intervened time and again to nudge the system ahead, often along new paths.

The land-grant colleges evolved across the hundred years between 1862/1872 and 1962/1972 into a complex, an American system of public higher education, that had nowhere been envisioned at the time the Civil War was raging, but that a wartime measure made possible as conditions changed, new impulses developed, and new leadership took hold: large, coeducational, multiracial, comprehensive research universities. The land-grant institutions did so in stages that can be seen as central tendencies, within regions or across regional boundaries: the first quarter century of tentative beginnings, down through around 1887; the launching of major new dimensions, by both race (most notably in the South) and function and funding (throughout the nation), between 1887 and World War II; and then a surge across all manner of dimensions into the 1970s.

This chapter has traced the tremendous long-term historical significance of the 1862 Morrill Land-Grant College Act—the origins of the measure, as well as its early post–Civil War reception, including the beginnings of three southern variations on the national pattern: a greater emphasis than outside the South on a military regimen, a legislated mandate for racial segregation, and a rejection of coeducation at the white land-grant schools. At greater length this chapter has explored how what typically began as

64Hugh Hawkins, *Banding Together: The Rise of National Associations in American Higher Education, 1887–1950* (Baltimore, 1992); Association of Land-Grant Colleges and Universities, 68th annual convention (November 1954), *Proceedings*, p. 86; "History of APLU," http://www.aplu.org/about-us/history-of-aplu/.

teaching institutions emphasizing engineering, agriculture, and the military, often with an entirely white male constituency, developed into public research universities, each with a comprehensive curriculum and a coeducational, multiracial, and largely (if not exclusively) civilian constituency.

Over half of the fifty states feature land-grant schools that are also their state's flagship school. Many of those combination universities—among them Maine, West Virginia, Tennessee, Minnesota, Nebraska, and California—had their origins in a state's putting the land-grant resources under the 1862 Morrill Act to effective use. Even when the two types of institutions have different identities and locations, the flagship school has come to look like the land-grant school as much as the other way around.

In one of the many ways that the land-grant institutions have proved significant, they came, by the closing decades of the twentieth century, to reflect American society in a far more robust and authentic manner than at any time before the Morrill Act's centenary in 1962. Moreover, work done at, by, and through the nation's land-grant institutions has increased agricultural productivity so much as to contribute mightily to feeding a rapidly growing human population, not only within the nation but around the globe. The work done in science and technology outside agriculture has been tremendously consequential as well. So, after a slower start, has the depth and breadth of research in the humanities and the social sciences.

But this chapter has emphasized the social laboratory of a democracy at work that the land-grant colleges inaugurated with one act of Congress in 1862. Across the years, from one generation to another, the "best idea" that started out as an ideal in embryo took its place in an institutionalized form as a reality crucial to higher education in every state in the nation.

Paul Finkelman

Military Conflict on the Minnesota Homefront

Lincoln's Humanitarian Concerns, Political Pressures, the Dakota Pardons, and the Future of U.S. Military Law

As the Civil war raged along the border between slavery and freedom, it was easy for Americans to forget that for most of American history, military activities had taken place on the frontier, usually between native populations and the ever-expanding white population. Even the War of 1812, which was ostensibly against Great Britain, had involved battles with Indians in the Mississippi, St. Lawrence, and Ohio valleys.[1] But the war to preserve the nation for the most part took the nation's eyes off the West. One major exception was the Dakota War in the late summer and early fall of 1862, which forced the Lincoln administration to shift some of its attention and resources to Minnesota, the scene of the most violent and bloody conflict between Indians and white settlers since the colonial period.[2] As

---

I initially wrote this chapter while I held the John Hope Franklin Chair in Legal History at Duke Law School and published an early version in the *William Mitchell Law Review*. I thank Daniel W. Stowell, the Papers of Abraham Lincoln; Shawn Rounds, the state archivist of Minnesota; the staff of the Minnesota Historical Society; and Jenny Bourne, Eric Carpenter, Jill Dupont, Amy S. Erickson, Tim A. Garrison, Meave E. Glass, Candace Gray, Alysa Landry, Karen Needles, H. Jefferson Powell, David Nichols, and Colette Routel for their perceptive readings of this chapter.

[1]See, for example, Robert V. Remini, *Andrew Jackson and His Indian Wars* (New York, 2001) for a discussion of the Creek War. On conflict in the Ohio Valley, see Roger L. Nichols, *Black Hawk and the Warrior's Path*, 2nd ed. (Chichester, UK, 2017).

[2]More Indians died in the Second Seminole War and the Red Stick Creek War, but these were essentially conflicts between the military and the Indians, rather than Indian–settler conflicts. The other exception in the Civil War was the Sand Creek

many as 600 or more white settlers, a few hundred soldiers, and somewhere between 100 (or less) and 300 Indians—almost all members of the Dakota nation (called Sioux at the time)—died in this conflict.[3] At the time, political and military leaders in Minnesota asserted that at least 1,000 whites died. While this number was an exaggeration, the fact that most white leaders believed the death toll was this high heightened emotions and increased demands for postwar punishments of the Dakota. Thus, after the war 300 or so Dakota would die, some through execution, but many more through harsh conditions in postconflict confinement.

As the conflict in Minnesota died down, General Henry Hastings Sibley (fig. 1) appointed a military commission that eventually tried 393 Indians for "crimes" connected to the conflict.[4] The trials began on September 28, 1862, and by November 5 the military commission had convicted 323 of the defendants. The speed of these trials was shocking. On the first day alone, sixteen men were tried, with ten being convicted and sentenced to death. This would have been one trial every thirty minutes, assuming eight full hours of hearing. As the trials wound down in November, the commission tried eighty-two men over two days.[5] Some of these trials must have lasted less than ten minutes. Some of the defendants spoke no English, and none

---

Massacre, which was shocking in its brutality, but did not involve nearly as many troops or as much time or have as great an impact on the national government.

[3]David A. Nichols, "The Other Civil War: Lincoln and the Indians," *Minnesota Historical Magazine* 44 (1974):2–15. Estimates of the dead vary from 400 to 800 (or more) white civilians and 200 or so soldiers. Philip Weeks, *Farewell My Nation: American Indians and the United States in the Nineteenth Century*, 3rd ed. (Chichester, UK, 2016), p. 132. Curtis A. Dahlin, *The Dakota Uprising: A Pictorial History* (Edina, Minn., 2009), p. 1 ("Estimates of the number of whites killed vary widely, with 600 being a conservative estimate"). Many sources estimate Dakota deaths at 300, although this may be too high. Carol Chomsky, citing a 1923 account of the events, puts the deaths at "77 American soldiers, 29 citizen-soldiers, approximately 358 settlers, and an estimated 29 Dakota soldiers." Carol Chomsky, "The United States–Dakota War Trials: A Study in Military Injustice," *Stanford Law Review* 43 (1990):13, 21–22. Chomsky also cites another source for fewer Dakota killed. I believe that Chomsky's figures, at least for the deaths of settlers, are far too modest.

[4]There is a large literature on the violence in Minnesota, but very little of it focuses on the trials, and even less on the pardons. The best work on the legal aspects of the trials is Chomsky, "The United States–Dakota War Trials," and Maeve Herbert, "Explaining the Sioux Military Commission of 1862," *Columbia Human Rights Law Review* 40 (2009):743, 780. On Dakota-white relations from the seventeenth century to the outbreak in 1862, see Gary Clayton Anderson, *Kinsmen of Another Kind: Dakota–White Relations in the Upper Mississippi Valley, 1650–1862* (St. Paul, Minn., 1984). See also David A. Nichols, *Lincoln and the Indians: Civil War Policy and Politics* (Columbia, Mo., 1978).

[5]Chomsky, "United States–Dakota War Trials," p. 25.

Fig. 1. Henry Hastings Sibley, 1862 photograph, Whitney's Gallery. *(Minnesota Historical Society)*

of them were afforded counsel. The commission sentenced 303 men to death and provided lesser punishments for twenty others who were convicted only of looting but were not involved in any combat or attacks on white settlers. Even before the trials were over, President Abraham Lincoln exercised his authority, and his obligation, under the Militia Act of 1862, ordering that no executions take place without his approval.[6] On November 7, Major General John H. Pope (fig. 2), the recently appointed commanding general of the brand new Department of the Northwest, sent Lincoln the list of those sentenced to death.[7]

Much to the shock of the military and civilian leaders in Minnesota, the president did not rubber-stamp these convictions and sentences. Instead, on November 10, Lincoln told General Pope to "forward as soon as possible the full and complete record of their convictions" and to "have a careful statement" indicating "the more guilty and influential of the culprits." After hearing of Lincoln's response, Minnesota Governor Alexander Ramsey (fig. 3) immediately expressed his "hope" that "the execution of every Sioux Indian condemned by the military court will be at once ordered." The governor warned the president that if all of the condemned Indians were not executed, "private revenge would . . . take place." Local sentiment clearly favored executions and perhaps vengeance on top of that, with one paper demanding "DEATH TO THE BARBARIANS."[8]

---

[6]"Act to Amend an Act Calling Forth the Militia to Execute the Laws of the Union, Suppress Insurrections, and Repel Invasions, Approved February Twenty-Eight, Seventeen Hundred and Ninety-Five and the Acts Amendatory Thereof, and for Other Purposes [Militia Act of 1862]," Act of July 17, 1862, 12 Stat. 597–598 (1862). Section 5 of the act provided that "no sentence of death, or imprisonment in the penitentiary, shall be carried into execution until the same shall have been approved by the President."

[7]Major General John Pope told General Henry Hastings Sibley, "The President directs that no executions be made without his sanction." Pope to Sibley, Oct. 17, 1862, quoted in Nichols, *Lincoln and the Indians*, p. 96; *Message of the President of the United States in Answer to A Resolution of the Senate of the 5th Instant in Relation to the Indian Barbarities in Minnesota*, Dec. 11, 1862, 37th Cong., 3d sess., Ex. Doc. 7, p. 1 (hereafter *Message of the President*); John Pope to Abraham Lincoln, Friday, Nov. 7, 1862 (telegram reporting the names of the 300 Sioux sentenced to death), Abraham Lincoln Papers at the Library of Congress (hereafter Lincoln Papers, LC). This collection is only available online, at http://memory.loc.gov/ammem/alhtml/malhome.html; Lincoln to Major General Pope, Nov. 10, 1862 (acknowledging receipt of the list of condemned men), in United States War Department et al., *The War of the Rebellion: A Compilation of the Official Records of the Union and Confederate Armies* (Washington, D.C., 1880–1901), ser. 1, vol. 13, p. 787 (hereafter *O.R.*).

[8]Lincoln to Major General Pope, Nov. 10, 1862; Alex. Ramsey to His Excellency Abraham Lincoln, Nov. 10, 1862; John Pope to His Excellency Abraham Lincoln, Nov. 11, 1862, all in *O.R.*, ser. 1, vol. 13, pp. 787–88; Stillwater *Messenger*, Nov. 11, 1862, quoted in

FIG. 2. "Portrait of Brig. Gen. John Pope, officer of the Federal Army (Maj. Gen. after Mar. 21, 1862)," Brady National Photographic Art Gallery (Washington, D.C.), ca. 1860–65. *(Library of Congress Prints and Photographs Division)*

FIG. 3. Alexander Ramsey in a photograph probably taken during his senatorial career (1863–75), Brady-Handy Photograph Collection. *(Library of Congress Prints and Photographs Division)*

On November 11, General Pope assured Lincoln he would send the trial records, but in fact they did not arrive until the end of the month. Perhaps Pope hoped that during this delay the president would let the matter drop

---

Chomsky, "The United States–Dakota War Trials," p. 29; see also Nichols, *Lincoln and the Indians*, pp. 101–11.

and allow the executions to move forward. Meanwhile, Pope lobbied Lincoln, assuring him that "the only distinction between the culprits is as to which of them murdered most people or violated most young girls. All of them are guilty of these things in more or less degree." Pope noted that in addition to the prisoners, he had in custody about "1,500 women and children and innocent old men prisoners"; and if the condemned Indians were not executed, there would be "an indiscriminate massacre" of those people. Pope said if civilians attacked the Indians in his custody, he did not believe he could control his own troops, who were "entirely new and raw, and are in full sympathy with the people on this subject."[9] It is hard to imagine how Lincoln reacted to General Pope's open admission of his incompetence to command the army under him. Pope had been sent to Minnesota after he had disgraced himself in the Second Battle of Bull Run, suffering about 15,000 casualties with nearly 1,800 men killed. Lincoln must have wondered, given Pope's admission in this letter, whether Pope was capable of any command.

Perhaps because he realized that confessing incompetence in commanding his troops was not productive for his military career, Pope sent the president a telegram, suggesting an alternative solution to the problem. He proposed that instead of the army executing the Sioux, "the Criminals be turned to the State Govt to be dealt with." In Pope's mind, this would take the onus off the president and resolve the issue. At the end of the month Governor Ramsey made a similar offer, telling the president, "If you prefer it turn them over to me & I will order their Execution."[10] Both the general and the governor were desperate to see the Indians executed. Neither understood that Lincoln's concerns for due process and fairness—and his discomfort with needless killing—would not be eliminated by substituting a state executioner for a federal hangman. Nor did either man apparently understand that Lincoln was not the kind of leader who would shift responsibility to someone else so that he would not have to make a distasteful decision.

Lincoln did not respond to the absurd idea of shifting the responsibility for the Dakota prisoners to Governor Ramsey and state authorities. Nor was

---

[9]*Message of the President*, p. 1; John Pope to His Excellency Abraham Lincoln, Nov. 11, 1862, in *O.R.*, ser. 1, vol. 13, p. 788.

[10]Telegraph from John Pope to Abraham Lincoln, Nov. 11, 1862, Lincoln Papers, LC; telegraph from Alexander Ramsey to The President, Nov. 28, 1862, Lincoln Papers, LC.

he impressed by the threats of vigilante violence against Indian women, children, and old men or pressures from Minnesota newspapers. Lincoln had seen so many newspaper attacks on him since he began his run for the presidency that he was likely unaffected by the wild harangues of Minnesota editors. However, he surely must have wondered why the major general he had appointed to command the newly created Department of the Northwest was incapable of preventing an unruly mob of civilians from attacking the Indians who were in his custody. He similarly might have wondered why Governor Ramsey was unable to prevent vigilante violence in his state. Ultimately, Lincoln would reprieve the overwhelming majority of the convicted Dakota, despite the pressure of his generals, the political leadership of the state, and the public press. Eventually all of those reprieved would go free,[11] and there would be no mob retaliation.

On December 26, 1862, the United States Army hanged thirty-eight Dakota men in Mankato, Minnesota, in the largest mass execution in American history (fig. 4). Many scholars and much of the general public focus on this horrific event. The event is made more horrific by the fact that many, perhaps most, of those executed were guilty of nothing that was recognizable as a war crime, and some had done nothing more than carry a weapon into battle. Furthermore, the trials themselves lacked any sense of due process or fairness. Modern scholarship has exposed that the trials of the Dakota were a horrendous miscarriage of justice that led to the hangings.

This chapter focuses on a narrow slice of those events: the decision by President Lincoln to prevent the execution of about 87 percent of those who were condemned to die. Lincoln's intervention and his decision to reprieve 265 Dakota—seven out of every eight who were condemned—constitute the largest mass clemency of people sentenced to death in American history.

---

[11]Technically Lincoln did not pardon any of the Dakota prisoners but merely refused to authorize their execution. However, at the time everyone understood that these were pardons, and contemporaries used that term in describing them. In reality, once the prisoners were reprieved, they were effectively pardoned and eventually released from custody. For use of the term "pardon," see, for example, a letter in which Judge Advocate General Joseph Holt told Lincoln that if he certified some of the convicted men to be executed, it was "merely an approval of the sentences, and a refusal to pardon." Joseph Holt to Abraham Lincoln, Dec. 1, 1862, in Lincoln Papers, LC.

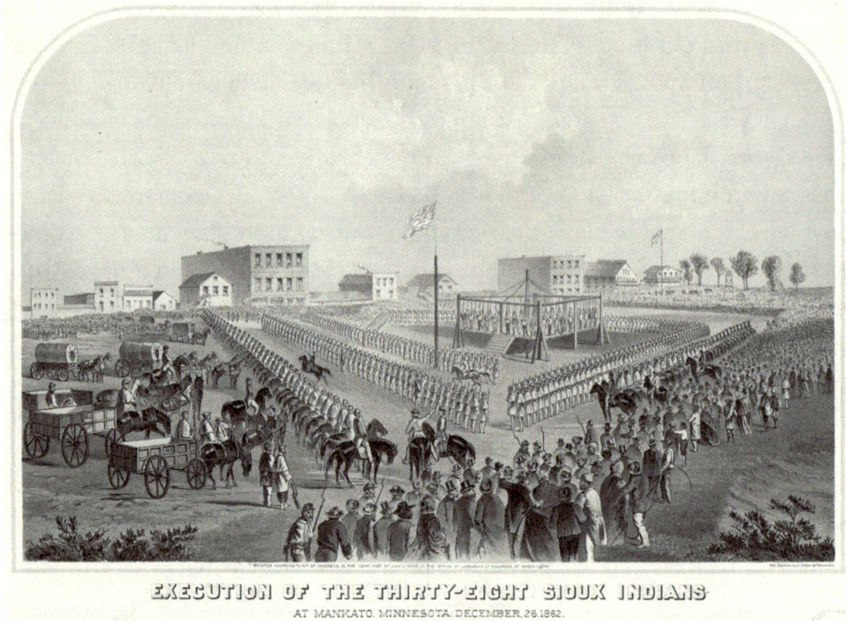

FIG. 4. "Execution of the Thirty-Eight Sioux Indians, at Mankato, Minnesota, December 26, 1862," color lithograph, Milwaukee Litho. & Engr. Co., 1883. *(Library of Congress Prints and Photographs Division)*

Political Considerations and the Pardon Issue

With the Civil War raging, Lincoln focused almost all of his attention on defeating the Confederacy and preserving the Union. With U.S. casualties already exceeding 100,000,[12] the fate of a few hundred Indians in Minnesota should not have been very significant to Lincoln. If anything, Lincoln had as much reason as the people in Minnesota to be furious at the

[12]Casualties refer to those killed, wounded, and missing. By the end of 1862 more than 15,500 U.S. soldiers had been killed in major battles (those in which the United States had more than 500 casualties), more than 69,000 U.S. soldiers had been wounded, and more than 52,000 were missing or captured. Tens of thousands of other soldiers had died or were incapacitated from disease related to the war. With high mortality rates from wounds and disease, many of those who had not died in battle would die later, as would many who were captured and sent to Confederate prison camps. A few thousand more soldiers had been killed or wounded in smaller engagements, including the battles in Minnesota. See Frederick Phisterer, *Statistical Record of the Armies of the United States* (New York, 1885), pp. 213–15.

Dakota who made war on the United States. They had been living peacefully in the state, they were reasonably well integrated into the society, and many of them knew and regularly interacted with whites. Thus, General Sibley asserted they were not "wild and ignorant savages" who could be excused for behavior that offended American law and culture.[13] Whatever their grievances, murderous attacks directed mostly at innocent civilians could hardly be justified.

The violence in Minnesota also threatened the larger security of the nation. The acts of the Dakota warriors forced Lincoln to devote troops, horses, arms, money, and time to pacify the frontier when he desperately needed these military assets for the ongoing war for the Union. In the end, the United States diverted only a few thousand troops to Minnesota, but when the violence began, Lincoln had no idea how many troops he would have to send there, and how long they would be there. Three days after the violence in Minnesota broke out, the United States suffered a humiliating defeat at the Second Battle of Bull Run. Lincoln faced a crisis in the military—as he searched for a new commander for the Army of the Potomac, to replace the disgraced Major General John H. Pope, who had been relieved because of his disastrous leadership at the Second Battle of Bull Run. The Indian conflict in Minnesota was an unanticipated complication for Lincoln that had the potential to divert huge resources from the war against the Confederacy.

The administration initially feared the events in Minnesota were part of a Confederate conspiracy to open up a new front on the western frontier.[14] Horace Greeley, the influential but not always accurate editor of the *New York Tribune*, published an unsigned editorial asserting that the Dakota were "stimulated if not bribed to plunder and slaughter their White neighbors" by agents "sent . . . by the Secessionists." Similarly, the *New York Times* reported that the "Indians are in league with the rebels."[15] While this proved not to be true, when the conflict began, the administration could not be certain

---

[13]Chomsky, "The United States–Dakota War Trials," pp. 91–92.

[14]The secretary of the interior made such claims in his report to Congress in December 1862. "Report of the Secretary of the Interior," in *Message of the President of the United States to the Two Houses of Congress at the Commencement of the Session of the Thirty-Seventh Congress*, Dec. 1, 1862, 37th Cong., 3d sess., Ex. Doc. 1, vol. 2, pp. 8–9.

[15]Gerald S. Henig, "A Neglected Cause of the Sioux Uprising," *Minnesota History* 45 (1976):109 (quoting the *New York Tribune*, Aug. 25, 1862, and the *New York Times*, Oct. 2, 1862, editorial titled "Are the Indians Allies of the Rebels?").

that this was not a Southern conspiracy. Even after the war in Minnesota was over, some people in the administration continued to believe it was part of a Confederate conspiracy that might break out again. On December 1, Secretary of the Interior Caleb Smith reported to Congress that "the chief cause" of the events in Minnesota "is to be found in the insurrection of the southern States."[16] Smith was certain that "southern emissaries"[17] had convinced the Dakota to go to war against the United States and the settlers. In retrospect, we know these claims were completely unfounded, but at the time some in the administration believed the events in Minnesota were part of a Confederate plot that harmed not just the people in Minnesota but the whole nation.

The violence in Minnesota also threatened Lincoln's larger goals for the nation. At the time of the outbreak Lincoln had written the Preliminary Emancipation Proclamation and was waiting for a decisive military victory to provide him with an opportunity to announce his plans for ending slavery in the Confederacy.[18] Shifting troops and resources to Minnesota could potentially have prevented Lincoln from winning a major battle that would allow him to announce emancipation. The events in Minnesota were not simply a distraction for the president: they threatened to derail—or at least delay—a major policy shift. For Lincoln, the outbreak of war on the Minnesota plains could hardly have come at a worse time. In the end the conflict in Minnesota did not require as many troops as Lincoln feared, and the administration needed only a few thousand troops to defeat the Dakota. But, shifting troops to the West, creating a whole new military district, and then focusing on the trials of the Dakota and their pending executions were distractions Lincoln could ill afford.

Lincoln also had strong political reasons for supporting the executions. On September 17, 1862, Lincoln issued the Preliminary Emancipation Proclamation. The war in Minnesota ended a week later. The trials in Minnesota began shortly after that. Just as the trials of the Dakota were winding

---

[16]"Report of the Secretary of the Interior."

[17]Ibid.

[18]Paul Finkelman, "Lincoln's Long Road to Freedom: How a Railroad Lawyer Became the Great Emancipator," in Paul Finkelman and Donald R. Kennon, eds., *Lincoln, Congress, and Emancipation* (Athens, Ohio, 2016), pp. 162–210; Paul Finkelman, "Lincoln, Emancipation, and the Limits of Constitutional Change," *Supreme Court Review* 2008 (2008):349, 361–62. See also Louis P. Masur, *Lincoln's Hundred Days: The Emancipation Proclamation and the War for the Union* (Cambridge, Mass., 2012).

down, Lincoln and his party had been badly bruised in the 1862 midterm elections, losing twenty-two House seats and holding control of the House of Representatives only with the help of a block of unionist Democrats. The Republicans lost control of state legislatures in Illinois and Indiana and the New York governorship. This backlash was caused by war weariness and the general weakness of the U.S. war effort in the East. Opposition to Lincoln's plans for emancipation, announced in late September, hurt the Republicans in some places, especially in the lower Midwest and among Irish Americans in New York City. Under these circumstances Lincoln could hardly afford to risk alienating voters in Minnesota, who at this time were overwhelmingly Republican. In Minnesota there was enormous popular support for executing all of the convicted Indians. In the calculus of good and evil, suffering and redemption, Lincoln might have easily concluded that the lives of a few hundred Indians—all of whom appeared to have made war on settlers—was a small cost to shore up support for saving the nation and reshaping the ongoing national conflict into a war for freedom and emancipation.

Yet, Lincoln rejected these obvious reasons for simply allowing the executions to go forward. Instead, he and his staff reviewed all of the convictions and concluded that many of the charges against the Dakota were exaggerated or bogus. As one historian has noted, "Early accounts of the uprising seized upon the occasional instances of torture and mutilation, exaggerated them, and conjured up a picture of wholesale atrocities unparalleled in the history of Indian warfare."[19] Minnesota Senator Morton S. Wilkinson and the state's members of the House detailed how the Indians had committed "fiendish brutality," murders in "cold blood," and gang rapes.[20] Lincoln politely replied to these three fellow Republicans that these "statements of fact" were "not found in the records of the trials."[21] Indeed, as the historian Roy Meyer notes, "[l]ike Falstaff's story of the men he battled . . . the closer these stories are scrutinized, the less foundation there seems to be for them."[22] Similarly, General Pope had told Lincoln, although

---

[19]Roy W. Meyer, *History of the Santee Sioux: United States Indian Policy on Trial* (Lincoln, Neb., 1967), p. 120.

[20]M. S. Wilkinson, Cyrus Aldrich, and Wm. Windom to The President of the United States, in *Message of the President*, pp. 2–4.

[21]*Message of the President*, p. 1.

[22]Meyer, *History of the Santee Sioux*, p. 120.

he knew better, that all of the men sentenced to death had murdered civilians and ravished women and girls "in more or less degree."[23] After his examination of the record, Lincoln discovered that the persistent assertions of rape and the slaughtering of women, children, and captives throughout the conflict and its aftermath were vastly overstated and mostly false. Lincoln concluded that only two of the condemned men had actually raped anyone,[24] although a number of other convicted men had killed civilians, including women and children. Ultimately, Lincoln refused to authorize the executions of 265 of the 303 men sentenced to die, effectively pardoning them.

On December 26, 1862, the army hanged thirty-eight Dakota men.[25] Some of those executed had in fact killed civilians needlessly, murdered captured prisoners, defiled dead bodies, and raped captured women and girls.[26] Under the rules of war at the time, the men who committed these acts were legitimately executed for what today we would call war crimes. However, the overwhelming majority of those sentenced to death, and many of those actually executed, were almost certainly innocent of such offenses. Despite the war crimes committed by some of those executed, the whole episode is rightly condemned as a barbaric blot on the nation. It is remembered as the largest mass execution in American history.

Given racial sensibilities in the nineteenth century and cultural hostility to Indians, we should probably not be surprised by the attempt to perpetrate this needless slaughter of Natives who were already incarcerated. The

---

[23]John Pope to His Excellency Abraham Lincoln, Nov. 11, 1862, in *O.R.*, ser. 1, vol. 13, p. 788.

[24]*Message of the President*, p. 1. Other Dakota may have been involved in rape and other barbarities, but either they were killed in battle or they escaped north with Little Crow, the leader of the Dakota during the conflict, and were not captured and tried at this time. Duane Schultz, *Over the Earth I Come: The Great Sioux Uprising of 1862* (New York, 1992), pp. 245, 249.

[25]H. H. Sibley to The President of the United States, Dec. 27, 1862, in *O.R.*, ser. 1, vol. 13, p. 880 ("I have the honor to inform you that the 38 Indians and half-breeds ordered by you for execution where hung yesterday at Mankato, at 10 a.m. Everything went off quietly, and the other prisoners are well secured.")

[26]At least one of those executed, a man named Chaskay, was clearly innocent; in fact, he had saved the lives of whites. Lincoln had attempted to reprieve him at the last minute, but another man with a similar name was reprieved instead. Meyer, *History of the Santee Sioux*, p. 130. This tragedy illustrates the arbitrary nature of the trials, the absurd rush to judgment by the military, the failure of the military to assess individual guilt, and the generally slipshod nature of the records of the trials.

303 death sentences were more vengeance than justice. The military and political leaders in Minnesota, as well as a majority of whites in the state, might very well have agreed with this analysis, but would have said that this vengeance was justified. As one "humble private citizen" wrote to Lincoln, "Not only does justice require the blood of these savages, but *vengeance will have it*," and if the Indians were not hanged, "[e]very man will become an Avenger."[27] Thus, the more interesting question is not why so many men were sentenced to die, or even why so many were executed, but why so many—seven times as many—were *not* executed. While we remember this as the largest mass execution in American history, it is worth considering why this was also the largest mass pardoning of condemned prisoners in American history. What was it about President Lincoln that led him to effectively pardon 87 percent of those who were sentenced to die?

What We Call the Conflict, and Why That Matters

Any discussion of the conflict in Minnesota in August and September 1862 is complicated by language, perception, and cultural values. Indeed, even what we call the conflict is contested. When the conflict began, the politicians and military leadership in Minnesota called it a war. But when the conflict was over it became known as the Great Sioux Uprising. Most modern scholars use the terms the "Dakota War" or the "U.S.–Dakota War." This takes the emphasis off the conflict as an uprising and implies that it was a war between two sovereignties.[28]

How we categorize the conflict affects how we see the trials. If it was an "uprising," then the Indian combatants were not "soldiers" but hooligans or criminals, a well-armed mob randomly causing violence and death. An uprising is a criminal act, perpetrated by malcontents who know they are acting illegally. Participants in an uprising are subject to trial and punishment. On the other hand, if it was a "war" between two sovereign nations,

[27]Thaddeus Williams to Abraham Lincoln, Nov. 22, 1862, Lincoln Papers, LC (emphasis added). Williams was a physician in St. Paul. His hysterical letter described numerous atrocities against settlers, including the beheading of prisoners, people nailed to trees, disemboweling of people, and other horrors that in fact had not taken place.

[28]For example, Minnesota History Center calls the conflict the U.S.–Dakota War. http://www.usdakotawar.org/.

then the captured Dakota soldiers should have been "treated as legitimate belligerents."[29] Once defeated, they were prisoners of war and not subject to criminal prosecution, unless they had actually committed war crimes.

None of these terms adequately describe the events of that fall. The vast majority of the Dakota in Minnesota did not take part in the conflict. "The Sioux were at no time united, at no time committed as a nation to the purposes of the hostile minority."[30] Most of the Dakota in Minnesota opposed resorting to violence on ethical grounds or practical reasons because they understood that a war with the United States was essentially suicidal. By this time, many Dakota had converted to Christianity, adopted Western dress and customs, become farmers, and were unwilling to return to their past lives. Most of the fighting was done by members of the lower Sioux, but "most of the principal chiefs of both the lower and upper Sioux, such as Wabasha, Wacouta, Traveling Hail (who had won the election for speaker), Red Iron, and Standing Buffalo, were opposed to the uprising and either took no part or joined very reluctantly in a few battles, meanwhile giving all the aid they safely could to white victims."[31] Because the Dakota Nation did not authorize the war and most leaders of the Dakota opposed it, it cannot exactly be seen as a war between two sovereignties. Thus, designations such as the Dakota War, or the U.S.–Dakota War might imply much greater support among the Dakota than there actually was.[32]

Nevertheless, the conflict had all the attributes of war, whether it was declared or not, and thus the term "war" seems far more accurate than "uprising." On the other hand, because the war involved only the Lower Sioux (and not even most of them) and was emphatically opposed by the Upper Sioux, the postwar response of the United States was clearly illegal and immoral. After the conflict was over, the military would punish all the Dakota in Minnesota, even those who had protected whites and did not join in the

---

[29]Chomsky, "The United States–Dakota War Trials," p. 15.

[30]Meyer, *History of the Santee Sioux*, p. 118.

[31]Ibid.

[32]An analogous naming issue can be seen in the "Red Stick War" of 1811, between the "Red Stick" Creeks and the United States. In that war the Lower Creeks, as well as the Choctaw and Cherokee, were allied with the United States against a separatist group of Creek known as the "Red Sticks." While earlier historians called this the Creek War, it is more properly called the Red Stick War or the Creek Civil War, recognizing that the Creek themselves were deeply divided in this conflict. For more information on the Red Stick War, see Remini, *Andrew Jackson and His Indian Wars.*

conflict. This is rightly condemned as punishing the group for actions of a small minority within the group, and more than that, punishing a large group—the Upper Sioux—who had absolutely nothing to do with the war. Oddly enough, because the United States punished the entire Dakota nation, it seems that the United States in fact recognized the right of the Dakota Nation "to make war."[33] Thus, trying the Dakota soldiers—and hanging thirty-eight of them—clearly violated the accepted law of war.

The army talked about it as a war and behaved accordingly *during* the war, but then immediately abandoned the law of war and accepted norms for the treatment of prisoners after the war. The events in Minnesota stood in marked contrast to the ongoing Civil War. In Minnesota, neither side followed accepted rules of behavior in a war. The Dakota killed mostly civilians and fought only a few engagements with the army. Similarly, as the conflict came to an end, the army rounded up thousands of noncombatants, including those who did not support the violence, and destroyed their crops and homes. There were three or four skirmishes between the Dakota warriors and the U.S. Army, and one decisive military engagement, the Battle of Wood Lake, on September 23, when somewhere between 700 and 1,200 Dakota were forced to retreat from a force led by Colonel Henry H. Sibley.[34] While a few hundred soldiers may have died in the war, most of the whites killed were civilians, including a significant number of women and children. These do not seem to be the statistics or the demographics of a traditional war. On the other hand, given the massive use of the army, and battles between combatants, it clearly was a war, and thus the United States was obligated to respond to the events according to existing rules of warfare.

After the war, the army violated almost every acceptable standard of behavior for the treatment of prisoners and civilians. Leaders in Minnesota, including General Pope, General Sibley, and Governor Ramsey, spoke of exterminating the Dakota, and while not actually embarking on a campaign of genocide, they hinted that this was their ultimate goal. Dakota civilians who had nothing to do with the conflict were rounded up, their crops were burned, their housing destroyed, and they were interned in camps that

---

[33] *Worcester v. Georgia*, 31 U.S. 515, 583 (1832) (McLean, J., concurring).

[34] Meyer, *History of the Santee Sioux*, pp. 115–23; Kenneth Carley, *The Sioux Uprising of 1862* (St. Paul, Minn., 1961), pp. 58–59.

were precursors of how the British would treat the Boers in South Africa a half century later.[35] Much of the behavior of the army after the war can be described only as racist vengeance perpetrated on innocent civilians who had taken no part in the conflict, and some of whom had provided shelter for fleeing white settlers. Meanwhile, in violation of the traditional rules of war, the military tried soldiers (including many who voluntarily surrendered to the army after the war was over) and, with no semblance of due process or even defense attorneys present, convicted the vast majority of them and sentenced them to death.

Alternatively, it might be more precise to call this Little Crow's War, after the Dakota chief who led the relatively small minority of the Dakota in their brief war.[36] Those Dakota who followed Little Crow (fig. 5) may have seen themselves as citizens of a sovereign nation fighting for their independence and defending their very existence against callous policies by agents of the U.S. government. They may have believed their actions were justified by desperate circumstances.

Whatever the terminology, there is yet one more way to analyze the events. The Dakota who fought against the army were involved in warfare, even if they represented only a minority of the Dakota Nation. Even if the technical rules of international law and conventional declarations of war were not present, the United States should have treated the Dakota soldiers as legitimate belligerents, just as it was treating Confederate soldiers, who fought an undeclared war for a putative nation that no other country in the world recognized as a legitimate sovereign state. The army never tried and hanged captured white Confederate soldiers merely for their participation in the War of the Rebellion. But the army applied different rules to Indians.

---

[35]The British used the term "concentration camp" for the facilities used to intern Afrikaan civilians during the Boer War. The camp at Pike Island, which held about 1,600 Dakota civilians, may in fact have been the world's first concentration camp. About 300 Dakota in this camp died from disease and malnutrition. Mark Joy, "U.S.–Dakota War of 1862," in Paul Finkelman and Tim Alan Garrison, eds., *Encyclopedia of United States Indian Policy and Law*, 2 vols. (Washington, D.C., 2009), 2:804.

[36]This would mirror the name of a handful of other wars between the United States and various Indian nations, such as Tecumseh's War (1811–13), Blacks Hawk's War (1832), Red Cloud's War (1866–68), Geronimo's War (1881–86), and the Posey War (1923), the last U.S.–Indian War.

FIG. 5. Little Crow, photographic print, ca. 1862. *(Library of Congress Prints and Photographs Division)*

What Caused the Conflict?

The Dakota who fought believed they had no choice, because their very existence was threatened by white settlers, Indian agents in Minnesota, and the policies of the national government. The initial cause was the delay in the annuity payments and the reality that the Dakota were facing starvation. As the Dakota leader Robert Hakewaste later recalled, "We were starving and in a desperate state of mind."[37] There were many underlying causes, including the corruption of the Indian agents and the often dishonest practices of the Indian traders, who persistently appeared to cheat the Indians out of much of their annuities. Beyond these economic issues were cultural conflicts. The Dakota who fought—mostly young men of the Mdewakanton band associated with Little Crow—felt squeezed by settlers and government policies, and they saw no future for themselves or their people. Dakota Chief Big Eagle (fig. 6), who opposed the violence, recalled that "the whites were always trying to make the Indians give up their life and live like white men," and this was something many Dakota had no interest in doing. Big Eagle thought the demands for change were coming too quickly and were accompanied by enormous white arrogance and racism.[38] These ongoing issues, combined with imminent starvation, the delay in annuity payments, and callousness on the part of the Indian agents and traders, led to the violence.

Under the treaties of 1851[39] and 1858[40] the Dakota had ceded most of southern Minnesota to the national government in exchange for annual "annuity payments" for fifty years. The Dakota were slowly transitioning to a

---

[37]Evidence for Defendants, *Sisseton & Wahpeton Bands v. United States*, 39 Ct. Cl. 172 (1904) (No. 22524), reprinted in Gary Clayton Anderson and Alan R. Woolworth, *Through Dakota Eyes: Narrative Accounts of the Minnesota Indian War of 1862* (St. Paul, Minn., 1988), p. 32. However, historian Gary Clayton Anderson argued that in mid-August the Dakota began to harvest what was the most abundant crop in memory, that they had an abundance of food, and that the serious food shortage that existed just a few weeks before no longer existed. Gary Clayton Anderson, "Myrick's Insult: A Fresh Look at Myth and Reality," *Minnesota History* 48 (1983):198, 200.

[38]Jerome Big Eagle, *A Sioux Story of War*, Collections of the Minnesota Historical Society 6, 1894, pp. 382–400, reprinted in Anderson and Woolworth, *Through Dakota Eyes*, p. 23.

[39]"Treaty with the Sioux" (Sisseton and Wahpeton Bands), July 23, 1851, 10 Stat. 949–51 (1855).

[40]"Treaty between the United States of America, and the Yancton Tribe of Sioux, or Dacota," Apr. 19, 1858, 11 Stat. 743–49 (1859).

Fig. 6. Waumacetanka (Big Eagle), carte de visite photograph by Simon & Shepherd, ca. 1863. *(Minnesota Historical Society)*

farming culture, and they lacked the land to survive by hunting and fishing.[41] They depended on the annuity payments for their very survival, but they were often cheated out of some of their money by corrupt Indian agents and Indian traders. In 1862, for instance, the Indian traders claimed half of the annuity for payment of goods previously given to the Dakota, even though some Dakota, such as Joseph Wabasha, had never agreed to this transfer of funds.[42] Although he opposed the violence, like many other Dakota, Wabasha believed he had been cheated out of his annuity by the Indian traders. He recalled that "the young men of the tribe . . . felt very angry" and "would not submit to having half of their annuity taken from them."[43] The conflict began in August 1862 at least in part because the annual payments "were months late in arriving."[44] Rumors were rife that they might never be paid because the federal government was bankrupt or because the Confederates had so disrupted the economy that there was no money to send.[45] There were also rumors that rather than being paid in gold, the Dakota annuities would be paid in newly printed greenbacks, which the Indian traders reportedly might not accept.[46] Gold coin had to be sent from Washington, but the Civil War impacted all government operations, including shipping gold west. The focus of the administration was on the ongoing War of the Rebellion. Transportation west was complicated by military requirements, and of course gold itself was more scarce than usual. Thus, the allotments the Dakota depended on for their very survival were very late. By late August they were desperately running out of food.[47]

The Upper Indian Agency at Yellow Medicine, fearful of violence from the Indians, and perhaps out of compassion for the Indians who faced starvation, began to distribute food in advance of the annuity payments. Officials at the Lower Agency at Redwood, however, lacked such foresight or

---

[41]Henig, "A Neglected Cause of the Sioux Uprising," p. 107.

[42]Anderson and Woolworth, *Through Dakota Eyes*, pp. 12–13.

[43]*Papers Relating to Talks and Councils Held with the Indians in Dakota and Montana Territories in the Years 1866–1869* (Washington, D.C., 1910), pp. 90–91, reprinted in Anderson and Woolworth, *Through Dakota Eyes*, p. 30.

[44]Ibid., p.13.

[45]Henig, "A Neglected Cause of the Sioux Uprising," p. 108.

[46]Meyer, *History of the Santee Sioux*, pp. 112–13; Chomsky, "The United States–Dakota War Trials," p. 17.

[47]Ironically, the gold for the annuities arrived in St. Paul on August 16 and arrived at Fort Ridgley on August 18, by which time the conflict had begun and a number of white settlers were dead. Meyer, *History of the Santee Sioux*, p. 113.

compassion. Even though the Lower Agency had plenty of food on hand to distribute to the Indians, the officials refused to allow the Dakota to purchase food on credit, in advance of the allotment. Some traders did not trust the Dakota to pay their debts, while others had absolutely no sympathy for the desperation of the Dakota. This attitude was famously expressed by an Indian trader named Andrew Myrick, who declared: "So far as I am concerned, if they are hungry, let them eat grass."[48] Little Crow's followers responded to this callousness with violence.

Frustrated and hungry, a few Dakota attacked a white farmstead near Acton, in Meeker County, on August 17, 1862, killing Robinson Jones, his wife, his adopted daughter, and two other white men.[49] Within a day the rebellion was in full force. Dakota swept through isolated farms and small towns. By mid-September large numbers of settlers—probably no fewer than 600 and perhaps as many as 800 to 1,000—had been killed, much of the town of New Ulm had been destroyed, and as many as 20,000 settlers in western Minnesota had fled to St. Paul.[50] These farmers, who were innocent of hostile acts toward the Dakota, lost their crops, which they had to abandon in the fields, and suffered enormous hardships. More than a hundred other settlers, the majority of them women and children, were captured by the Dakota. A few were murdered after capture, and some of the women may have been raped. The conflict was effectively over on September 23, when the Minnesota militia and federal troops defeated the Dakota at the Battle of Wood Lake. After the battle, hundreds of Dakota immediately surrendered, and most of the rest were quickly captured, although their leader, Little Crow, managed to escape into Canada.[51]

---

[48]Myrick was killed on the first day of the conflict, and grass was stuffed into his mouth. Curt Brown, "In the Footsteps of Little Crow: 150 Years after the U.S. Dakota War," *St. Paul Star Tribune*, Aug. 15, 2012. This quotation is found in almost every account of the conflict. Anderson's "Myrick's Insult" provides a history of the story of Myrick's insult and suggests that it may not have taken place or that it was not one of the precipitating events leading to the violence.

[49]Meyer, *History of the Santee Sioux*, p. 115.

[50]Hank H. Cox, *Lincoln and the Sioux Uprising of 1862* (Nashville, Tenn., 2005), pp. 103–4, describes the burning of much of New Ulm. See also various descriptions of the military conflict in Nichols, "The Other Civil War"; Dahlin, *The Dakota Uprising: A Pictorial History*, p. 1; Meyer, *History of the Santee Sioux*, p. 120; and Schultz, *Over the Earth I Come*, pp. 245, 249.

[51]In July 1863, Little Crow returned to Minnesota with his teenage son. While foraging for food he was shot and killed by a local farmer, Nathan Lamson, who received a $500 bounty for killing Little Crow and turning his scalp over to the state. Little Crow's son

The Politics of the Conflict

Almost immediately after the conflict began, Governor Alexander Ramsey appointed Henry Hastings Sibley to organize a defense of the state. Sibley had been the first governor of the state of Minnesota, and in 1862, and at the outbreak of violence, he was appointed a colonel in the state militia, making him the highest-ranking military officer in the state.[52] On August 21, Governor Ramsey telegraphed Secretary of War Edwin M. Stanton asking for help[53] while Minnesota's secretary of state asked Assistant Secretary of War Christopher P. Wolcott for authorization to raise a cavalry force of 1,000 men and to purchase a sufficient number of horses for them to ride into battle.[54] Five days later, Governor Ramsey begged Major General Henry W. Halleck, the general in chief of the army, to create a military district in the Northwest as a prelude to sending sufficient troops and leadership to fully crush the Indians in the region.[55] Halleck bluntly told the governor that the "War Department is not prepared at present to create a new military department in the West."[56]

But Halleck missed the political significance of this issue, which President Abraham Lincoln did not miss. Facing midterm elections, Lincoln doubtless saw creating a military department in Minnesota as politically useful even if it was not fully necessary to restore peace on the northwestern frontier. Governor Ramsey asked Lincoln to order the War Department to supply horses or mounted troops for the conflict, arguing that this "is not our war, it is a National War." There is some evidence that Lincoln and others in the administration initially may have agreed with Ramsey, believing, or at least fearing, that the Indian violence was the result of Confederate

(Wowinape, also known as Thomas Wowinape Wakeman) was captured and scheduled for execution, but this never happened. Ultimately he was released from custody, perhaps reflecting that even in Minnesota people lacked the stomach to execute a child for the "crimes" of his father. Wowinape later founded the first Sioux YMCA.

52. Kenneth Carley, "The Sioux Campaign of 1862: Sibley's Letters to His Wife," *Minnesota History* 38 (1962):99. By the end of September, Sibley had been promoted to brigadier general of volunteers within the regular army. Sibley would later be promoted to brevet major general and command the Department of the Northwest. Ibid., pp. 109, 114.

53. Alexander Ramsey to Hon. E. M. Stanton (by telegraph), Aug. 21, 1862, at 4:00 P.M., in *O.R.*, ser. 1, vol. 13, p. 590.

54. J. H. Baker to Hon. C. P. Wolcott, Aug. 21, 1862, in *O.R.*, ser. 1, vol. 13, pp. 590–91.

55. Alexander Ramsey to Major-General Henry Halleck (by telegraph), Aug. 26, 1862, at 2:00 P.M., in *O.R.*, ser. 1, vol. 13, p. 597.

56. H. W. Halleck to Governor Ramsey, Aug. 29, 1862, in *O.R.*, ser. 1, vol. 13, p. 605.

machinations, and thus a stronger military presence in Minnesota might be truly necessary for the safety of the nation. Minnesota's secretary of state told Assistant Secretary of War Wolcott that the Dakota violence was the result of a "deep-laid plan." This was actually not true, but the Lincoln administration could not know this at the time, and feared that Confederate agents were trying to start a wholesale Indian war in the West. Secretary of Interior Caleb B. Smith later claimed to have evidence that "southern emissaries" had encouraged the Dakota.[57] Thus, for both military and political reasons, Halleck was forced to do a quick about-face, and on September 6, Secretary of War Stanton ordered Major General John H. Pope to "proceed immediately" to St. Paul, where he was to assume command of the newly created Department of the Northwest and "take such prompt and vigorous measures as shall quell the hostilities and afford peace, security, and protection to the people against Indian hostilities."[58]

The decision to send Pope to Minnesota was curious, but perhaps predictable. Pope was a West Point graduate who had had some initial success in the West, defeating Sterling Price in Missouri and helping capture a key island in the Mississippi. He was then transferred to the East, where he suffered a humiliating defeat at the Second Battle of Bull Run just days after the outbreak of violence in Minnesota. His failure at Bull Run, combined with his almost insufferable arrogance, made it impossible to put him in combat against the Confederates. At the same time, Pope did have combat experience and logistical skills. The new department in the Northwest provided General Halleck with a place to send Pope while enhancing Lincoln's support in the West. Pope initially saw his removal to Minnesota as a demotion (which after Bull Run he should have expected), but quickly used the new post to lead an aggressive campaign against the Dakota that he doubtless hoped would lead to a new command in the *real* war against the Confederates.

Pope and Sibley quickly organized a defense of the state, and within a few weeks defeated the Dakota. The conflict was essentially over after the Battle of Wood Lake, on September 23. Hundreds of Dakota were soon

---

[57]Alexander Ramsey to Abraham Lincoln, Sept. 6, 1862, Lincoln Papers, LC; J. H. Baker to Hon. C. P. Wolcott, Aug. 21, 1862, in *O.R.*, ser. 1, vol. 13, pp. 590–91; Nichols, "The Other Civil War," p. 5; see also Nichols, *Lincoln and the Indians*, p. 78.

[58]Edwin M. Stanton to Major-General John Pope, Sept. 6, 1862, in *O.R.*, ser. 1, vol. 13, p. 617.

surrendering to the army, and those who had not participated in the conflict were coming forward with whites they had sheltered or rescued from other Dakota who had captured them. Sibley continued to pursue some Dakota into early October, rounding up Indians who had not been involved in the conflict. Indeed, the Indian population of Minnesota suffered more after peace was restored than during the conflict. On October 9, General Pope sent a dispatch to General Halleck stating that "[t]he Sioux war may be considered at an end."[59]

The Trials

Following the restoration of peace, the army tried 393 Indians for the "crime" of going to war with the United States. On October 3, Colonel Sibley, who by then was actually a brigadier general,[60] reported that a military tribunal was already at work "engaged in the trial of between 20 and 30 of the Indians . . . suspected of participating in the murders and outrages committed on the frontier."[61] Sibley admitted that 90 percent of the Indians in his custody "have not been actively engaged in the war," but he had to ferret out those who had. Sibley already assumed he would execute those found guilty, but would not order any executions until he could persuade all the Indians not in his custody to surrender. He understood that if they heard about death sentences "they might be deterred from returning." General Pope agreed with this strategy, telling General Halleck "it will be necessary to try and execute many of those engaged in the late horrible outrages, and also some of the Winnebagoes."[62]

---

[59]John Pope to Major General Halleck, Oct. 4, 1862, in *O.R.*, ser. 1, vol. 13, p. 709, noting that Sibley was still pursuing Indians and that he wanted to disarm the Winnebagoes, which Pope and Sibley incorrectly asserted had been "engaged in the recent outrages with the Sioux." See also H. H. Sibley to Maj. Gen. John Pope, Oct. 5, 1862, in *O.R.*, ser. 1, vol. 13, pp. 711–12, describing his attempts to capture all remaining Sioux, disarm them, and arrest "the men, except the older ones." John Pope to Maj. Gen. H. W. Halleck (by telegraph), Oct. 9, 1862, at 10:45 P.M., in *O.R.*, ser. 1, vol. 13, p. 722.

[60]Sibley did not find out about this promotion until October 7. See H. H. Sibley to Maj. Gen. John Pope, Oct. 7, 1862, in *O.R.*, ser. 1, vol. 13, p. 717. Technically he was brevet brigadier general until April 7, 1864, when Congress confirmed this promotion. Carley, "The Sioux Campaign of 1862," p. 109.

[61]Col. H. H. Sibley to Maj. Gen. John Pope, Oct. 3, 1862, in *O.R.*, ser. 1, vol. 13, p. 707.

[62]Ibid.; John Pope to Maj. Gen. H. W. Halleck (by telegraph), Oct. 7, 1862, at 1:30 P.M., in *O.R.*, ser. 1, vol. 13, p. 716.

These trials were swift and summary. The Dakota were not provided with counsel, as would have been done in a true court martial, and most of the trials were shams. Without counsel the defendants lacked any due process protections, since none of the Dakota had any experience with American legal procedure. Some of those prosecuted knew little or no English, but this did not deter the military from trying them without defense counsel. But even those who were fluent in English probably did not understand the proceedings or that they were even on trial for their lives. None of the defendants seemed to have had any idea of the legal right against self-incrimination. Indeed, many probably believed that honest answers would lead to fair treatment. This would have comported with Native American notions of justice and with the understanding of Indian soldiers operating in a traditional honor culture. Thus, many of the defendants admitted to something, such as firing a weapon, for example, or riding with Little Crow, the leader of the rebellion. However, they were not always given the opportunity to explain what they did—in effect to testify on their own behalf and explain their circumstances.[63]

These admissions were used to convict many defendants. Generals Pope and Sibley believed that *any* participation in the rebellion was enough to merit a conviction. This logic flew in the face of General Pope's own assertions to Lincoln after the trials: "[T]hat the only distinction between the culprits is as to which of them murdered most people or violated most young girls. All of them are guilty of these things in more or less degree."[64] In fact, Pope knew better. But it did not matter, because the military tribunal essentially operated on the assumption that any participation in the rebellion was an offense and that there was no meaningful distinction between those who committed what might be regarded as war crimes and those who were merely soldiers or fellow travelers in Little Crow's makeshift army.

In the next six weeks the army tried 393 men, convicting 323 and sentencing 303 to death. Many of these hearings—it would be too much to call them trials—lasted no more than five or ten minutes. On the first day alone, sixteen men were tried, with ten being convicted and sentenced to death. On November 3, forty-two men were tried,[65] and on November 5, the last

[63]Chomsky, "The United States–Dakota War Trials," pp. 52–53. See also Herbert, "Explaining the Sioux Military Commission," and Nichols, *Lincoln and the Indians*, p. 100.

[64]John Pope to Abraham Lincoln, Nov. 11, 1862, in *O.R.*, ser. 1, vol. 13, p. 788.

[65]Ibid., p. 27.

day of the proceedings, forty men were tried. Assuming an eight-hour day, with no pauses between hearings or recesses, this meant that each trial lasted an average of twelve minutes or less. The standard of guilt was quite simple: anyone who fired a rifle in any form of combat was considered guilty and subject to a death penalty.[66]

Sibley's motivations are not clear. Some scholars suggest that the trials were mostly an act of vengeance by a victorious army.[67] Surely there is an element of that. The soldiers under Sibley had just fought for a month, many of their comrades were dead or wounded, and revenge is a common human emotion. This level of vengeance was also present in the civilian community in Minnesota, as refugee settlers streamed into St. Paul and it became apparent that hundreds of white settlers had been killed. The civilian community was also inundated with stories (mostly untrue) of "outrages" committed against settler women and girls. All of this was enough to lead to calls for vengeance and executions.

But the trials and attempted executions went beyond mere vengeance. These procedures also dovetailed with Sibley's larger goal of removing or killing all the Dakota in Minnesota. Sibley, who had been one of the first white settlers in Minnesota and had served as the first governor of the state,[68] expressed the hope, from the very beginning of the conflict, that his forces would "overtake and kill a thousand or more of the savages . . . and drive the remainder across the Missouri [River] or to the devil."[69] He told his

---

[66]Nichols, *Lincoln and the Indians*, pp. 99–101; Chomsky, "The United States–Dakota War Trials," pp. 25, 27; Meyer, *History of the Santee Sioux*, p. 127; Herbert, "Explaining the Sioux Military Commission."

[67]See Nichols, *Lincoln and the Indians*, pp. 125–26.

[68]In the late 1830s and early 1840s, Sibley had been virtually, although not legally, married to an Indian woman, Red Blanket Woman, and fathered a child with her, Helen Hastings Sibley. This relationship, known as a marriage "a la façon du pays," lasted two or three years, and Sibley never denied his paternity of Helen. He paid for her education, helped support her, and gave her away at her wedding in 1859. Sibley later married Sarah Jane Steele, the daughter of a commanding general at Fort Snelling. Sarah Sibley apparently hated that her husband maintained a relationship with his half-Dakota daughter. It is difficult to know how this earlier relationship affected his views of Indians. It is possible that given his earlier relationship with the Dakota, Sibley felt he had to go to extra lengths to prove his bona fide hostility to the Dakota after the rebellion began. Jane Lamm Carroll, "Who Was Jane Lamont? Anglo-Dakota Daughters in Early Minnesota," *Minnesota History* 59 (2005):192–93.

[69]Henry H. Sibley, Colonel, Commanding Military Expedition, Minn. State Militia, to Sarah Sibley, Aug. 24, 1862, in "Extracts from General Sibley's Letters to his Wife, Written on the Indian Campaign" (R. J. Holcombe, ed., 1893), microform in Henry H.

wife, "My preparations are nearly completed to begin my work upon them with fire and sword, and my heart is hardened against them beyond any touch of mercy." He referred to them as "miserable hounds," "fiends," and "devils in human shape." On September 10 he vowed to "pursue" the "red devils" with "fire and sword."[70] As the conflict was coming to an end, Sibley asked General Pope to replace him with a "strictly military commander" who "would be better fitted" to "follow up the Indians vigorously and exterminate them."[71] The trials were a first step in Sibley's larger goal of exterminating the Dakota. Executing a large number of young men would clearly undermine and weaken the entire Dakota society.

Major General John H. Pope also supported the trials and executions because they dovetailed with his larger goals. Near the end of the Dakota War, Pope predicted that he had the firepower to "put a final stop to Indian troubles by exterminating or ruining all the Indians engaged in the late outbreak."[72] After the decisive Battle at Wood Lake, Pope told Sibley that "[n]o treaty must be made with the Sioux." Instead, Pope was determined to "utterly . . . exterminate the Sioux if I have the power to do so and even if it requires a campaign lasting the whole of next year." Calling the Sioux "wild beasts," he asserted they deserved "punishment beyond human power to inflict," and urged Sibley to "[d]estroy everything belonging to them."[73] During the trials, Pope wrote the secretary of war that he was "anxious to execute a number of them." Pope had destroyed the crops of not only the offending Dakota but also other Dakota who had not been involved in the combat and also the Winnebagoes, who had nothing to do with the conflict.[74]

When faced with the reality of the postconflict trials, Sibley vacillated between wanting swift punishment and having mild concerns about fairness. With over 250 prisoners in his care he admitted that "[s]ome of them are probably innocent" but believed "by far the greater part will be found guilty

Sibley Papers, Film M164, Reel 11 (Yale University), quoted in Herbert, "Explaining the Sioux Military Commission," p. 753.

[70]Sibley to his Wife, Aug. 24, 1862; Sibley to his Wife, Aug. 28, 1862; Sibley to his Wife, Sept. 10, 1862, all quoted in Carley, "The Sioux Campaign of 1862," pp. 99, 101, 102, 106.

[71]H. H. Sibley to General John Pope, Sept. 27, 1862, in *O.R.*, ser. 1, vol. 13, p. 680.

[72]John Pope to H. H. Sibley, Sept. 17, 1862, in *O.R.*, ser. 1, vol. 13, p. 649.

[73]John Pope to H. H. Sibley, Sept. 28, 1862, in *O.R.*, ser. 1, vol. 13, p. 686.

[74]Gideon Welles, *Diary of Gideon Welles: Secretary of the Navy under Lincoln and Johnson*, 2 vols. (Boston, 1911), 1:171.

of murder, rape, etc." This was a significant change from his assertion to General Pope just a week earlier that the vast majority of the captured Indians were innocent of any crime. At this point he was planning to send most of these captured men to Fort Snelling and regretted that he would "be deprived of the gratification of strangling the guilty ones." Two days later he told his wife that "the Indian prisoners are being tried as fast as a due regard for justice will permit. I have to review all the proceedings and decide the fate of each individual."[75]

As a young man, Sibley had read law under the tutelage of his father, Solomon Sibley, the first chief justice of the Michigan Territory. Henry Sibley was the first justice of the peace in the Minnesota Territory.[76] But, for all this legal background, Sibley clearly had no respect for due process or fair trials, as he reviewed trials that lasted a few minutes and sentenced men to death for noncapital offenses on the basis of virtually no evidence. His earlier legal training and his practical experience served him poorly in 1862 and again afterward when he tried to justify his actions.[77] At the beginning of the trials he did not bother to review the findings of his commission, telling General Pope that "the proceedings . . . may not be exactly in form in all the details," but he fully expected him to approve all the sentences and "hang the villains." Pope would have agreed. He had already told Sibley that he doubted it was possible to assess individual guilt and "discriminate between Indians who say they are and have been friendly, and those who have not."[78]

---

[75]Henry H. Sibley to his wife, Oct. 13, 1862, in Carley, "The Sioux Campaign of 1862," p. 110; H. H. Sibley to Maj. Gen. John Pope, Oct. 5, 1862, in *O.R.*, ser. 1, vol. 13, pp. 711–12 (noting that most of the Indians in his custody were not guilty of anything); Henry H. Sibley to his wife, Oct. 17, 1862, in Carley, "The Sioux Campaign of 1862," pp. 110–11.

[76]See Robert J. Sheran and Timothy J. Baland, "The Law, Courts, and Lawyers in the Frontier Days of Minnesota: An Informal Legal History of the Years 1835 to 1865," *William Mitchell Law Review* 2 (1976):6 n. 33.

[77]See Chomsky, "The United States–Dakota War Trials," p. 93 (arguing that Sibley's legal training led him to use military commissions to provide a semblance of due process); Herbert, "Explaining the Sioux Military Commission," pp. 794–97 (describing Sibley's postexecution justifications and his desire to bring new hearings and have new executions in March 1863).

[78]Henry H. Sibley, Brigadier General, to John H. Pope, Major General, Oct. 7, 1862, in *O.R.*, ser. 1, vol. 13, p. 717; John H. Pope, Major General, to Henry H. Sibley, Brigadier General, Oct. 2, 1862, quoted in Herbert, "Explaining the Sioux Military Commission," p. 774.

Sibley admitted to his wife that the "power of life and death is an awful thing to exercise," telling her "it makes me shudder" to "think [that] more than three hundred human beings are subject to that power." But, shudder or not, he was prepared to do his "duty" and make sure that "judgment [would be] visited upon the guilty."[79] By the end of the trials, Sibley had long abandoned any notion of due process. "A military commission," he told Bishop Henry Whipple, "is not expected to enter into details of a technical character" or function like "ordinary criminal tribunals" or even like "regular courts-martial."[80] This was certainly how Sibley set them in motion, with Pope's acquiescence. But this was not in fact how they were *supposed* to operate. In Missouri, the scene of the most violent guerilla warfare in the Civil War, the army declared that military commissions "should be . . . constituted in a similar manner and their proceedings be conducted according to the same general rules as courts-martial in order to prevent abuses that might otherwise arise."[81] Congress applied this logic to the entire nation in the Militia Act of 1862 by providing for the "same post-conviction review in both military commissions and courts-martial."[82]

Some scholars suggest that Sibley and Pope used the trials to "protect" the incarcerated Dakota from lynching by the local populace. Pope and Sibley made this argument, claiming that without the summary trials, mobs of civilians would have massacred many Dakota women, children, and old men in Sibley's custody. By this time more than 1,000 Indians were under military control. Trying and executing a sufficient number of combatants might have been enough to satisfy the bloodlust of most Minnesotans, as articulated by one newspaper's demand that the Indians be "exterminated."[83] Sibley and Pope may have believed this was what they were doing, but their arguments were transparently self-serving. The Indian noncombatants were

---

[79]Henry H. Sibley to his wife, Oct. 17, 1862, in Carley, "The Sioux Campaign of 1862," p. 111.

[80]Henry H. Sibley to Henry B. Whipple, Dec. 4, 1862, quoted in Herbert, "Explaining the Sioux Military Commission," p. 771.

[81]Gen. Orders No. 1, Headq. Dept. of the Missouri, Jan. 1, 1862, in *O.R.*, ser. 2, vol. 1, p. 248.

[82]Militia Act of 1862, Sec. 5–8, 12 Stat. 597–598; Louis Fisher, "Military Commissions: Problems of Authority and Practice," *Boston University International Law Journal* 24 (2006):15, 27 n. 97.

[83]Chomsky, "The United States–Dakota War Trials," pp. 93–94; Schultz, *Over the Earth I Come*, p. 243. See Meyer, *History of the Santee Sioux*, p. 124, for other examples of popular demands for "extermination" of the Dakota.

in custody only because Sibley had been so busy rounding them up and forcing them off their lands. Moreover, the military was surely powerful enough to protect the Dakota. That Sibley and Pope made these arguments illustrates their own vacillation over the fate of the Dakota. Both Sibley and Pope had been calling for the extermination, annihilation, or total removal of the Dakota. Yet, when faced with the reality of the slaughter of women, children, and old men, they stepped back. They may have wished for genocide, but they lacked the stomach for it.

Sibley complained that the newspapers thought he was too "tender hearted" and that the trials and executions were not moving fast enough. He insisted he would not "murder any man, even a savage, who is shown to be innocent of the 'great transgression,' or permit of the massacre of women and children."[84] But in fact he was pushing the trials along as fast as possible and showed little concern for due process, fairness, or actual guilt. Sibley may have been annoyed at pressure from newspapers or the civilian public, and he may have formally opposed killing native women and children, but he was still planning further military expeditions to force these women and children to leave Minnesota; and he had little regard for any fair investigation of the alleged "crimes" of their husbands, fathers, sons, and brothers, whom he was planning to execute as quickly as possible.

General Pope told Lincoln that vigilantes were preparing to massacre the Dakota. Governor Ramsey similarly warned Lincoln in a telegram that "[n]othing but the Speedy execution of the tried and convicted Sioux Indians will save us here from Scenes of outrage."[85] Civilians made two attempts to attack Indian prisoners in November, but the army easily prevented any significant violence, capturing some of the vigilantes and forcing them to march with the Indians to Mankato.[86] The fears of Pope and Ramsey were clearly exaggerated, and Lincoln did not take them at face value. He must have intuitively understood that both Pope and Ramsey were trying to force him to let the executions go forward. Clearly, the military had more than sufficient force to protect all Indian captives from

---

[84]Henry H. Sibley to his wife, Oct. 20, 1862, quoted in Carley, "The Sioux Campaign of 1862," p. 111.

[85]John H. Pope to Abraham Lincoln, Nov. 24, 1862, quoted in Nichols, "The Other Civil War," p. 10 n. 34; Alexander Ramsey, Governor, State of Minnesota, to Abraham Lincoln, President, United States of America, Nov. 28, 1862, Lincoln Papers, LC.

[86]Attacks by civilians on the Indian prisoners are described in Carley, "The Sioux Campaign of 1862," pp. 112–13.

vigilantes, and Pope, as a career officer, should have had the skill and backbone to make sure his soldiers did their duty.

Another reason for the trials, the demands for mass executions, and the incarceration of even friendly and cooperative Indians involved land and money. Final removal of the Indians would open more land to settlers and remove any fear of future violence.[87] Secretary of the Navy Gideon Welles believed that the vengeance against the Dakota was part of a larger plan to remove other Indians from the state. This was especially the case when it came to the arrest of non-Dakota. He noted that "the Winnebagoes have good land which white men want and mean to have."[88]

In reality there was no need for the trials. Once the Dakota had surrendered and were under military control they certainly posed no threat to the people of Minnesota. The conflict was over, and there was no chance it could resume, given the army's decisive victory and the overwhelming military force General Pope had in Minnesota. The threats from civilian vigilantes were exaggerated. The U.S. Army could surely have protected the Indians from a mob of angry farmers, and in fact it did so. Governor Ramsey's fear of "[s]cenes of outrage" was either an admission of his utter incompetence as a chief executive (which seems unlikely) or an exaggeration of the threats to pressure Lincoln to allow the executions to take place as quickly as possible. Ramsey was surely using the threats of violence to accomplish his real goal: highly popular vengeful executions. Indeed, after civilians attacked Indians under army guard, and were repulsed, Ramsey issued a public proclamation "to avert the disastrous consequences of a collision" between the people of Minnesota and the United States.[89] He urged all citizens to refrain from attacking U.S. troops or Indians in the custody of the troops, and there were no more outbreaks of vigilante violence.

The terminology for the events comes directly into play when we consider the motivations for the trials. Throughout the military campaigns against the Dakota, both Pope and Sibley referred to the "war" with the Dakota. Pope was a military man at war with the enemy. As such, he and Sibley should have known that trying prisoners—except for very specific war crimes—was not acceptable behavior. It was not a "crime" to go to war

[87]Meyer, *History of the Santee* Sioux, pp. 124–25.

[88]Welles, *Diary*, 1:171.

[89]Alexander Ramsey, "Proclamation to the People of Minnesota," Dec. 6, 1862, Lincoln Papers, LC.

against an enemy. Many Dakota were convicted of shooting at U.S. soldiers. This was surely not a crime under normal rules of war.

While Pope and Sibley did not understand their own hypocrisy, Secretary of the Navy Gideon Welles did. As Lincoln contemplated what to do with the convicted Dakota, he had to cope with letters from Pope and Sibley, editorials, and the demands of Minnesota's congressional delegation that the sentences be swiftly carried out against *all* the convicted Indians. Secretary Welles was especially annoyed by the behavior of Senator Morton S. Wilkinson and the state's two representatives. He wondered how these "Representatives of a State can deliberately besiege the Government to take the lives of these ignorant barbarians by wholesale, after they have surrendered themselves prisoners." He thought the aggressive and almost bloodthirsty "sentiments of the Representatives were but slightly removed from the barbarians whom they would execute."[90] The point was clear to Welles—if the Indians were soldiers who had surrendered, they could not then be executed for having been soldiers. It was a position President Lincoln would accept as well.

The Administration and the Dakota Trials

When President Lincoln received General Pope's list of condemned men, he immediately asked for the full records of the trials. Lincoln was a wartime president, and by the end of 1862 he was no longer shocked by the human cost of warfare. But he was also deeply troubled by unnecessary killing. Throughout his presidency he often commuted sentences of soldiers charged with desertion or other infractions. He understood that warfare cost lives, but he was also always reluctant to be the instrument of death for people already in custody who posed no threat to anyone. He reviewed about 1,600 court-martial cases and, much to the annoyance of his generals, issued pardons or commutations to almost all the enlisted men charged with desertion or most other military offenses. He also issued at least 331 clemency orders for civilians convicted in federal courts.[91]

---

[90]Welles, *Diary*, 1:186.

[91]"Pardons & Clemency," Mr. Lincoln's White House, http://www.mrlincolnswhitehouse.org/inside.asp?ID=226&subjectID=3. P. S. Ruckman Jr. and

Many of Lincoln's military and civilian pardons were clearly part of his own military strategy. His humane attitude toward the troops certainly increased morale. For example, Lincoln never signed a warrant for the execution of a common soldier convicted of falling asleep while on guard duty.[92] In 1864 he issued a wholesale pardon for "all deserters, who have been condemned by Court Martial to death." He later issued a wholesale pardon to all deserters who were not in custody if they would return to their units within two months of his proclamation.[93] Lincoln almost always asked himself the pertinent question whenever a military execution came up: "[W]hether this soldier can better serve the country dead than living."[94] While Lincoln almost never signed an execution warrant for soldiers charged with military infractions like desertion or sleeping on duty, and regularly pardoned deserters, he rarely commuted sentences for nonmilitary crimes, such as murder or rape. Lincoln famously issued pardons when lobbied by members of Congress, state politicians, and other "respectable" and "honorable" citizens. He was equally susceptible to the entreaties of mothers, wives, and sisters seeking to save a son, husband, or brother. Attorney General Edward Bates complained he was "unfit to be trusted with the pardoning power." However, it is also clear that Lincoln signed death warrants "only after he had examined the facts of each case and determined that the sentence was appropriate."[95]

Given this record of issuing pardons, it is perhaps not surprising that Lincoln wanted more information from General Pope before he was willing to authorize the executions of 303 men. Lincoln was troubled by a single execution, and so the thought of 303 at one time must have boggled his mind. He worried about blood on his hands from the shooting of a teenage deserter; he was surely concerned about the blood of more than 300 men.

David Kincaid, "Inside Lincoln's Clemency Decision Making," *Presidential Studies Quarterly* 29 (1999):84.

[92]Ruckman and Kincaid, "Inside Lincoln's Clemency Decision Making," pp. 84–85.

[93]E. D. Townsend, "Order Commuting Sentence of Deserters," General Orders No. 76, Feb. 26, 1864, in Roy P. Basler, ed., *The Collected Works of Abraham Lincoln*, 9 vols. (New Brunswick, N.J., 1953–55), 7:208 (hereafter *CW*); Abraham Lincoln, "Proclamation Offering Pardon to Deserters," Mar. 11, 1865, in *CW*, 8:349–50.

[94]"Pardons & Clemency"; *CW*, 8:349–50.

[95]Townsend, "Order Commuting Sentence of Deserters"; Lincoln, "Proclamation Offering Pardon to Deserters"; Ruckman and Kincaid, "Inside Lincoln's Clemency Decision Making," pp. 85, 88–90.

But these were captured enemies, not American soldiers who failed to fully do their duty. They were accused of barbaric treatment of civilians—Lincoln's own constituents—and they had also killed a substantial number of American soldiers before they were finally subdued. And they were Indians, not whites. Lincoln's relationship with Indians was complicated. His grandfather had been killed by Indians in Kentucky, and his only military experience—in which he never saw combat—was in Black Hawk's War.[96] As a lawyer in Illinois, Lincoln had had black clients, which helped him better understand the need for emancipation and a reduction in discriminatory laws. But in Illinois he had had very few, if any, interactions with Indians. They were truly foreign to him.

Politically, there was little advantage to issuing pardons. The Indians were not constituents. Lincoln could not score points with voters or soldiers by issuing pardons. Indeed, he would offend voters and soldiers in Minnesota and perhaps Wisconsin. Lincoln had received political pressure from the army, the civilian leadership in Minnesota, Senator Wilkinson, and the state's congressmen. Had Lincoln made a narrow and expedient political calculation, he would have approved all the executions and ordered General Pope to move swiftly to eliminate the problem of the Indian prisoners.

Instead, Lincoln remained consistent in his general opposition to executions and military trials, and insisted on reviewing every one of the trial records. The many military pardons Lincoln had already issued had convinced him that military trials were notoriously unfair and often without any meaningful due process. As a trial lawyer, the president was particularly sensitive to the unfairness of military trials. In addition, Lincoln and members of his cabinet were skeptical of the reports of many generals, who constantly wanted more troops and equipment, consistently overestimated Confederate troop strength, and then did not perform in battle. General Pope, who had just embarrassed the administration with his disastrous defeat at the Second Battle of Bull Run, had little credibility with the administration. His reports of Indian atrocities in Minnesota did not impress Secretary of the Navy Welles, who believed the tales of Indian "barbarities" were "greatly exaggerated."[97]

---

[96]Nichols, "The Other Civil War," p. 3.

[97]Welles, *Diary*, 1:186.

While the generals, politicians, and citizens from Minnesota pressed Lincoln to let the executions go forward, Lincoln also heard from a few people on the other side of the issue. There was a memorial from a group of Quakers in Pennsylvania, but that was to be expected. Most scholars who write about the pardon process assert that Bishop Henry B. Whipple (fig. 7), the head of the Episcopal Church in Minnesota, convinced Lincoln to pardon most of the convicted Dakota.[98]

How much influence Bishop Whipple had over Lincoln is uncertain. Scholars cite Whipple's autobiography, in which he describes his meeting with Lincoln while he was in the East to attend the Episcopal General Convention. At the meeting with Lincoln, Whipple discussed the corruption of the entire Indian Agency system, explaining how Indian agents, Indian traders, and others systematically cheated the Indians while lining their own pockets. Whipple claims in this book that Lincoln was "deeply moved" by their conversation, and that later Lincoln told someone that Whipple "talked to me about the rascality of the Indian business until I felt it in my boots."[99] However, this meeting took place in mid-September, before the conflict in Minnesota was over, and of course before any Dakota had been put on trial. Whipple was in Washington at about the time of the Battle of Antietam, where he preached to the First Minnesota Volunteer Regiment and met General George B. McClellan.[100]

Because this meeting took place before the conflict was over and before any Indians were being tried for crimes, Whipple could not have lobbied

---

[98]See speech of Senator Wilkinson, *Congressional Globe*, Dec. 5, 1862, 37th Cong., 3d sess., p. 13; see also Herbert, "Explaining the Sioux Military Commission," p. 780; Chomsky, "The United States–Dakota War Trials," p. 30; Nichols, "The Other Civil War," p. 9.

[99]Henry B. Whipple, *Lights and Shadows of a Long Episcopate* (New York, 1899), pp. 136–37. Many historians quote this story, but there is no source for it beyond Whipple's recollection. However, Whipple wrote about this in 1899, thirty-seven years after the events took place.

[100]Bishop Henry Whipple Diary, box 42, Whipple Papers, Minnesota History Center (hereafter WP/MHC). The Abraham Lincoln papers at the Library of Congress contain an undated calling card from Secretary of the Treasury Salmon P. Chase to Lincoln, introducing Lincoln to Bishop Whipple. Chase was active in the Episcopal Church and would have been a natural contact for Whipple. The library erroneously dates this calling card as "December 1862." This dating is incorrect since Whipple was in Minnesota at that time. The footnote to this document also erroneously claims Whipple talked to Lincoln about the Dakota prisoners at this time; however, this would have been impossible, because there were no prisoners yet and because the meeting would have taken place in September, not December.

Fig. 7. Bishop Henry Whipple, photograph by J. Russell & Sons, ca. 1860. *(Minnesota Historical Society)*

Lincoln to pardon anyone. His conversations probably touched on the cause of the conflict in Minnesota. But they were mostly about general Indian policies and the corruption of Indian agencies. This would have comported with a long letter Whipple sent Lincoln in March 1862 about the failures of

Indian policies and the dishonesty of Indian agents. In that letter he complained that Indian agents were "often men without any fitness, sometimes a disgrace to a Christian nation; whiskey-sellers, bar-room loungers, debauchers."[101] When Whipple met with Lincoln in September, with the conflict in Minnesota still raging, he probably continued to denounce the entire system of Indian agents. But, there is one oddity about this meeting with Lincoln: Whipple made no mention of meeting the president in his personal diary,[102] although he did record many of the people he met, including General McClellan, noted churches he preached at, and towns he visited. It seems incomprehensible that he would not have noted this meeting in his diary. Thus, his discussion of this meeting in his memoirs, published thirty-seven years later, makes one wonder whether the meeting actually took place. Moreover, in Whipple's memoirs he offers no source or explanation of how he heard that Lincoln said Whipple had made Lincoln feel the "rascality" of the Indian agencies in his "boots."[103] Whipple's discussions of the corruption of the Indian agency system would probably have affected Lincoln's views of the causes of the violence in Minnesota, but Whipple could not have been lobbying Lincoln for leniency before any trials took place.

After the trials Whipple lobbied Lincoln from a distance, but he was clearly ambivalent about what should happen to the convicted Dakota warriors. He wrote to Senator Henry M. Rice on November 12, asking him to deliver a letter to Lincoln on the proposed executions. He praised Rice as "the only public man who has at all times recognized the wickedness of our Indian system." He told Rice: "We cannot hang men by the hundreds." Whipple argued that the captured Indians were "prisoners of war" and that it would violate "our own premises" to hang them.[104] But it does not appear that this letter was directly about the executions and trials. On November 20, Senator Rice sent Lincoln a petition from eighteen Episcopal bishops and twenty or so other leaders of the church,[105] asking for a comprehensive reform of American Indian policy. The petition began with a reference to the

---

[101]Bishop Henry Whipple to The President of the United States, Mar. 6, 1862, in Whipple, *Lights and Shadows*, pp. 510–14.

[102]Bishop Henry Whipple Diary, box 42, WP/MHC.

[103]The lack of any mention in his diary or in any other source corroborating this meeting does not prove Bishop did not meet with the president, but it does weaken the case for it.

[104]There does not appear to be an actual copy of this letter in existence, only the cover letter Whipple sent Rice. Whipple to Rice, Nov. 12, 1862, box 40, letterbook 4, WP/MHC.

[105]Henry M. Rice to Abraham Lincoln, Nov. 20, 1862, Lincoln Papers, LC.

"recent Indian attack" but then immediately went to a discussion of needed reforms in Indian policies. Whatever Whipple and the other bishops thought about the executions, they wanted the tragedy to lead to significant reforms.[106] Rice delivered the petition to Lincoln, met with the president, and on November 27 reported back to Whipple that the president would advocate reform of the Indian agency system in his annual message to Congress. However, Rice did not indicate that he discussed the convictions of the Dakota soldiers with the president.[107]

A few days later Whipple reiterated his "demand" for "a reform" of the entire Indian agency system.[108] But then Whipple clarified his views on the trials and executions, which Rice had apparently misunderstood from Whipple's earlier objection to "hang[ing] men by hundreds."[109] Whipple flatly declared that when it came to the convicted Dakota soldiers he did not "desire to screen the guilty murderers." He objected to the irregularities in the commission's work and feared for the many innocent Dakota in federal custody because of the public "cry to exterminate every one who had a red skin." But "as a law abiding man" he was prepared to "bow to the supremacy of all decisions lawfully conducted." His only concern was whether the convicted Dakota had been given fair trials "such as to carefully scrutinize between the guilty and the innocent."[110] Thus, even the most committed friend of the Indians in Minnesota was, in the end, not troubled by executing some Dakota soldiers, even though he had initially argued that the captured Indians were "prisoners of war" and that it would violate "our own premises" to hang them.[111]

Whipple's concerns were mostly about the Indian system, and only tangentially about the condemned Dakota. On December 4, Whipple wrote Lincoln directly, thanking him for supporting a reform of the entire Indian

---

[106]Protestant Episcopal Church to Abraham Lincoln, Nov. 20, 1862, in Lincoln Papers, LC.

[107]Senator Henry M. Rice to Bishop Henry B. Whipple, Nov. 27, 1862, box 3, WP/MHC.

[108]Bishop Henry B. Whipple to Senator Henry M. Rice, Nov. 29, 1862, box 40, bk. 3, WP/MHC.

[109]Bishop Henry B. Whipple to Senator Henry M. Rice, Nov. 12, 1862, box 40, bk. 4, WP/MHC.

[110]Bishop Henry B. Whipple to Senator Henry M. Rice, Nov. 29, 1862, box 40, bk. 3, WP/MHC.

[111]Bishop Henry B. Whipple to Senator Henry M. Rice, Nov. 12, 1862, box 40, bk. 4, WP/MHC.

system, which was "a stupendous piece of wickedness." Whipple enclosed a "history of the causes of the late fearful massacre," but he did not urge Lincoln to pardon the Dakota.[112]

The petition from Whipple and the other Episcopal bishops surely had some impact on Lincoln's thinking. By this time Lincoln fully understood that the Indian agents and traders in Minnesota had been outrageous in their greed, incompetence, and callous indifference to Indian welfare. He also fully understood that many of those sentenced to die were innocent of any "outrages." Along this line, Lincoln received a letter from Stephen R. Riggs, a missionary and the chaplain to General Sibley's command. He noted that "among those condemned there are various grades of guilt from the men who butchered women and children to the men who simply followed with a party for the purpose of taking away spoils from the homes of settlers who fled." But Riggs also admitted that most of the convicted men "were condemned on general principles, without any specific charges proved." Riggs told Lincoln "there is room for the exercise of your *clemency*."[113] Riggs then suggested some specific men who should be pardoned.

The petitions of Whipple and the other clergymen, Senator Rice's conversations, and other communications condemning the trials doubtless affected Lincoln. He told Rice he would raise the issue of Indian reform in his annual message to Congress (the nineteenth-century equivalent of the State of the Union Address), which led Bishop Whipple to profusely praise and thank Lincoln.[114] But communications on the other side, including lobbying by Governor Ramsey, Senator Wilkinson, and General Pope, urging speedy execution of all the Dakota also must have weighed on Lincoln's mind.[115] Bishop Whipple, and to some extent Rev. Riggs, argued for justice

---

[112]Bishop Henry B. Whipple to Abraham Lincoln, Dec. 4, 1862, box 40, bk. 3, WP/MHC. The actual letter to Lincoln is found in Record Group 48: Records of the Office of the Secretary of the Interior, Entry 649: Records of the Indian Division, 1828–1907, General Records, 1838–1907, Letters Received, 1849–1880, National Archives College Park, College Park, Md.

[113]Stephen R. Riggs to Abraham Lincoln, Nov. 17, 1862, in Lincoln Papers, LC (emphasis in the original).

[114]Bishop Henry B. Whipple to Abraham Lincoln, Dec. 4, 1862 (see note 112 for full cite).

[115]M. S. Wilkinson, Cyrus Aldrich, and Wm. Windom to Abraham Lincoln, President of the U.S., in Staff of the Senate Committee on Indian Affairs, 37th Cong., *Message of the President*, pp. 2–4 (Comm. Print 1862). Morton S. Wilkinson was a U.S. senator from Minnesota, and Aldrich and Windom were the state's two House representatives. All three were Republicans.

and humanitarian concerns for the Dakota; Ramsey and others argued for justice for the dead settlers and for the good of the Republican Party in the state. Ultimately, however, the concerns of those in Minnesota were only part of the process that led Lincoln to pardon the overwhelming majority of the Dakota soldiers who were sentenced to death.

Francis Lieber, the Law of War, and the Dakota War

The Dakota trials and Lincoln's effective pardon of the vast majority of those sentenced to death must also be seen in the context of the emerging law of war within the administration. On April 24, 1863, the administration would promulgate General Orders 100, known since then as Lieber's Code.[116] This code, or even a draft of it, was not available to Lincoln in December 1862. Lieber (fig. 8) began the project just as Lincoln was dealing with the Dakota convictions, but did not have a draft of the code until February, and therefore had nothing to give the president before the pardons were issued.[117] However, Lieber influenced Lincoln in other ways.

After the First Battle of Bull Run, on July 21, 1861, the administration was uncertain what to do with captured Confederate prisoners. If secession was illegal, as Lincoln contended, then the Confederates were little more than brigands, or perhaps some form of land-based pirates, making war on the general populace, and might be sent to hard labor, imprisoned, or even summarily executed. Such a solution, however, would lead only to retaliation by the Confederacy against U.S. soldiers and encourage barbaric behavior on both sides. But if the captured Confederates were treated as soldiers in battle, Lincoln and Attorney General Edward Bates worried this would be a de facto recognition of the Confederacy as a legitimate nation.

[116]"Instructions for the Government of the Armies of the United States in the Field, Revised by a Board of Officers, General Order 100, April 24, 1863," in Daniel C. Gilman, ed., *The Miscellaneous Writings of Francis Lieber*, 2 vols. (Philadelphia, 1881), 2:245.

[117]Richard Shelly Hartigan, *Lieber's Code and the Law of War* (Chicago, 1983), pp. 13–14, 20. Paragraph 5, Special Orders No. 399, War Department, Adjutant General's Office, Washington D.C., Dec. 17, 1862, in *O.R.*, ser. 3, vol. 2, p. 951; see also John Fabian Witt, *Lincoln's Code: The Laws of War in American History* (New York, 2012), p. 3; Paul Finkelman, "Francis Lieber and the Modern Law of War," *University of Chicago Law Review* 80 (2013):2071–132.

Fig. 8. "Prof. Francis Lieber," ca. 1855–65, Brady-Handy Photograph Collection. *(Library of Congress Prints and Photographs Division)*

On August 19, 1861, Lieber published a letter to consider the nature of Confederate prisoners. He examined the treatment of captured Confederates—whether they were soldiers or pirates—and also how captured U.S. soldiers might be treated. In arguing that traditional rules of war should be applied to prisoners, he asserted that this was not a formal or diplomatic recognition of the Confederacy but was merely "the recognition of reality." Lieber offered an analogy that set the issue out clearly: "When a highway robber asks my purse, and I, being unarmed, consider it expedient to give it, I certainly recognize the robber, it is no more than recognition of a fact." For humanitarian reasons it was also important that Confederate prisoners be treated as legitimate belligerents under international law. This would not be a recognition of the Confederacy and would not even prevent a subsequent prosecution for treason. But it would be a practical solution to the problem, since both sides had captured each other's soldiers. Eventually Lieber's theory would lead to prisoner exchanges. In this letter Lieber noted, but dismissed, the idea of executing prisoners of war. Executing prisoners would in effect reduce the United States to the level of the Jacobins during the French Revolution, who "guillotined . . . the prisoners they made."[118] Lieber's point was clear: civilized, humane nations did not execute prisoners of war.

In a subsequent essay published in 1862, Lieber set out rules for dealing with guerrilla soldiers and other irregular forces. Here he argued that "guerrillamen, when captured in fair fight and open warfare, should be treated as the regular partisan is, until special crimes, such as murder, or the killing of prisoners, or the sacking of places, are proved upon them." Lieber argued that this was the precedent of "the most humane belligerents in recent times."[119]

These two theories were available to Lincoln when he considered the cases of the Dakota warriors. Lincoln acted on both theories. In reviewing the cases, Lincoln made a sharp distinction between Indian soldiers, who simply participated in combat, and those who raped, killed women and children, or killed prisoners. This last point would have been particularly important to a careful and logical attorney like Lincoln. If it was wrong (a war crime) for Indians to kill prisoners, then would it not have been equally wrong (equally a war crime) for the United States to execute prisoners?

[118]F[rancis] L[ieber], "The Disposal of Prisoners," *New York Times*, Aug. 19, 1861, p. 5.

[119]Francis Lieber, *Guerrilla Parties Considered with Reference to the Laws and Usages of War, Written at the Request of Major-General Henry W. Halleck* (1862), reprinted in Lieber, *Miscellaneous Writings of Francis Lieber*, vol. 2: *Contributions to Political Science* (Philadelphia, 1881), pp. 275, 290.

"I Could Not Afford to Hang Men for Votes"

In the end, Lincoln was pulled in many directions by the Dakota conflict. A humane chief executive, he was unable to even consider the mass hanging of hundreds of men.[120] The Civil War was bloody enough, and there was no end in sight. Lincoln had no stomach for what the generals and politicians in Minnesota wanted. From the moment he heard of the push for mass executions, he made it clear that he was skeptical about the idea.

Lincoln first heard about the possibility of mass executions in mid-October. On October 9 General Pope informed General Halleck that the "Sioux war may be considered at an end," but that the bloodletting was not over. Pope reported that he had 1,500 prisoners and that many of them were being "tried by military commission . . . and will be executed." He reported that he had seized "a number of Winnebagoes" and that he had "destroyed all the fields and property of the Sioux," even though most of the Sioux had not participated in the violence and the Winnebagoes had not been involved at all. He told Halleck he planned to renew his attacks on the Sioux in the spring and that "[t]he Indians are greatly terrified."[121] However we characterize the events of the fall of 1862—insurrection, war, or rebellion—Pope was planning to escalate the violence. For Pope, the mass execution of prisoners was the beginning of a process that can be described only as a war of genocide.

Secretary of War Edwin M. Stanton presented Pope's report to the cabinet on October 14. Secretary of the Navy Welles was "disgusted" with Pope's report, the "tone" of which was "discreditable." It was at this meeting that Welles noted that the Winnebagoes had "good land which white men want and mean to have."[122] Welles also observed that there was nothing in the reports to indicate *why* this violence had erupted, and he suspected—correctly—that the Indians in Minnesota had legitimate grievances.

We do not know what the rest of the cabinet thought about this, but Lincoln immediately informed the military authorities that there would be no hasty executions. A disappointed General Pope told General Sibley that

[120]Alexander Ramsey, Diary (Nov. 23, 1864), quoted in Nichols, *Lincoln and the Indians*, p. 118.

[121]Jno. Pope, Major Gen., to H. W. Halleck, Major Gen., Oct. 9, 1862, in *O.R.*, ser. 1, vol. 13, p. 722.

[122]Welles, *Diary*, 1:171.

"[t]he President directs that no executions be made without his sanction."[123] When the Dakota were sentenced, Pope dutifully sent Lincoln a list of those to be executed, and as we know, Lincoln immediately asked that all the records of the trials be forwarded to him.

Meanwhile, Lincoln was pressured to approve the executions. We have seen how Governor Ramsey, Senator Wilkinson, and Minnesota's congressmen urged the president to facilitate speedy executions. Even Chaplain Riggs, who urged Lincoln to exercise clemency, expressed "a great necessity . . . to execute the *great majority* of those who have been condemned by the Military Commission."[124]

The more moderate advice of Bishop Whipple and other clergymen reminded Lincoln of the corruption of the Indian system, the failure of the allotments to arrive, and the real threat of starvation among the Indians. Their desperate situation may not have justified killing civilians, but going to war with the United States was not totally unjustified. Lincoln also heard from William P. Dole, the commissioner of Indian Affairs, whom he sent to Minnesota. Dole communicated to Secretary of the Interior Caleb B. Smith,[125] who passed the letter on to Lincoln, "concurring in the humane views" of Dole.[126] In his letter, Dole condemned the "indiscriminate punishment of men who have laid down their arms and surrendered themselves as prisoners." He suggested that the trials and the planned executions were merely "revenge" rather than "the infliction of deserved punishment," and thus they were "contrary to the spirit of the age, and our character as a great, magnanimous and christian [*sic*] people." Dole urged Smith to pass his letter on to Lincoln to "prevent the consummation of an act which I cannot believe would be otherwise than a stain upon our national character, and source of future regret."[127]

In pardoning the vast majority of those condemned to death, Lincoln accepted the recommendation of his own Indian commissioner. It dovetailed with his own persistent opposition to needless killing and his lifelong commitment to due process of law. Lincoln was doubtless shocked by the lack of

[123]John Pope to Henry Sibley, Oct. 17, 1862, quoted in Nichols, *Lincoln and the Indians*, p. 96.

[124]Stephen R. Riggs to Abraham Lincoln, Nov. 17, 1862, Lincoln Papers, LC.

[125]William P. Dole to Caleb B. Smith, Nov. 10, 1862, Lincoln Papers, LC.

[126]Caleb B. Smith to Abraham Lincoln, Nov. 11, 1862, Lincoln Papers, LC.

[127]William P. Dole to Caleb B. Smith, Nov. 10, 1862, Lincoln Papers, LC.

specific evidence for many of those convicted, the lack of due process and respect for legal rules in the trials, and the apparent unwillingness of the military to even attempt to treat the prisoners individually and assess their guilt or innocence on an individual basis.[128] In the early stages of the trials, General Sibley had admitted that "the proceedings . . . may not be exactly in form in all the details."[129] But this lack of due process clearly did not bother him. Perhaps if only a handful of Dakota had been sentenced to death after such proceedings, as Confederate guerillas had been in Missouri,[130] Lincoln might not have been too concerned either. But Lincoln refused to approve the bloodbath that Sibley, Pope, and Ramsey wanted on the basis of such shoddy evidence and suspect proceedings.

Lincoln also understood that there was a significant difference between the war in Minnesota and the guerilla warfare in Missouri. Missouri guerillas fought secretly, without uniforms, and then after their attacks on soldiers and civilians melted back into their community to strike again.[131] But in Minnesota the Dakota War was over. Almost the entire Dakota nation was in military custody or had fled the state. There was no chance of a revival of hostilities, and there was no need to execute the Dakota to prevent them from resuming the conflict.

Lincoln's decision to review the proceedings and spare the lives of the overwhelming majority of those convicted also comported with the emerging views of the War Department on the role of law in military affairs. Lieber's arguments about prisoners of war and guerillas probably played into this. So too did the realization that the nature of the Civil War itself was changing. On July 17, Lincoln had signed two laws that allowed for the enlistment of black troops: the Second Confiscation Act and the Militia Act of 1862.[132] A week later, Secretary of War Stanton authorized General Rufus

---

[128]At least one of those who was eventually executed, a man named Chaskay, was clearly innocent, and was reprieved, but was nevertheless executed when a man with a similar name was reprieved. Meyer, *History of the Santee Sioux*, p. 130. This tragedy underscored the arbitrary nature of the trials and the inability or unwillingness of the military authorities in Minnesota to distinguish one prisoner from another.

[129]Henry H. Sibley to John H. Pope, Oct. 7, 1862, in *O.R.*, ser. 1, vol. 13, p. 717.

[130]Herbert, "Explaining the Sioux Military Commission," pp. 791–93 (discussing drumhead prosecutions and summary executions of guerillas in Missouri).

[131]Daniel E. Sutherland, *A Savage Conflict: The Decisive Roles of Guerrillas in the American Civil War* (Chapel Hill, N.C., 2009).

[132]Act of July 17, 1862, 12 Stat. 589, 592 (1862), secs. 11 and 12; Militia Act of 1862, secs. 12 and 13, 12 Stat. 599.

Saxton, who was based at Hilton Head, South Carolina, to begin to enlist black troops.[133] Now that the United States was enlisting and training black soldiers, Lincoln had to be even more concerned about the fate of captured prisoners. Confederates might soon seek to execute or enslave black soldiers they captured. This would turn the war into one of unmitigated barbarism as the United States would then have to retaliate by executing captured Confederates. These were real possibilities. Executing enemy soldiers—even Indian enemy soldiers—not only was immoral but also would set a dangerous precedent. If Lincoln allowed the execution of Indian soldiers on the grounds that the Indian attacks on the frontier were barbaric, then the Confederates could respond that from their perspective putting free blacks and former slaves in uniform and giving them guns was also barbaric. The military and civilian authorities in Minnesota wanted to execute the Dakota because they believed such executions would prevent future frontier warfare and thus save the lives of civilians and soldiers. But Lincoln's view from the White House was the opposite. Executing Indian prisoners of war would serve only to justify Confederate executions of black U.S. soldiers (and their white officers). Rather than saving lives, a mass execution in Minnesota could have cost lives in the larger Civil War that was more important to Lincoln.

On December 1, Lincoln asked Judge Advocate General Joseph Holt of the U.S. Army for advice on how to deal with the convicted men. He was clearly planning to pardon many of the Indians. He asked Holt "whether I should conclude to execute only a part of them, I must myself designate which, or could I leave the designation to some officer on the ground?"[134] Holt replied that day, telling the president he could not delegate his pardon power "and that the designation of the individuals, which its exercise involves, must necessarily be made by yourself." Holt said that he knew of no instance where any president had attempted "the delegation of this delicate and responsible trust." Holt then made the observation that was obvious to others in the administration, including Lincoln, that "[i]n view of the large amount of human life involved in these proceedings, [it would] be well—if this step has not already been taken—to submit them to the Attorney

[133]Edwin M. Stanton to Brigadier-General Saxton, Aug. 25, 1862, in *O.R.*, ser. 1, vol. 14, pp. 377–78.

[134]Abraham Lincoln to Joseph Holt, Dec. 1, 1862, in *CW*, 5:537–38.

General for the purpose of more satisfactorily determining the question of their regularity."[135] The point seems clear: the leaders of the army were concerned about the lack of due process, the rush to judgment, and the large amount of life at stake. In the midst of America's bloodiest war, even the leaders of the army were concerned about executing more than 300 men after trials that on their face were, at best, parodies of the legal process.

Lincoln, following his own humanitarian instincts and his lawyerly training, and backed by members of his cabinet, his commissioner of Indian Affairs, and the judge advocate general of the U.S. Army, moved to mitigate, as much as possible, the barbarism of hanging more than 300 men, especially when it was obvious that most of them were not guilty of any crimes. Thus, the president ordered his subordinates to divide the convicted Dakota into two groups: those "who were proven to have participated in *massacres*," which were "distinguished from participation in *battles*."[136] In doing so, Lincoln was forced to accept some of the findings of the military commission, even though he knew those hearings were deeply flawed and jurisprudentially scandalous. Carol Chomsky argues that Lincoln's "judgments" to allow any executions were "questionable" because all the trials were "flawed."[137] But this argument ignores the fact that some of those executed had openly bragged about killing civilians, and that some of the evidence for what amounted to war crimes was persuasive and compelling. Moreover, in the world of 1862, with the Civil War raging, with a miniscule staff, and with the issues of the real war constantly pressing him, Lincoln may have done as much as he could have done—and spent as much time as he could afford—to correct the miscarriage of justice that took place in Minnesota.

Furthermore, Lincoln tried to balance justice with military concerns, issues involving the ongoing War of the Rebellion, and fear of renewed violence in Minnesota. As he told the Senate, he was "[a]nxious to not act with so much clemency as to encourage another outbreak, on the one hand, nor with so much severity as to be real cruelty, on the other."[138] In the end, he spared seven out of every eight of the convicted men. In hindsight, he should have pardoned more and required new trials—fair trials—for anyone going

[135]Joseph Holt to Abraham Lincoln, Dec. 1, 1862, in Lincoln Papers, LC.

[136]*Message of the President*, pp. 1–2.

[137]Chomsky, "The United States–Dakota War Trials," p. 15.

[138]*Message of the President*, p. 1.

to the gallows.[139] Even if some of the Dakota were guilty of war crimes, such as murdering civilians or raping women, their crimes had not been proved in the military commission with its sham trials. Clearly, Lincoln and his advisers understood the many problems with the trials and the lack of due process. But the lack of due process for those who were executed was swallowed up by the complexities of the Civil War, the distance between Washington and St. Paul, and the myriad other demands on Lincoln's time and attention. In December 1862 he had other things on his mind—the ongoing campaign against the Confederacy and the implementation of the final Emancipation Proclamation on January 1, 1863. Thus, on December 6, he sent General Sibley a list of forty men who would be executed.[140] By the time of the executions this would be reduced to thirty-eight, as two more men were reprieved.

Lincoln expected there would be a huge political cost for this massive commutation. He may have allowed a certain amount of rough justice, and rough injustice, to settle the matter, but he fully understood that his massive commutation—which would effectively be a massive pardon—would probably not satisfy the demands for vengeance and mass executions in Minnesota. But, Lincoln was willing to accept these political costs because the alternative was to acquiesce in the executions of over 300 men, most of whom had not committed any recognizable crime.

Ultimately, the political cost was not as great as Lincoln had feared. Minnesota troops continued to fight bravely and gallantly against the Confederacy. The people of Minnesota remained mostly loyal to the Union cause. In 1864 Lincoln carried Minnesota by 7,000 votes. This was not as large as his 10,000-vote majority in 1860, and given that the state had a larger population by 1864, the decline in his margin of victory was even greater. He had carried 63.5 percent of the popular vote in 1860 but only 59.1 in 1864.[141] This decline was noticeable, but hardly a threat to Lincoln or his party's

---

[139]At least one Dakota scholar sees the executions as "a political decision in order to appease the angry and vengeful Minnesota citizens." Interview by Deborah Locke with Dr. Eldon Lawrence in New Ulm, Minn., Apr. 12, 2011 (transcript available at http://collections.mnhs.org/cms/web5/media.php?pdf=1&irn=10248274).

[140]Abraham Lincoln to Brigadier General H. H. Sibley, Dec. 6, 1862, in *CW*, 5:543.

[141]Center for the Study of Politics and Governance, "Minnesota Presidential Election Results, 1860–2008," Humphrey Institute of Public Affairs, pp. 8–9, http://lgi.umn.edu/centers/cspg/research/election_data_archive/pdf/MN_Presidential_Election_Results.pdf.

power in the state. After the results were in, Alexander Ramsey, who by then was a U.S. senator, told Lincoln "that if he had hung more Indians, we should have given him his old majority." It is difficult to know whether Ramsey was attempting to make a joke, or whether he was offering serious political advice. Lincoln replied with a more sober point that reflected his own legal and moral standards: "I could not afford to hang men for votes."[142]

---

[142]Diary of Alexander Ramsey, entry for Nov. 23, 1864, quoted in Nichols, *Lincoln and the Indians*, p. 118.

Jean H. Baker

Behind the Scenes

Abraham Lincoln's Life in the White House

MONDAY, MARCH 4, 1861, was the busiest and certainly the most important day in Abraham Lincoln's life. He awoke early, as was his habit, in the National Hotel, where the Lincoln family had been staying ever since their arrival in Washington ten days earlier. The president-elect then waited at the hotel until his predecessor, James Buchanan, escorted him to the still-domeless United States Capitol for the official ceremony. The two men rode stiffly side-by-side in the open carriage. At some point along Pennsylvania Avenue the sixty-nine-year-old Buchanan turned to Lincoln and acknowledged that if Lincoln was as happy entering the White House as Buchanan was leaving it, then the new president was indeed a happy man.[1]

On the East Front portico of the Capitol, Lincoln delivered his wistful inaugural address, closing with words of reconciliation and poetic expression that fell on deaf ears in the South: "We are not enemies but friends. We must not be enemies. Though passion may have strained, it must not break our bonds of affection. The mystic chords of memory, stretching from every battlefield, and patriot grave, to every living hearth stone, all over this broad land, will yet swell the chorus of the Union, when again touched as surely they will be by the better angels of our nature."[2]

---

[1]Jean H. Baker, *James Buchanan* (New York, 2004), p. 140.

[2]"First Inaugural Address of Abraham Lincoln," Monday, Mar. 4, 1861, The Avalon Project, Lillian Goldman Law Library, Yale Law School, http: //avalon.law.yale.edu/19th _century/lincoln1.asp.

After various festivities—including a dinner for seventeen mostly Todd relatives and a short rest at the White House (by this time a relieved James Buchanan was long gone to his home in Lancaster, Pennsylvania)—the new president attended the evening's sole inaugural ball. For the second time that day he heard the Marine Band play the stirring "Hail to the Chief" in his honor. By then he had also heard the ominous news from Fort Sumter in Charleston Harbor that the Union commander there—Major Robert Anderson—needed more supplies. Even for a man of great stamina, Abraham Lincoln was surely exhausted when he finally tumbled into bed in the new home that he would inhabit for the next four years and five weeks—until that fateful night in April 1865 when he and Mrs. Lincoln went to Ford's Theatre to see Laura Keene in *Our American Cousin.*

The subject of this essay is Lincoln and his family in the White House—their lives behind the scenes in what some nineteenth-century Americans called in homely democratic fashion the People's House. Others dubbed it the Executive Mansion, and Lincoln sometimes called it the President's House or the White House, though it would not officially be called the latter until Teddy Roosevelt's administration. I have no grand theme to present, only the idea that the White House, with its multiple functions as a family residence, an executive office, and the location of endless ceremonies and rituals, complicated the sixteenth president's tenure in many, not always positive, ways.

And for his wife and three sons—one son, Eddie, had died in Springfield in 1850 before the Lincolns came to Washington—the presidential years magnified the anguish of what Mary Lincoln called "her vanishing circle." While the founders of the American republic had successfully divided political power and authority among various institutions of government in the United States Constitution, they had done nothing to provide living quarters for the president and his family that were separate from his office and the grand ceremonial rooms of the White House.

From its beginnings the White House (fig. 1) had been intended as a magnificent structure, though George Washington, who wanted a stone building "designed for the ages" and who never lived in the Washington White House, had disagreed with Thomas Jefferson, who favored brick simplicity. In a people's republic that had just thrown off the yoke of a monarchy, the home of this new functionary called a president must not be too grand. On the other hand, it must be spacious enough to symbolize the new nation's

FIG. 1. "White House, Washington, D.C., 1861–1865," Brady National Photographic Art Gallery. *(Still Picture Records Section, Special Media Archives Services Division, National Archives and Records Administration, College Park, Md.)*

power in the dangerous international world of European governments unwilling to surrender their expansive claims to territory in the Western Hemisphere. The home of the president also must mirror the future world-class expectations of the United States of America.[3]

Yet, like the new instruments of government created by the Constitution, there were no precedents to follow in the construction of what soon became, along with its neighbor, the Capitol, a national symbol for a new type of government. By Thomas Jefferson's administration there were complaints that the great stone house designed by James Hoban, an Irish immigrant who had won the architectural design competition, was "big enough for two emperors, one pope and the grand lama."[4] Later the building was refigured and its grounds improved by the great architect of the new republic, Benjamin Henry Latrobe. First inhabited by John and Abigail Adams, who moved in before it was completed, the building had its exterior structure in place by

[3]Jean H. Baker, *Benjamin Henry Latrobe: Architect and Engineer of the Republic* (New York, forthcoming).

[4]Quoted in John Whitcomb and Claire Whitcomb, *Real Life in the White House* (New York, 2000), p. xix.

1800, which remained unchanged during the nineteenth century, save for the addition of the porticos on the north and south, some revision of its internal rooms, and its refurbishing after its destruction during the War of 1812.

By the time of the Lincolns' arrival, the interior of the White House was in deplorable condition—circumstances readily apparent to Mary Todd Lincoln and her cousin Lizzie Grimsley, both sharp-eyed and strong-voiced housewives from Springfield, when they toured the mansion the day after the inauguration. Still, its huge transverse halls, large windows, high ceilings, and the grandiose proportions of the East Room revealed its imposing possibilities. In the first decade of the nineteenth century Dolley Madison had made extensive improvements to the interior. But after the British invasion of Washington in 1814, on the interior only her red velvet curtains had survived the burning of the White House. Thereafter Congress proved stingy in providing appropriations.

By 1861 there was general agreement with Lizzie Grimsley's determination that it resembled a "seedy and dilapidated" third-rate hotel. Of course, the Executive Mansion was the grandest house and with its thirty-one rooms the largest home the Lincolns and their children had ever lived in. Such would be the case for all Americans. But for the president it was a far cry from the humble wattle and daub cabins of his childhood and youth in Kentucky, Indiana, and Illinois. And this president, with his simple tastes, yearned for little more than shelter, privacy, and modest meals.

But Mary Lincoln had grown up in aristocratic Lexington, Kentucky, and she, not her husband, noticed the stained upholstery, abominable furniture, and peeling wallpaper, along with the threadbare rugs and faded curtains. Even Lincoln's young secretary, John Nicolay, soon to reside in a small bedroom on the second floor of the East Wing of the White House, wondered how long "a great nation would compel its ruler to live in a small dilapidated shanty and in such shabby genteel style." Meanwhile, William Stoddard, another White House secretary, was reminded of an "old and unsuccessful boarding house." And as for Washington correspondent Noah Brooks, he wanted Congress to appropriate enough money to buy paintings from American artists to hang in the White House. But Brooks's visionary plan took another century to reach fruition.[5]

[5]William Stoddard, *Inside the White House in Wartime*, ed. Michael Burlingame (Lincoln, Neb., 2000), p. 49; Harry Pratt and Ernest East, "Mrs. Lincoln Refurbishes the White

It soon became Mary Lincoln's self-appointed project—an especially important one during the Civil War and one that she accomplished with distinction—to make the White House into an elegant statement of Union power. Even as the wives of other public officials fled home in the face of a possible Confederate attack across the Potomac River, the First Lady traveled to New York within weeks of the inauguration to buy rugs and curtains. In a record one day's shopping at Alexander Stewart's new department store, she spent $2,000 of the $20,000 allowance for White House repairs and refurbishing. The First Lady traveled to both New York and Philadelphia several times during the year, always spending too much money, though it is worth remembering that she had no power of the purse.

Rather, it was the commissioner of public buildings, William Wood, and later after he was fired, Benjamin B. French, who signed the vouchers. Both men evidently approved of her new decorations and the reasons for them, though she took the blame for extravagance—however tasteful the results—in the press, among Washington officials, and later to an unforgiving fraternity of historians. Ever oblivious to his surroundings, her husband, on the other hand, left such activities to his wife until she overspent the budget and made Lincoln angry: "It would stink in the nostrils of the American people to have it said that the President of the United States had approved a bill over-running an appropriation of $20,000 for flub-dubs for this damned house when the soldiers cannot have blankets."[6] While the Lincolns, who had been married twenty years, generally were congenial partners despite his melancholy and her tempers, certainly one of the things they argued about behind the scenes during their years in the White House was her excessive spending.

In examining the private lives of Lincoln and his family in the White House we must remember that peculiar American arrangement placing three essential purposes under one roof in a way that no other nations do. Wisely, in European capitals, palaces were never the location of all three functions. Yet the White House was—and still is—the place where the executive business of the nation takes place. Lincoln worked from home—in

House," *Lincoln Lore* 47 (February 1945):12–22; Mary Todd Lincoln to Alex Williamson, Jan. 26, 1866, in Justin Turner and Linda Turner, eds., *Mary Todd Lincoln: Her Life and Letters* (New York, 1972), p. 330; Elizabeth Grimsley, "Six Months in the White House," *Journal of the Illinois State Historical Society* 19 (October 1926–January 1927):47.

[6]Jean H. Baker, *Mary Todd Lincoln: A Biography* (New York, 1987), pp. 188–89.

an office he called "the shop," which measured twenty-five feet by thirty feet and had a marble fireplace, large windows that faced south, a desk between the windows, and a stained carpet. (Years later President Ronald Reagan, who was born in a small apartment over a general store in Tampico, Illinois, told his wife when they moved into the White House that he was still living above the store.)[7]

At the beginning of the war, the flags of the Confederacy flying high atop the buildings in Arlington and Alexandria could be seen from Lincoln's office. For four years Abraham Lincoln spent most of his time in this simple room, furnished with a couch, a table, enough chairs for his cabinet of seven, a few books including the Statutes of the United States, the United States Constitution, some Shakespeare plays, and a portrait of the Democratic president Andrew Jackson on the wall—which Lincoln, an instinctive bipartisan soon to be the leader of a wartime coalition called the Union Party, did not bother to replace. There was also an uncomfortable, soiled horsehair sofa. The only new furnishing that Lincoln requested was a large rack for the war maps that the president closely studied as he rapidly took on the role of an involved commander in chief and military tactician.

In this era before the commodious West Wing addition in the twentieth century, Lincoln met in his office with the cabinet twice a week, discussed personnel matters involving military appointments, and crafted the letters that carried his policy messages to private citizens. Here he wrote both the preliminary and final Emancipation Proclamation, began the Gettysburg Address, and wrote in its entirety his Second Inaugural Address. He also interviewed Republican Party leaders intent on the federal patronage jobs that exploded from 1,200 in 1861 to nearly four times that number by 1865. Of course, partisans knew who dispensed these political plums, which meant that the White House swarmed with men and a few women seeking jobs. The president was an astute student of party politics and spent time making appropriate choices that would aid the new Republican Party and, in 1864, his own reelection.

Still, none of the family knew whom they might encounter in the second-floor hallway when they left their bedrooms, as the job seekers overflowed the waiting room outside Lincoln's anteroom. Even for the times, observers from Europe, where public buildings were better protected and no one

[7]Whitcomb and Whitcomb, *Real Life in the White House*, p. xvii.

dreamed of walking into a minister's home, noted the lack of security at the White House. There was, concluded one English visitor, not a "dog on the watch," as Edward McManus and Thomas Burns, the porters, paid little attention to monitoring the north portico entrance. When Napoleon's nephew arrived for a state dinner, no one was at the front door, and so young Willie Lincoln did the honors, after which the prince confided to his diary that "one goes right into the [White House] as if entering a café."[8] After all, according to an editor of the *New York Times*, the people had paid for the house and thereby earned the right to see him in it.[9]

In his second-floor office, Lincoln also met with delegations of endless associations and groups from Sioux Indians to temperance advocates. In one instance he listened to the zealous advocacy of a temperance group, observing from the corner of his eye the attention that his tipsy carriage driver was giving to this call to abandon the temptations of alcohol. And it was in this office that shortly before he issued the Emancipation Proclamation, the president harshly harangued a delegation of African Americans, proclaiming that they would never be the equal of white men, that they were the cause of the war, and that colonization was the best answer for their future: "You and I are different races. . . . It is better for us both therefore to be separated."[10] The president also gave his limited time to widows seeking pensions and mothers who came with desperate pleas to save their deserting sons from the firing squad.

One of the criticisms of Abraham Lincoln's presidency was that he lavished far too much time, according to one of his secretaries, on "the endless requests of poor widows who wanted to work in the Treasury Department, the brigadiers who wanted a promotion, the inventors after a contract, and the curiosity seekers with an autograph book."[11] For example, he spent hours on the especially troubling case of a civilian from Norfolk, Virginia, Dr. David Wright, who had shot the white commanding officer of a black Union regiment because the black soldiers had not moved off the sidewalk in Norfolk to make way for white civilians. This murder arrived on Lincoln's

---

[8]Baker, *Mary Todd Lincoln*, p. 199.

[9]James Conroy, *Lincoln's White House: The People's House in Wartime* (Lanham, Md., 2017), p. 2.

[10]Roy P. Basler, ed., *The Collected Works of Abraham Lincoln*, 9 vols. (New Brunswick, N.J., 1953–55), 5:370–75.

[11]Noah Brooks, *Washington in Lincoln's Time* (New York, 1895), pp. 248–49.

desk as "an unprovoked assassination," followed by a guilty verdict and death sentence by a military commission. Eventually Lincoln declined to pardon the man, but he carefully considered whether Wright could be called insane and therefore not put to death, even sending an investigator to Norfolk before rejecting such a defense.[12]

Additionally, as president, Abraham Lincoln ran the nation's foreign affairs, defining its policies such as the naval blockade of the Confederacy and the proper reaction to the *Trent* affair and the *Alabama*—the cruiser built in Scotland and delivered to the Confederacy. Along with his secretary of state, he also oversaw the choice of personnel. Almost everyone who knew Abraham Lincoln, particularly those who worked with him, such as his secretaries, appreciated, as William Stoddard wrote, "his vast capacity for work and also the exceedingly valuable faculty of putting his work upon others. He could load up to their limit or beyond it his cabinet officers, generals, legislative supporters and others."[13] In an underappreciated trait of Lincoln's leadership, this president knew how to delegate authority.

Lincoln's executive office lacked the very thing he might have appreciated the most: a telegraph line. As a result, the president frequently left the White House to walk the block to the War Department, which was fitted out with a telegraph, the latest technological marvel. But given the perpetual busyness of the White House, this sometimes became a blessing. Lincoln once told Thomas Eckard, chief of the War Department Telegraphic Division, that "he had been able to work at [Eckard's desk] more quietly and command his thoughts better than at the White House, where he was frequently interrupted."[14] These interruptions, often from his wife and his two young sons and sometimes from the household staff and frequently from patronage seekers, came from the failure to separate the functions of the White House.

Mostly, Lincoln worked in the White House and to that extent he had no private life beyond its walls and outside of his family, though he did move in the late summers and early fall to the Old Soldiers Home, returning daily to the White House. He visited hospitals in Washington and the

---

[12]For an account of this case, see William Lee Miller, *President Lincoln: Duty of a Statesman* (New York, 2008), pp. 273–88.

[13]Ibid., p. 230.

[14]Harold Holzer, ed., *Lincoln as I Knew Him: Gossip, Tributes, and Revelations from His Best Friends and Worst Enemies* (Chapel Hill, N.C., 1999), p. 237.

fortifications around the city. At Fort Stevens, one of the forts on the periphery of the city, both the president and the First Lady, standing on the parapet, came under fire from advancing Confederates only 150 yards away during General Jubal Early's raid in the summer of 1864. A young lieutenant, probably Oliver Wendell Holmes, not recognizing his commander in chief shouted "get down, you damn fool, before you get shot." "With his long frock coat and plug hat on," concluded another observer, "he made a conspicuous figure."[15]

The president traveled several times to the Virginia battlefront and, of course, as we all know, once to Gettysburg to consecrate the national cemetery there. In 1864 he spoke briefly about the meaning of the word "liberty" and the massacre of black soldiers at Fort Pillow at a fund-raising event for the Sanitary Commission in Baltimore.[16] He took carriage rides with his wife, and he went to the theater over a hundred times during his years in Washington. But there is no behind-the-scenes Lincoln who socialized with Washington society or, like Warren Harding, hosted poker games with friends in the family quarters or talked politics, as Lincoln himself had done so avidly in his early years in Springfield at Joshua Speed's store. He had no kitchen cabinet; he also had no privacy.

Instead, most mornings Lincoln got up early, ate an apple or a boiled egg, drank some coffee at 8:30 with his wife and sons, and then worked late into the night with breaks in his day only for a light lunch and a hearty dinner. He never drank wine or what this generation of Americans called spirits. Surely he was one of the hardest working and simplest—in his domestic demands—of all our presidents. His wife once wrote a friend that she was "lucky if by eleven o'clock he was ready to join me in my chamber."[17] Those who had known him in Springfield and saw him later during the war recognized the toll that the presidency had taken physically, though Lincoln had always been gaunt and underweight.

Besides serving as the workplace for the president, in its second function the White House was where ceremonial occasions of the nation took place (figs. 2–4). Again, most European governments separated the two purposes to spare overworked officials from the commotions, pressures, and for some

---

[15]David Herbert Donald, *Lincoln* (New York, 1995), p. 519.
[16]Basler, *Collected Works*, 7:301–3.
[17]Turner and Turner, *Mary Todd Lincoln*, p. 187.

FIG. 2. "New Year's Reception at the White House, Washington," *Illustrated London News*, Feb. 1, 1862. *(Courtesy Donald R. Kennon)*

FIG. 3. "Grand Reception at the White House, January 1862," *Harper's Weekly*, Jan. 25, 1862. *(Courtesy Donald R. Kennon)*

FIG. 4. "Grand Reception of the Notabilities of the Nation at the White House, 1865," lithograph print of the reception for Lincoln's second inauguration, Major and Knapp Engraving, Manufacturing and Lithographic Co., [1865]. *(Library of Congress Prints and Photographs Division)*

public officials, pleasures of social occasions. But in the United States, in the downstairs rooms of the White House—especially the grand East Room, with its twenty-two-foot ceilings, but also the smaller Blue and Red Rooms, the latter, with its crimson and gold upholstery and curtains, being Mary Lincoln's favorite—the president and his lady met "the people" as well as congressmen, judges, and foreign dignitaries. Immediately after the inauguration, the First Lady had initiated her expensive process of White House rehabilitation and redecoration that eventually turned these rooms into elegant public spaces.

Mary Lincoln did not wait to entertain until after the new, elegant pale green rug for the East Room had arrived, and in time she and her husband used all the great rooms on the first floor for an array of receptions and public events, to which a great cross-section of Americans came. Their first function, on March 28, took place amid the smell of paint and varnish, as many of the downstairs public rooms were undergoing a refurbishing. "Mrs. Lincoln bore the fatigue of the two and a half hour siege with great patience," wrote one observer. "She appeared remarkably well and performed her part of the honors, in response to the grand ovation paid to her as well as to her honored husband with an unreserved dignity which is much more becoming for the wife of a Republican president than it would be an attempt to ape the sycophantic haughty manner of European courts, as has been done in the past."[18]

Soon the lines for public receptions stretched out the door, and the Washington pickpockets discovered their best targets in the unguarded White House coatrooms. "Mrs. Lincoln and the President," wrote Commissioner of the Public Buildings Benjamin B. French about an event in 1863, "had such an event as I have never seen in the daytime. Mrs. L. appeared lively and gracious and received with an air of grace and dignity."[19]

During the Civil War these receptions took up private family time and certainly some of the president's energy, even as they sustained public morale. "I met the president and his lady," wrote one soldier who, fresh from the Virginia battlefield in 1862, was inspired by the president's easy manner and his wife's graciousness. He was surprised that "every person has a right to go through the rooms of the White House."[20] But this was the democratic way in the People's House.

European travelers were surprised as well at the inclusiveness. Ernest Duvergier de Hauranne was astonished that no one needed a formal invitation or a frock coat to be admitted, as was the case in his native France: "The servants don't have the authority to refuse admittance on the ground of muddy boots or disreputable clothes to any patriotic citizen eager to meet his president."[21] Yet both Lincolns understood the importance of opening the White House to the public, and they did so with a frequency and a style that had not been seen since Dolley Madison's tenure. As William Crook, a doorman who served in five administrations, wrote about the Lincoln White

---

[18]Esther Singleton, *The Story of the White House*, 2 vols. (New York, 1907), 2:71–72.

[19]Journal of Benjamin French, Feb. 15, 1863, Benjamin French Papers, Manuscript Division, Library of Congress, Washington, D.C.

[20]William C. Davis, *Lincoln's Men: How President Lincoln Became Father to an Army and a Nation* (New York, 1999), p. 59.

[21]Ernest Duvergier de Hauranne, *A Frenchman in Lincoln's America*, trans. and ed. Ralph H. Bowen (Chicago, 1947–50), p. 357.

House, "by design no matter what it did to the president's concentration, never was the House so entirely given over to the public as during Lincoln's administration. The times were too tense to make of social affairs anything other than an aid to more serious matters."[22]

Thus, even on such social occasions that might have provided relaxation, the private Lincoln merged with the wartime leader, always on call, always engaged in some public duty. At these receptions, the president stood patiently for three and four hours shaking hands with the citizenry. But as the French visitor Hauranne noted, "Lincoln was a farmer and his hands can take the terrible punishment."[23] But because the White House mixed private and public functions, the Lincolns were on constant public display.

What Lincoln earlier thought frivolous now emerged as confidence-raising affairs intended to build the optimism of the people and symbolically show foreign ministers from Confederate-leaning nations like Britain's Lord Lyons and France's Henri Mercier that the United States was no weak, debilitated, failed nation that could not even pay for improvements to the president's home. These social events—what the president called his "Handshake Days"—became moments when serious matters of state were discussed, and with a simple handshake he could honor a soldier's commitment to the nation.

But the largest events could not begin until the soldiers who were billeted during the spring of 1861 in the East Room, to Willie and Tad's delight, had left and Washington seemed secure from a Confederate attack. Thereafter, with the Marine Band stationed in the hall and lanterns outside marking even the smallest Union victory, former Washington snobs who believed the Lincolns unmannered rural folk from the frontier agreed with French's observation about Mrs. Lincoln's grace and dignity.

At these events the First Lady scintillated in her elegant dresses (figs. 5–6)—some borrowed, others created by her talented seamstress, Elizabeth Keckley. A reporter from *Frank Leslie's Illustrated News* described her "lustrous white satin robe with a train a yard in length, trimmed with one deep flounce of the richest black chantilly lace. Mrs. Lincoln possesses that rare beauty which rendered the empress of the French so celebrated as a grand dame

[22]William Crook, *Through Five Administrations: Reminiscences of Colonel William H. Crook*, ed. Margarita Spalding Gerry (New York, 1910), p. 17.

[23]Hauranne, *A Frenchman in Lincoln's America*, p. 357.

FIG. 5. Carte de visite photograph of Mary Todd Lincoln standing, Brady's National Photographic Portrait Galleries [1861]. *(Library of Congress Prints and Photographs Division)*

FIG. 6. Carte de visite photograph of Mary Todd Lincoln seated holding flowers, Brady's National Photographic Portrait Galleries [1861]. *(Library of Congress Prints and Photographs Division)*

woman."[24] A senator from Oregon, James Nesmith, was more down to earth. Having met Mrs. Lincoln at an evening party, he described his hostess as having "a flower pot on her head and her milking apparatus on display."[25]

---

[24] *Frank Leslie's Illustrated Newspaper*, Feb. 5, 1862.

[25] Senator Nesmith to my wife, Feb. 5, 1862, Ruth Randall Papers, Manuscript Division, Library of Congress.

The third essential function of the White House was to serve as the home of the president's family—in this case his wife and the three surviving Lincoln sons: Robert, who was mostly away as a student at Harvard, eleven-year-old Willie, and the irrepressible nine-year-old Tad. The family quarters of eight rooms were on the west side of the second floor of the mansion, with the library or family room and the parents' adjoining bedrooms on the south side and the boys' bedrooms across the hall on the north side. A staff of over ten African Americans served as cooks, cleaners, and doorkeepers. Lincoln had brought William Johnson, a young black man from Springfield, whom the president described as "honest, faithful, sober industrious and handy as a servant."[26] Most respected was William Slade, the keeper of the White House keys, a factotum who served as a messenger, arranged functions, and even brought his sons to play with the Lincoln boys.

The boys, considered spoiled and ill mannered by some visitors, roamed everywhere in their new home, once disrupting the bell system used to call the servants who staffed the White House. On another occasion the boys dressed Nannie and Nanko, their pet goats, in festive outfits and led them proudly through a reception in the East Room. And there was the time when Tad somehow discovered a Confederate flag, climbed to the roof of the White House, and was seen waving the flag. But that was early in the war. The behind-the-scenes White House included episodes of hilarity with Tad and Willie, and at the time Americans reveled in reports of the antics of these boys, for the Lincolns were the first presidential couple to bring young children to the White House since John Tyler's ten-year-old son had lived there twenty years before.

The boys were homeschooled by tutor Alexander Williamson, who came even on Sundays, and by their mother. Like their parents they spent most of their days in the White House or on the grounds with their ponies. One of the few unalloyed pleasures the president had was being with his sons (fig. 7). He wrestled with them, he read to them, he chased them, and he never reprimanded them when they hid under the table when the cabinet was meeting, or in the provocative Tad's case, pulled the beards of his cabinet officers. The motto of the Lincolns, according to one observer, was "Let the Children have a good time."[27]

---

[26]John Washington, *They Knew Lincoln* (New York, 1942), p. 127.

[27]Julia Taft Bayne, *Tad Lincoln's Father* (Boston, 1931), p. 107.

FIG. 7. Abraham Lincoln, seated and holding a book, with his son Tad (Thomas) leaning on a table, photograph by Alexander Gardner, Feb. 5, 1865. *(Library of Congress Prints and Photographs Division)*

Among the unfortunate legacies of this tricentric White House was the inability of the Lincolns to avoid the patronage seekers who were often aligned on the grand staircase with its mahogany handrail waiting to see the president in what Lincoln called "the Great Beggar's Opera." It was necessary for Mary Lincoln to climb over them on her way to her bedroom. The only structural change that Lincoln made to the White House was to cut a door between his anteroom and the library, which served as the family living room on the south side of the mansion, so that, at least on the second floor, he could avoid the public. Given the location of these functions in one building, it is obvious that the president could never expect the distance and privacy he might have attained in another setting.

Two episodes reveal the joys and sorrows of Lincoln's life in the White House, just as they also reveal the interaction among Lincoln's work, his social occasions, and his family life. An impatient Lincoln had reason to believe that General George McClellan might never move his soldiers beyond the parade grounds, where all of Washington gathered to watch the snappy drills on what is now the Washington Mall. The Lincolns observed them as well from the south portico. In January 1862 the president signed a special command designated as the President's War Order No. 1. It required a general forward movement of the Union forces to take place on February 22.

Ignoring the president's orders, General McClellan instead decided on an oblique advance to Richmond by way of the peninsula between the York and James rivers. And so began the Peninsula Campaign—an intricate and in some ways foolish operation involving over 100,000 troops, by sea down the Potomac River to Norfolk and then by land to the Confederate capital of Richmond. Lincoln was apprehensive about the scale of an operation that left Washington undefended, and he was especially worried during the winter months of 1862.

His wife had her own reasons to be nervous. With her typical élan she was organizing a grand party to raise the spirits of those in this dreary winter, planned for February 5. She had invited officers, ambassadors, congressmen, and their families. A caterer from New York had been hired, thus irritating the local Washington tradesmen, and the flowers came from Philadelphia. The Marine Band played the new "Mary Lincoln Polka," composed especially for the occasion, along with selections from operas. But there was no dancing during wartime at the White House. Instead, the hostess had planned a splendid scene in the dining room with vases of flowers and delicacies made of sugar—one was a replica of Fort Pickens—roast pheasant and beef. Lincoln was suspicious of the scale of the party, but his wife, like other middle-class women in the republic, nearly always made the decisions about social affairs in this age of domestic feminism.

There was a great deal of sickness in Washington during the Christmas season, and in late January 1862 Willie Lincoln fell ill with a cold that soon turned into fever and chills. Mary Lincoln wanted to cancel the party, but her husband discouraged this. On the day of the reception, Willie took a turn for the worse and both Lincolns sat by his bedside during most of the party. A local doctor encouraged the parents to go downstairs, though they were as often in Willie's room as at the party. The next day, along with some newspaper reports that it was inappropriate to have such an extravagant party during wartime, one newspaper reporting on Willie's illness included the news that his younger brother Tad was sick as well.

For days the Lincolns sat by both boys' beds, though it was Willie who was wasting away. Having already lost their second son Eddie from tuberculosis, the Lincolns were especially apprehensive. There were remissions and relapses as typhoid fever cruelly assaulted the eleven-year-old boy's body. Most likely the bacteria had come from the contaminated water now piped into the mansion from the Potomac River, a supposed improvement that had turned lethal once the Union army began using the river as a latrine.

On February 20, 1862, Willie Lincoln died, and no one in the family was ever the same. John Nicolay remembered the president coming to his bedside and saying, "'Well, Nicolay, my boy is gone—he is actually gone!' And then the president burst into tears."[28] While the president might meld his loss into the grief of other parents who were losing their sons on the battlefield, for Mary Lincoln there would never be any consolation. And so on the grim, cold day of the funeral four days later, Abraham Lincoln and his eldest son, Robert, helped Mary Lincoln down the stairs into the Green Room, where they stayed for half an hour, saying their private farewell to the dead boy. In Washington they gossiped that Mary Lincoln believed her son's death a judgment for her party, but it was not gossip that she had turned to the spiritualists for comfort.

---

[28]Elizabeth Keckley, *Behind the Scenes; or, Thirty Years a Slave and Four Years in the White House* (1868; reprint ed., New York, 1968), pp. 46–48.

A later episode also gives some of the flavor of the Lincoln White House. It too stands at the intersection of the ceremonial, familial, and executive functions of the White House. Throughout the war Mary Lincoln, with her Kentucky roots and drawl, had been accused of being a Southern spy. When the First Lady's half brothers joined the Confederate army and her half sister married a Confederate general (earlier Lincoln had offered him a commission as an army pay master for the Union), the gossip intensified. Lincoln's brother-in-law Ben Helm chose the Confederacy and was killed at the battle of Chickamauga in 1863. Needing to go through Union lines to return home to Lexington, Kentucky, his widow, Emilie Todd Helm, Mary Lincoln's favorite half sister, was required to take an oath of allegiance to the Union government—which she refused to do. Informed of this, Lincoln telegraphed "Send her to me."

And so Emilie Helm, a rabid Confederate, arrived at the White House with a military escort in December 1863. It is a measure of Lincoln as a loyal family man that he met his half sister-in-law "with the warmest affection." In her diary Emilie wrote that "we were all too grief-stricken at first for speech. I have lost my husband and they have lost their fine little son Willie."[29] In the family quarters Emilie provided some solace to Mary Lincoln, but there were political consequences to having a Confederate in the White House.

One evening two Union generals came to confer with Lincoln. One was General Daniel Sickles, the former congressman from New York who had lost a leg at the battle of Gettysburg. Sickles was a notable womanizer who shared Mary Lincoln's interest in séances and who wanted to meet the lovely Emilie in the family quarters, perhaps even to flirt with her. But instead an angry exchange in the Blue Room between Emilie, Sickles, and Congressman Ira Harris, who had just lost his son in the Union army, ensued. Responding to a comment about recent rebel defeats at Chattanooga, Emilie retorted that this "was the example you set for them at Bull Run and Manassas." "If I had twenty sons they would all be fighting yours," said Emilie as tempers flared.[30]

When Sickles and Harris complained to the president that he should not have a rebel living in the White House, Lincoln responded that "my wife

[29]Katherine Helm, *The True Story of Mary, Wife of Lincoln* (New York, 1928), p. 221.

[30]Ibid., p. 230.

and I are in the habit of choosing our own guests."[31] In this episode the configuration of the White House—its public rooms for entertainment, its position as the official office of the executive, and its family rooms all located in the same building—denied privacy to the family.

Certainly a separate home away from the business of the republic would have shielded Mary Lincoln from the intense scrutiny that included the reports that she was having séances in the White House. A well-known spiritualist had been seen entering the White House, and it was no secret that Mary Lincoln went to Georgetown to consult with spiritualists. On several occasions mediums organized séances in the Green Room, and as Mary told Emilie Helm, Eddie and Willie sometimes returned as comforting spectral presences. As a Presbyterian, the First Lady believed that when she died she would join her two sons in heaven through the process of resurrection, but in the meantime the mediums could place a bereaved mother in immediate touch with her sons.

For the rest of her life Mary Lincoln accepted the essential doctrine of the spiritualist that there was "a very slight veil separating us from the loved and lost" and that with the proper suggestion, attitude, and circumstances, the departed could return.[32] Such convictions emerged as a popular phenomenon during the Civil War when the deaths of young soldiers encouraged bereaved families to try to communicate with the dead. But for other Americans, such goings-on in the White House sullied the dignity of the mansion and directed more criticism at the First Lady.

On April 14, 1865, Abraham Lincoln spent his last day in the White House. He had arisen early and breakfasted with his wife and his son Robert on nothing more than an apple. Then he returned to his office, where he conducted several interviews, signed papers, and met with the cabinet. It was a typical day, though his spirits were high. The president had already traveled to Richmond, the defeated capital of the Confederacy, and he told his wife that he felt that the war was finally over. Lincoln ate no lunch, but in the afternoon he and Mary took a carriage ride. She noted how cheerful he seemed, and they spoke of their future together with the terrible burden of the war lifted. Abraham Lincoln had an early dinner, and a little later picked up his top hat and joined his wife for their carriage ride to Ford's

[31]Ibid., p. 231.

[32]Turner, *Mary Todd Lincoln*, p. 256; Baker, *Mary Todd Lincoln*, p. 220.

Theatre. He never returned to the home where he had lived for more than four years.

In the last analysis, when Mary and her two sons Tad and Robert left the White House six weeks later in May 1865, every member of the diminished Lincoln family could remember their enjoyment of some aspect of the White House—its parties, its grounds, even the spacious grandeur of its rooms and corridors. One time Lincoln had reminded a regiment of soldiers on their way home to Ohio that he was not a permanent resident of the White House: "I happen temporarily to occupy this big White House. I am a living witness that any one of your children may look to come here as my father's child has. And like my father's son, your son may live here."[33] The constitutional arrangement that ensured a constant turnover of White House occupants was part of the nation's birthright and one of the reasons Lincoln believed that the war was being fought. The states of the Confederacy had, after all, denied the legitimacy of his right to live there.

In different ways, these four years had devastated the little band of five who had taken up residence in March 1861. One Lincoln son had died, leaving his parents and younger brother bereft. Meanwhile, Mary Lincoln had worked hard in her ceremonial role, only to lose a son and a husband during her residence. And while Lincoln was not assassinated in the White House, its lack of security surely emboldened potential conspirators. Like thousands of other Americans during the Civil War, the Lincoln family had endured wartime casualties and, now depleted, faced a bleak future beyond the White House.

---

[33]Basler, *Collected Works*, 7:512.

Guy Gugliotta

A National Icon Comes of Age

SHORTLY AFTER NOON on December 2, 1863, architect Thomas U. Walter ordered his construction crew to winch the last piece of the bronze statue *Freedom* to the top of the United States Capitol and bolt it into place (fig. 1). It was a cold, clear, still day: no wind, which was important for Walter's ironworkers, perched on a small wooden platform 300 feet above the Capitol's front yard. When Walter first came to work at the Capitol in 1851, the Capitol grounds were well manicured and elegant. Not now. On this day they were a chill, muddy mess, churned up by countless wagons loaded with stone, lumber, pipe, bricks, and multi-ton pieces of cast iron. Derelict sheds, scattered marble boulders, piles of trash, and other assorted junk dotted the grounds, seeming to underscore the grim reality of a city beset by war for more than two and a half years.

Vicksburg and Gettysburg had put the Union in a better military position than it had enjoyed for some time, but winter had brought no jubilation in Washington, and Walter had no illusions. He had two sons in the Union army and one son who had repudiated the Union and joined the Confederate army. "Should that be the case," he wrote to a friend, "I shall never again acknowledge him as belonging to me.[1]

[1]Walter to John Rice, May 8, 1861, Thomas Ustick Walter Collection, Archives of American Art, Athenaeum, Philadelphia, roll 4140.

FIG. 1. "West front of the U.S. Capitol in Washington, D.C., as it appeared the moment the statue [of *Freedom*] was completed, and placed in position by Charles F. Thomas," December 2, 1863, photograph. *(Library of Congress Prints and Photographs Division)*

By mid-1862 the prodigal had repented, but Walter would "let bygones be bygones," he wrote, only if he took a loyalty oath.[2] His wife and younger children were living in Philadelphia, leaving him to rent a beat-up house at exorbitant rates. Housing in wartime Washington was at a premium.

Civility was not. Neighbors routinely dumped garbage in the vacant lot next door to Walter's digs. Teenage rock throwers had broken the windows in his bathroom.[3] A few months earlier a rabid dog had stumbled into his kitchen and terrorized the help.[4] His houseman clubbed it to death in the cellar. Walter, a natural Panglossian, had once regarded the war as a petty, stupid dustup between headstrong brothers. He knew better now. He no longer speculated on outcomes, but he expected a fight to the death.

With Walter's considerable help, the Capitol during his tenure had tripled in size from a glorified town hall to a rambling colossus that on this day dominated the D.C. landscape. Walter had designed the new Senate and House wings and the new cast-iron dome, and he well knew that the

---

[2]Walter to Thomas Walter, Aug. 16, 1862, ibid.
[3]Walter to Amanda Walter, June 28 and July 22–25, 1862, ibid.
[4]Walter to Olivia Walter, June 11, 1863, ibid., roll 4141.

Capitol was the greatest achievement of his long and already illustrious career. Mounting *Freedom Triumphant in War and Peace*[5] was the finishing touch, and he welcomed it. But he had told his workers there would be no ceremony to mark the event. He did not like ceremonies as a rule, and he saw no justification for any sort of celebration in these difficult times. He would treat *Freedom*'s final assembly as part of the workday. He instructed his crew: there would be no waving of hats, no speeches, no brass bands, no prayers. Lincoln would not show up. He was ailing and, of course, had other things on his mind. Reporters wanted to write stories about the dome, but Walter had given no interviews. He did, however, make one concession. He put a notice in local papers for those who were interested: barring inclement weather, the crowning of the Capitol would take place at noon.

Now the moment had arrived. As Walter looked out his office windows, he could see thousands of people gathered silently in the muck below him, gazing upward as *Freedom*'s head and feathered headdress rose to the highest point in Washington. When the last screw was bolted in place at 12:25 P.M., twelve forts around the city, taking turns, fired a succession of thirty-five-gun salutes: one gun for each state—including those in the Confederacy.[6]

This starkly simple display of solidarity and hard-bitten defiance marked the coming of age of a national icon. Henceforth the Capitol would serve as a rallying point and a symbol of the growing reach of the federal government and the people it served. Eventually it would become the most prestigious emblem of representative democracy in the world—one of the most easily recognized buildings on earth. December 2, 1863, was the day that course was set.

It had taken a long time to reach that starting point, and the travails undergone by the project known as the Capitol Extension closely tracked the changing fortunes of the country it served and the changing attitudes of the three men who built it. When Walter (fig. 2) began work at the Capitol in 1851, he was a slavery sympathizer and had even briefly owned a slave. By 1863 he had become a fire-and-brimstone abolitionist who welcomed the opportunity to hire a young freedman to work on his beloved project.[7]

---

[5]*Freedom Triumphant in War and Peace* was the name sculptor Thomas Crawford gave to his statue. History would come to know it simply as *Freedom*.

[6]Guy Gugliotta, *Freedom's Cap: The United States Capitol and the Coming of the Civil War* (New York, 2012), pp. 365–67.

[7]Ibid., p. 366.

Fig. 2. Thomas U. Walter, photograph, ca. 1860–65, Mathew Brady Photographs of the Civil War, Record Group 111: Records of the Office of the Chief Signal Officer. *(National Archives and Records Administration, Still Pictures, College Park, Md.)*

Montgomery C. Meigs (fig. 3) was a lowly captain in the Army Corps of Engineers when he was ordered to build the extension in 1853. Ten years later he was quartermaster general of the Union army, a logistical genius who built the supply lines that enabled Grant and Sherman to destroy the Confederacy.

The third member of this triumvirate, oddly enough, was Confederate President Jefferson Davis (fig. 4), who had embraced the idea of a new, expanded Capitol and had obtained the project's first appropriation in 1850 as a junior U.S. senator from Mississippi. From that moment until he left Washington forever in 1861, Davis drove the project forward both as a senator and as secretary of war under President Franklin Pierce. In December 1863 he was in Richmond, planning the Confederacy's future after disastrous defeats at Lookout Mountain and Missionary Ridge in Tennessee. Meigs had personally supervised logistics during the campaign. In Washington ten years earlier, Davis had mentored Meigs and the younger officer had esteemed Davis without reservation. Now Meigs wanted to see him hanged.

The project that began in 1850 generated minimal enthusiasm at first. The United States at that moment was a loose agglomeration of disparate, selfish provinces and districts defined by parochial interests. Congress showed up a few weeks before Christmas for the legislative session each year, and usually managed to finish its business before the following summer, when Washington's weather became intolerable. Congress regarded the Capitol as an uncomfortable but necessary evil—site of the public trough where members of the Senate and House obtained federal money to build post offices, dig canals, and dredge harbors. Congress's only certifiably enduring "national" concern at the time was the future of slavery, and even in 1850 there was enough bitterness to infect virtually every important question of public policy from international trade (high tariffs to protect Northern industry or low tariffs to allow cheap imports to the rural South and keep markets in Europe open to Southern cotton?) to the annexation of states (if a free state was admitted, should there also be a new slave state to balance it?). Enlarging the Capitol was a sideshow with a virtually nonexistent priority.

But in the ensuing fourteen years, the fortunes of the United States and its most important building took divergent paths. The dispute over slavery worsened from irritation, to dismay, to despair, to desperation, and finally

Fig. 3. "Quartermaster General Montgomery C. Meigs of the U.S. Army General Staff in uniform, holding papers," March 1861, carte de visite. *(Library of Congress Prints and Photographs Division)*

FIG. 4. Jefferson Davis, three-quarter-length portrait facing right, Mathew Brady photograph, ca. 1858–60. *(Library of Congress Prints and Photographs Division)*

to rage and civil war. At the same time, however, enthusiasm for the new Capitol grew among both free-staters and slave-staters.

Reasons for this change in attitude are difficult to quantify, but an argument can be made based on the very nature of the Capitol and its city, and on the increasingly frustrated impulses of the United States Congress, an institution filled with men interested in accomplishing things, rather than simply doing nothing.

The biggest disadvantage that the Capitol had during the initial phase of the expansion was that it was in the District of Columbia, which had no voice, no vote, and, thus, no politics. No senator or representative could get anything he could use by doing something for Washington—and favors for the District would simply mean less largesse for states and districts. The city was easy to ignore, and lawmakers paid no political price for doing so.

But as the decade wore on, this disadvantage became an advantage. Washington had no stake in the slavery dispute. It would be whatever the winners wanted it to be. As such, investing in the Capitol became attractive. Senators and representatives always wanted to build big things and put their names on them, and the Capitol was the rare big thing in the 1850s that did not carry any political baggage. Lawmakers could go home during the recess and show their constituents that even if they could not agree on a transcontinental railroad (southern route or northern route?) or an isthmian canal (slavery in Nicaragua?) they could at least do something big somewhere.

And finally, as despair deepened during the late 1850s, the Capitol began to acquire the first hints of a mystique. As a seat of government and a large public work, it became a symbol of American aspirations and enterprise. Americans were arrogant, and lawmakers, even if they acted petty and small, thought big, dreamed big, and built big. Also, during impossibly hard times, the new Capitol became an emotional statement of hope. This was what the United States *could* be, Congress seemed to say, if only "we" could resolve "our" differences.

These attitudes evolved slowly. In 1850, Washington, D.C., had just 40,000 inhabitants. It was a made-up place—a ten-miles-square grid of perpendicular streets and diagonal avenues designed by French-born city planner Peter L'Enfant (he changed his name from Pierre to Peter when he settled in the United States) and installed between the slave states of Virginia and Maryland just across the Potomac River from George Washington's Mount

Vernon home. The federal government moved to the District of Columbia in 1800, but greatness did not follow; and, as Charles Dickens noted during a visit in 1842, the "city" remained an amalgam of wide avenues "that begin in nothing and lead nowhere" and streets "that only want houses, roads and inhabitants."[8]

"Congress House" had been conceived in 1792 by President George Washington and then–Secretary of State Thomas Jefferson, who immediately renamed the building the Capitol.[9] Over the next thirty-six years a succession of designers, architects, and contractors built it and rebuilt it (after British soldiers torched it during the War of 1812). It had a central rotunda, flanked by a Senate chamber and committee offices on the north side and a House chamber and committee offices on the south side. The building was faced with Aquia sandstone from Virginia and topped with a copper-sheathed wooden dome that almost everyone agreed was both hideous and too tall. By 1850 nothing of substance had been done to enhance the building for twenty-two years.

Mississippi Senator Jefferson Davis used three arguments to sell the Capitol Extension to his congressional colleagues. The first was mundane yet compelling, at least to the House of Representatives. The House chamber was universally regarded as a beautiful room, but it had dreadful acoustics; they were so bad that the place was almost unusable. Many years later this feature would become an entertaining curiosity for tourists visiting what came to be known as Statuary Hall, but it was not amusing in 1850. A congressman seated in the middle of the chamber could easily overhear a lobbyist talking to one of his House colleagues across the room, but a floor speech taking place ten feet in front of him would be drowned in a bedlam of shouting and white noise. Several congressional observers had suggested—and not in jest—that the reason that members were routinely at one another's throats over slavery was because they spent most of their legislative day screaming in one another's faces in order to be heard.[10] A

---

[8]Charles Dickens, *American Notes* (1842; reprint ed., New York, 1992), pp. 156–61.

[9]William C. Allen, *History of the United States Capitol: A Chronicle of Design, Construction, and Politics*, Senate Doc. 106-29, 106th Cong., 2d sess. (Washington, D.C., 2001), p. 8.

[10]Robert Mills to the Senate and House of Representatives, Feb. 22, 1850, in Robert Mills, *The Papers of Robert Mills 1781–1855*, ed. Pamela Scott (Wilmington, Del., 1990), microfilm, reel 10, item 2731A.

Capitol extension would bring a new chamber. Davis, not surprisingly, had plenty of House support.

The second reason for expansion was also obvious. The United States in 1848 had won a huge new tract of territory as spoils of the recently concluded Mexican War. A year later gold was discovered in the westernmost part of it. By 1850, California had 90,000 people and needed to become a state. That said nothing about the vast expanses of mostly empty, still unannexed territory from the Louisiana Purchase. There were thirty states in the Union when 1850 dawned, and thirty-three by the end of the decade (California, Minnesota, and Oregon), with several others standing in line. Congress needed a bigger Capitol because the existing building was simply too small.

These arguments, however, did not kindle much urgency, especially in the Senate, which had good acoustics and plenty of room. Building a new Capitol put money in Washington and kept it out of individual states. It was self-evident that the United States would get bigger and that the government would inevitably grow, but there was no reason to do anything now. Expanding the Capitol was the sort of long-term necessity that could be easily ignored and—in typical congressional fashion—kicked down the road. Let somebody else worry about it.

But it was Davis's third reason that turned out to be prophetic, even though Congress hardly noticed it at the time, and greeted it with skepticism, if not outright derision. The United States needed a bigger Capitol, Davis told his Senate colleagues, because a great nation needed a great seat of government. As the Mexican War had proved, the country was putting on muscle every day, and immigrants were flooding in amid robust national economic growth. The United States could not have a House chamber that was unfit for intelligent debate, and it would not do to have increasing numbers of senators and representatives crammed into overstuffed committee rooms and chambers. The United States was destined to become a global force. It was time to act like it.

It is not clear that Davis intended to make this argument when his proposal for an initial appropriation of $100,000 for the Capitol Extension came up for debate, and he did not articulate it in so many words. But there was no mistaking his meaning. He was a forceful man, a formidable debater, and a vicious rhetorical counterpuncher. He did not easily abide people who disagreed with him, and he was not shy about saying so.

The debate opened on September 20, 1850, and lasted four days. There was plenty of opposition. Michigan's Lewis Cass, loser to Zachary Taylor in the 1848 presidential election and a sour-voiced Democratic Party elder statesman, remarked that the Capitol was the "worst building on the face of the earth for the purpose to which it is devoted," and he had no interest "in voting for the creation of another like it."[11]

Several senators reminded their colleagues that government programs, once born, seldom die, and what appeared to be a modest investment today would inevitably be seen in retrospect as just the first drop in what would become a very big bucket.

Davis, who at first had carefully described his request as "just an estimate" of the cost, but one that "will approach very nearly the amount required," then took the floor.[12] He agreed with his critics. It was true that the final cost "will be limited only by the degree of the extension." But that was beside the point: "if this Union continues together, and this continues to be the seat of Government, I have no idea that any plan which may now be suggested will finally answer all the wants of the country." In the context of burgeoning U.S. power, he suggested, the Capitol represents who we are, and in the end Congress might need to "cover the whole square with buildings, and I think it is likely."[13] He carried the vote, but it was a near thing, 24–21.

From that day until January 19, 1861, when he left Washington to join the Confederacy, Davis was the political driving force behind the expansion of the U.S. Capitol. It is probably safe to say that Davis is the reason the modern Capitol looks the way it does. What is not clear is how Davis came to this leadership position, and, even more puzzling, how he came to have such an overriding national vision at a time when the horizon for most Americans—including members of Congress—was the ridgeline that defined the border of their county or state.

Virtually all of Davis's personal correspondence was destroyed when Union forces raided his Mississippi plantation in 1863, so there is no record of how his thinking evolved during the period before the Civil War. But one

---

[11]U.S. Congress, House of Representatives, *Documentary History of the Construction and Development of the United States Capitol Buildings and Grounds*, House Rep. no. 646, 58th Cong., 2d sess. (Washington, D.C., 1904), p. 442.

[12]Ibid., p. 441.

[13]Ibid., p. 443.

aspect of his early biography seems instructive. He was the youngest child of a frontier Mississippi planter, but spent perhaps half of the first forty years of his life away from home. His family sent him to boarding schools, including the United States Military Academy at West Point, and he spent a good piece of his early adulthood in the army, either as a young subaltern on the western frontier or as the regimental commander of Mississippi volunteers during the Mexican War. By the time he arrived in the Senate in 1848, he had seen and lived in the South, the East, the Midwest, and the Southwest. He undoubtedly had a far better idea of the immense territory and potential of the United States than the vast majority of his countrymen.[14]

He cultivated this national perspective and coaxed it forward throughout the 1850s while overseeing the Capitol project. At the same time, by contrast, he used the decade to cement his reputation as an outspoken advocate for slavery and an eloquent opponent of federal encroachments on states' rights. He did as much as anyone to promote the Union's destiny as a great nation; and he did as much as anyone to cripple the Union's path to nationhood. There is no evidence that he ever saw the contradiction in his two competing personae, and there are no overt clues showing how he concluded that nationalism and sectionalism could coexist indefinitely—which, in the end, they could not.

Once again, however, there is a hint. Davis had a close, almost filial relationship with his former father-in-law Zachary Taylor, his commander during the Mexican War and his dear friend up until Taylor, elected president in 1848, died suddenly two years later. Although Taylor was one of the biggest slave owners in the country, he was utterly convinced that slavery would never extend beyond the states where it already existed. He had flatly told Davis that he would never argue for slavery in new states.[15] Davis categorically disagreed with Taylor's stance but never challenged him publicly, and perhaps harbored the wish that sectionalism and nationalism might finally find common ground—that the future of slavery could somehow be resolved to everyone's satisfaction, or at least papered over somehow and ignored.

---

[14]See Gugliotta, *Freedom's Cap*, pp. 39–42, for a discussion of Davis's early travels.

[15]Zachary Taylor to Jefferson Davis, Aug. 16, 1847, in Lynda Lasswell Crist et al., eds., *The Papers of Jefferson Davis*, 15 vols. (Baton Rouge, La., 1971–2015), 3:208–15.

Regardless of his motivations or hopes, it was quickly obvious that Davis's patronage was crucial in the Capitol Extension's early years, for without it, the project nearly foundered. After Congress passed the initial appropriation, Davis and, later, President Millard Fillmore undertook contests to choose a design and pick an architect to execute it. Davis went home when Congress recessed in March 1851 as this process unfolded and later allowed Democrats to induce him to run for governor of Mississippi in an attempt to resurrect party fortunes after a disastrous campaign by the initial candidate. Davis made up lost ground but could not overcome his early disadvantage and lost narrowly. He had resigned his Senate seat and so in late 1851 "retired" to his riverside plantation.

Both Davis and Fillmore advocated a horizontal design for the Capitol Extension, putting new Senate and House wings on the north and south ends of the existing building to create a rambling, broad facade—giving it a welcoming and open aspect, despite its immense size. Fillmore, a Whig, hired Walter, also a Whig, as his architect.

The final design (fig. 5) was an amalgam of concepts developed during the contests. Walter had authored none of the preferred drawings, but he nevertheless proved a masterful choice for the job. He was a brilliant draftsman, an innovative designer, a quick worker, and an able synthesizer, well equipped to turn the preferences and ideas of clients—including politicians—into art. The precocious son of a Philadelphia bricklayer, Walter, at forty-six, was at the height of his powers. He had designed more than 300 structures by his own estimate and had become probably the most highly paid architect in the country. He was aggressive, smart, and tough, and he needed all these attributes almost immediately.

Walter's problem was that Fillmore, his patron, was a lame duck, and Congress had Democratic majorities in both houses. The Capitol Extension was a way to smear both the administration and the Whigs generally. The opportunity arose at the end of 1851, when the initial appropriation ran out and Walter, because of either inexperience or carelessness, forgot to apply for new money. Construction stopped, workers were laid off, the Capitol grounds were a mess, and Congress began to question both the wisdom of the project generally and Walter's competence and honesty.

Several of the arguments during these early days reflected lawmakers' dismissive attitude toward government and toward anything—even a building—that appeared to enhance federal power. This view could embrace

FIG. 5. "North east view of the Capitol at Washington, with the new extension," engraved by J. Steel, the original by T. U. Walter [Philadelphia, 1852]. *(Library of Congress Prints and Photographs Division)*

many prejudices. Political concerns back home prescribed public disdain for an elaborate building that could be said to reflect European "decadence" or "pretentiousness." Anything that did not extol the backwoods virtues of industry and Puritan simplicity was seen—at least publicly—as an extravagance and an embarrassment.[16]

Other opponents had a different idea. Why lavish public moneys on a building that should be somewhere else? The nation was growing, spreading westward. It was time to move the capital city—and the Capitol—to Ohio, St. Louis, or Chicago. This argument had a veneer of nationalism, but those who made it were usually from the states that had a chance to host the proposed new venues.[17] Building a new Capitol, and especially a new capital city, meant jobs. Why should Washington, D.C., get them?

The third argument was never forthrightly articulated, but it was clear that several Southerners wished to halt Capitol construction because, even in 1852, they did not want to put money into a building in the capital of a country that they intended to abandon. This, perhaps, was the motivation for a prolonged and quite brilliant attack on additional Capitol Extension funding mounted by Arkansas Democratic Senator Solon Borland, a noted

---

[16]*Documentary History*, p. 498.
[17]Ibid., p. 488.

proslavery hardliner. He was ultimately unsuccessful but managed to smear the project and rally opposition to it without ever explaining his true objective.[18]

The motives for the personal attacks on Walter were more transparently political and self-interested. He was a Whig appointee in a dying Whig administration who, at one point, in 1851 had more than 800 men working for him digging the foundations. After the government itself, Walter was undoubtedly the biggest single employer in the district. There were a dozen rivals—many of them contest losers—who wanted his job for the prestige it brought, and just as many congressional hacks and lobbyists who wanted the job for the patronage it brought. Walter endured a constant stream of criticism and vilification for supposed incompetence and corruption throughout 1852, but it was never really possible to tell whether these assaults arose from a desire to throw mud at the Whigs or from simple greed. None of the charges ever amounted to anything, but serious damage was done to Walter's reputation, and his days—and, perhaps, the days of the Capitol Extension—appeared numbered when the new Democratic administration of President Franklin Pierce arrived in March 1853.

The Capitol's rise from a legislative sideshow to a point of congressional pride began with the advent of Pierce and was pushed forward by Jefferson Davis, who returned to Washington as secretary of war and shortly became one of the new president's closest advisers. Within days of Davis's arrival, the secretary of the interior, who was in charge of the Capitol, contacted him to see if he would send an army engineer to run the project. Walter, already bruised, was about to take an even more severe beating from congressional investigators, and regardless of his ultimate fate, the project itself appeared to be in great jeopardy.

Davis lost no time in taking action. It was a superb idea, and Davis liked it so much that within days he had induced Pierce to transfer authority over the project to the War Department. A few days after that, Davis named Captain Meigs as engineer in charge, reporting directly to him. Now he "owned" the project, and his man was running it. He left Walter in place but had him working under Meigs.[19]

---

[18]Ibid., pp. 498–502.

[19]See Gugliotta, *Freedom's Cap*, pp. 136–40, for a discussion of Meigs's selection.

It was a bureaucratic masterstroke. The sharks in Congress had been focused on Walter, but suddenly Walter no longer mattered. He could stay or depart. He was no longer hiring the workforce or signing the checks. Opponents of the project and patronage seekers lost interest in ousting him practically overnight.

Now there was Meigs, but, as a lowly captain, he did not matter either. If lawmakers wanted to make trouble, they were going to have to take on Davis, arguably the second-most powerful man in Washington. This was not a task to be undertaken lightly. Davis was smart, acerbic, intimidating, and capable of terrible rages, holding grudges, and ruthlessly taking retribution. He was very hard on anyone who crossed him. The chairman of the House Committee on Buildings and Grounds, a Capitol Extension advocate whom Davis had ignored during the 1850–51 planning for the extension, early in the Pierce administration mounted a campaign against "military rule" over civilian public works projects.[20] Very shortly thereafter he lost his committee chairmanship.

The added benefit during this period of change was that Meigs turned out to be just as tough and smart as Davis and Walter. He was only thirty-six when he took over at the Capitol, and, like many of his Corps of Engineers colleagues, he had spent most of his career building forts and doing surveys in the country's nether reaches. He did not have much of a résumé at the time, but the corps regarded him as an up-and-comer and had also assigned him the job of building the Washington Aqueduct, bringing fresh water to the district from Great Falls on the Potomac River. Meigs embraced both assignments and quickly became a Davis favorite.

In the four years that they worked together, Davis, Meigs, and Walter defined the Capitol for posterity. Meigs, the army engineer, believed in building things to last. He faced the new wings with thicker, heavier, and more durable marble than Walter and Fillmore had envisioned, mandated that new columns be made from one-piece marble monoliths, had windows and doorframes made of iron instead of wood, and ordered the sash cords to be fashioned from wire rope instead of hemp. All of this cost much more money than had been originally predicted, but Meigs wanted the best and Davis agreed with him and was willing to pay for it. And Congress, cajoled by

[20]See Montgomery C. Meigs, *Capitol Builder: The Shorthand Journals of Montgomery C. Meigs, 1853–1859, 1861,* ed. Wendy Wolff (Washington, D.C., 2001), p. 32.

Walter, earnestly proselytized by Meigs, and berated when necessary by Davis, appropriated the money.

Not everything was easy. Meigs decided to change Walter's original second-floor design by moving the Senate and House chambers to the interior of the new wings. Each would be enclosed, without windows, and would have to be heated and ventilated artificially. No longer exposed to street noise and natural light, the new Congress would lose some of the raucous openness that had characterized it for sixty years. Instead, the new chambers would be quieter, more intimate, clubby—and dignified. The design was controversial for decades, but it was an effect that Davis liked. As a senator he argued against allowing lobbyists, cabinet members, and ambassadors inside the chamber and wanted them confined in rooms set aside for their use.[21] His views did not prevail at first, but they did later. Davis wanted government that was more formal, and the new chambers moved it in that direction.

Meigs's other key design decision was to abandon the austere neoclassic, whitewashed interiors favored by Walter and Fillmore in favor of an opulent Pompeiian style epitomized by the elaborate frescoes and wall decorations of his chosen resident artist, Italian immigrant Constantino Brumidi (fig. 6), who had trained at the Vatican. The work of Brumidi and his assistants gave the interior of the new Capitol wings (especially the Senate wing) spectacular dazzle, bordering on, and perhaps at times crossing the line into, excess. Protestant lawmakers clucked their disapproval, but throngs of tourists and congressional families visited the extension to see Brumidi's paintings or watch him and his acolytes at work. One Brumidi–designed committee room was such a popular spot that the House Speaker had to keep a permanent guard on duty to manage the multitudes.[22]

Controversy mattered little to Davis, who ran roughshod over all opposition, brazenly claiming at one point in his annual message to Congress that it was Congress that had chosen this "higher style" of decoration for its new wings.[23] This was a patent lie. Davis and Meigs chose it, and consulted no one.

---

[21] *Congressional Globe*, Jan. 10, 1859, 35th Cong., 2d sess., pp. 288–90.
[22] Meigs, *Capitol Builder*, pp. 389, 429.
[23] *Documentary History*, p. 664.

FIG. 6. Photograph of Constantino Brumidi, ca. 1855–65. *(Brady-Handy Photograph Collection, Library of Congress Prints and Photographs Division)*

By mid-1854 the triumvirate was building a colossus, and Congress could like it or not. Then Walter gave lawmakers an overriding reason to embrace the project. When members of Congress returned after the midyear recess in December 1854, they saw a seven-foot-long color drawing tacked to the wall outside the first-floor Capitol Extension office. It showed the new wings completed, with elegantly clad ladies and gentlemen in the foreground climbing the eastern stairs, arriving in fancy coaches, or conversing in groups.

But in place of the old, leaky worn-out wooden dome, Walter had drawn a spectacular cast-iron replacement stretching to the sky with a colonnade, a row of high windows, a tapered top, and a statue—as yet undefined—standing at the pinnacle (fig. 7). It was a powerful image, as Meigs found out when he walked a group of congressmen past it, hinting that the dome was a future possibility—once the wings were finished. Why not build it now? the congressmen asked.[24] The dome and Walter's drawing, perhaps, had for the first time given members of Congress the opportunity to see exactly how immense and how spectacular their new headquarters was going to be. And Walter, who knew his audience, had put them in the picture. They were the top-hatted dignitaries lingering with their beautiful wives on the staircase. With the dome on the drawing board, the Capitol became a congressional necessity and started to become a national monument.

All of this occurred at a time when the country's tenuous unity was rapidly crumbling. Pierce was weak, and his administration was dominated by the disastrous piece of legislation known as the Kansas-Nebraska Act. Refusing to take a stand on whether states-to-be would have slavery, Congress decided to leave the decision up to the settlers—a notion known as "popular sovereignty." No sooner had the act been signed into law than rival gangs of proslavery Missourians and armed free-state settlers streamed into Kansas Territory to impose their will.

The result was the national catastrophe known as "Bleeding Kansas." The Whigs, already split over slavery, were finished, but Kansas cost the Democrats most of their Northern support and left the party in the hands of increasingly hardline Southerners. Antislavery Northerners formed the Republican Party, which had no Southern support. The sectional schism had opened wide. In one five-day stretch during late May 1856, abolitionist

[24]Meigs, *Capitol Builder*, p. 164.

Fig. 7. "Original Design of New Dome on the U.S. Capitol," by Thomas U. Walter, 1854. This period photograph of the lost seven-foot-long drawing of the architect's proposed new cast-iron dome attracted much attention when it hung in Walter's office. *(Architect of the Capitol)*

firebrand Senator Charles Sumner gave a vicious speech against slavery's defenders, attacking two senators by name. The next day proslavery gunmen wrecked the town of Lawrence, Kansas, an antislavery stronghold. The day after that, South Carolina Representative Preston S. Brooks, a cousin of one of the senators denounced by Sumner, nearly beat Sumner to death on the Senate floor with a cane. And two nights later, abolitionist John Brown and his followers hacked five proslavery settlers to death with broadswords.

Although Davis had long opposed what he called "squatter sovereignty," he was nevertheless instrumental in getting Pierce to support the Kansas-Nebraska Act. He also did nothing when old school chum and former Missouri Senator David R. Atchison wrote him a letter promising to "shoot, burn and hang" antislavery settlers.[25] And he sent a message of solidarity to a group of South Carolinians who were putting on a banquet to celebrate Brooks's caning of Sumner.[26] As secretary of war he did not comment directly on the chaos embracing the country, but the middle ground evaporated during the Pierce administration, and Davis bears some responsibility for helping it happen.

Davis's views on slavery also played a role in the odd events surrounding the selection of a design for the statue of *Freedom*. Meigs had given the

[25]Quoted in William W. Freehling, *The Road to Disunion*, vol. 2, *Secessionists Triumphant, 1854–1861* (New York, 2007), pp. 72–73.

[26]Davis to South Carolina Citizens, Sept. 22, 1856, in Crist et al., *Papers of Jefferson Davis*, 6:44.

contract to Thomas Crawford, an American sculptor living in Rome, and Crawford had produced the figure of a woman wearing a laurel wreath in her hair that both Davis and Meigs approved. Meigs, however, needed the statue to stand on a pedestal so she would not be bolted directly to the top of the dome and asked Crawford to modify the design. Instead, Crawford sent back an entirely new *Freedom*—a gorgeous, wraithlike figure wearing a "liberty cap," the symbol from classic antiquity of a manumitted slave (fig. 8). Davis, as Meigs knew, did not like liberty caps, an opinion he said was an anachronism in America, a country where people "were always free, not freedmen."[27] This came from a man who owned one hundred slaves himself in a country that, in all, held four million people in bondage. Meigs, who was against slavery but a dutiful subordinate, sent Crawford a noncommittal letter passing on Davis's opinion, taking no position of his own and leaving Crawford to figure out by himself what to do. Meigs clearly did not want his own bureaucratic fingerprints on the decision. The final design, approved by Davis and Meigs (fig. 9), was a robust nineteen-foot Indian princess–Roman goddess with a buckskin skirt, classical drapery above the waist, European features, and a bird purporting to be an American eagle sitting on her head with its mouth open. *Freedom Triumphant in War and Peace*, bolted in place atop the Capitol dome during the depths of the Civil War, was the design preferred by the president of the Confederacy.

THE ADVENT OF new president James Buchanan in 1857 brought no relief from the political crisis. Buchanan, a career politician, public servant, and Pennsylvanian, was probably the only Democrat of stature still relatively unblemished by the slavery controversy, having spent the Pierce years as U.S. ambassador to Great Britain. Still, it was clear that the party would have great difficulty finding a consensus candidate in 1860. Failure to do so would give the Republicans a substantial opening, and if their candidate won, secession by at least some Southern states was all but certain.

Buchanan's task was to find a way out of this mess, and he wagered his presidency on the Supreme Court's upcoming decision in the case of Dred Scott, a Missouri slave suing for his freedom. In later years, the Dred Scott ruling would earn notoriety for holding that slaves "had no rights which the white man is bound to respect," but the more trenchant finding at the time

[27]Meigs, *Capitol Builder*, p. 66.

FIG. 8. "Statue of Freedom maquette, for the dome of the U.S. Capitol, T. Crawford, sculptor, Rome, Oct. 1855," photograph by Robert Macpherson. This design met with Jefferson Davis's disapproval. *(Library of Congress Prints and Photographs Division)*

FIG. 9. Crawford's final design for the statue of *Freedom* replaced the liberty cap (see fig. 8) with an eagle's head and feathers. The plaster model from which the statue was cast in bronze was displayed for many years in the Old Hall of the House of Representatives in the Capitol, as seen in this photograph created ca. 1859–78. *(Library of Congress Prints and Photographs Division)*

was that Congress had no right to exclude slavery from the territories.[28] Buchanan expected Dred Scott to defuse the Kansas crisis by providing a comprehensive legal solution that would trump sectional politics.

Instead, Republicans were outraged, regarding Dred Scott as a legal subterfuge cooked up by Buchanan and the court to give slavery the advantage in any territorial dispute, and the decision triggered an economic panic later in the year. The Buchanan administration, having painted itself into a corner in its opening days, spent most of the rest of its time in a futile attempt to pass a proslavery constitution for Kansas.

Apart from this policy debacle, Buchanan performed as an old-style pol, big on deal-making, patronage, and cronyism. He was also an entertainer of note, whose fancy parties, as the country's woes deepened, marked a Nero-like contrast to the austerity of the equally ineffectual Pierce, a recovering alcoholic who wandered his White House neighborhood at night looking for a cup of coffee and chitchat at the houses of old friends like Davis.

Pierce's departure prompted Davis to make a smooth, preplanned transition back to the Senate, where he acquired a reputation for moderation in the slavery dispute at a time when many of his Southern colleagues were daily threatening secession. The congressional atmosphere was becoming so rancorous that lawmakers from the different sections could scarcely speak civilly to one another. Davis's ability to mute his tone as the crisis advanced in these last prewar years probably gave him the stature that eventually won him the Confederate presidency. One of his best friends during the Buchanan administration was New York abolitionist William H. Seward, Abraham Lincoln's leading rival for the 1860 Republican presidential nomination.

Despite the continued presence of all its members, the Capitol Extension triumvirate was not nearly as powerful in the Buchanan years. The principal reason was a sharp rift between Meigs and Walter, whose monstrous egos could no longer maintain the uneasy equilibrium that had guided them for years. Meigs enraged Walter by altering the inscriptions on early Walter drawings to give himself more credit for their execution. Walter enraged Meigs by plotting to have the Buchanan administration fire him. Meigs had Davis's help, but Walter was allied with new Secretary of War John B.

[28] "The Dred Scott Decision," Digital History ID 293, http://www.digitalhistory.uh.edu/disp_textbook.cfm?smtID=3&psid=293.

Floyd of Virginia, a notorious political hack but also a close Buchanan crony.[29] Meigs eventually lost the battle and left the Capitol in late 1859.

Despite this intrigue, the Capitol Extension in these last, grim prewar years began to acquire a charisma it would never lose. The mystique probably claimed Walter first. When he began working in Washington, he had maintained his Philadelphia practice and had taken on several outside jobs. In an 1854 letter to one of his sons he said he had abandoned everything else to commit himself to the Capitol full time.[30] Meigs was right behind him. He earned only $1,800 per year as an army captain when he began working on the project and needed a $300 yearly stipend from his father, a well-to-do Philadelphia doctor, to make ends meet. But in 1854 he turned down job offers to dig a canal in Baltimore for $3,500 per year and to run a lead mine in North Carolina for $5,000 per year. He was in charge of the "greatest work of a civil engineer in the country," he wrote in his diary, and would not give it up.[31]

For Davis, the enthusiasm never waned, and during the Buchanan years, his congressional colleagues joined him. The new House had gone into service in late 1857. Its acoustics were widely praised, and by themselves were enough to term the new wing a success; but the lack of sunlight and the fancy Brumidi-inspired decorations were a bit too avant-garde for many members. The new Senate, with a more muted decor, opened to high praise from the tenants in early 1859 and won generally favorable press reviews. By the end of the year, both "new" chambers were well on their way to becoming, once again, simply "the Senate" and "the House."

In 1860, with Davis directing legislative traffic, the Senate effortlessly and almost urgently passed appropriations ensuring that there would be enough money to finish the dome, to move the Supreme Court into the old Senate chamber, and to comfortably fund Capitol construction through the arrival of the new administration the following year.

In 1859, the entire South Carolina congressional delegation, which would abandon Congress within two months of Lincoln's election, successfully lobbied the Buchanan administration to ensure that fellow South Carolinian Clark Mills won the contract to cast *Freedom* at his new foundry on the

---

[29]See Gugliotta, *Freedom's Cap*, pp. 274–90, for a detailed discussion of the feud. See Allen, *History of the Capitol*, pp. 268–74, for another view.

[30]Walter to Thomas Walter, Aug. 19, 1854, Walter Collection, roll 4137.

[31]Meigs, *Capitol Builder*, p. 82.

district's eastern edge.[32] And during House debate on the 1860 Capitol appropriations for Capitol construction, Georgia Representative Joshua Hill told colleagues he would "never hesitate" when offered a chance to promote the "embellishment of the Capitol of my country, to vote for it with pleasure." He resigned from Congress in 1861 after Georgia seceded.[33]

MEIGS RETURNED TO the Capitol in the opening days of the Lincoln administration, reclaiming his post as engineer in charge and, with the help of former Senator Seward, now Lincoln's secretary of state, becoming the Union army's leading supply officer. He tried but failed to fire Walter, who had the ear of Secretary of War Simon Cameron, a fellow Philadelphian. Then, on May 19, 1861, Meigs shut down Capitol construction altogether, citing changing priorities prompted by the war.

For the first three months of the war, with Congress in recess, the Capitol—the new Senate and House chambers, the congressional offices, and even the rotunda—served as a transient barracks for newly mustered regiments of Union soldiers on their way to battle. The Commissary General opened a bakery in the basement, and soot from the ovens wafted out the west front windows and back into the Library of Congress stacks. Mess cooks left sides of meat and other perishables on the tiled floors of the committee rooms, and idle soldiers spent their days holding mock debates in the Senate and House chambers, swinging back and forth over the rotunda, and using every dark corner in the building for a privy. The worst of this had been cleaned up by the time Congress convened for an emergency session in July, but it was not until early 1862 when lawmakers took a close look at the building—still needing completion of the dome and a lot of exterior work. Walter had sat on his thumbs briefly in Philadelphia at the beginning of the war, but by the time the special session began, he and some of his contractors began lobbying the congressional leadership for a resumption of construction. This, Walter and his co-conspirators argued, could most easily be accomplished through the simple expedient of transferring stewardship of the project from the War Department back to the Interior

[32] Walter to J. Ames, Jan. 1, 1860, Walter Collection, roll 4139.

[33] *Documentary History*, p. 768.

Department, where it rightfully belonged and where it had been before the traitor Davis hijacked it in 1853.[34]

This was not a hard argument to make. Lawmakers had gotten the troops out of the building, but the bakery lingered for months, wearing out the army's welcome. Meigs's plan to put the Capitol Extension on ice until after the war generated little enthusiasm. The building was not finished, had been sorely used in recent months, and, at a minimum, needed maintenance. Meigs had too much to do, crafting a supply system for a Union army that had 16,000 men in 1861 and would grow to more than two million over the next four years.

But most important for Congress, finishing the Capitol made a statement about Union resources, Union resolve, and the future of the United States. On March 25, 1862, Vermont Senator Solomon Foot, president pro tempore of the Senate and chair of the Committee on Public Buildings and Grounds, made the argument, telling his colleagues to vote for a resolution transferring the Capitol back to Interior Department jurisdiction and resuming construction:

> This national Capitol of ours, in its present condition, instead of being the boast and the pride of the country, instead of being an ornament and a credit to the country, stands to-day, after 12 years, an unfinished and an unsightly pile. . . . [W]e are strong enough yet, thank God, to put down this rebellion and to put up this our Capitol at the same time. And when the rebellion shall have been suppressed—as suppressed it soon will be; when this war shall have been terminated—as terminated it soon will be; and when this Union of ours shall have been restored—as restored it soon will be; it will furnish a fitting and appropriate occasion to celebrate that welcome event by crowning the American Capitol with the statue of the Goddess of Freedom.

The joint resolution passed both houses of Congress with fewer than ten votes in opposition.[35]

---

[34]Walter to Fowler, Mar. 17, 1862, Walter Collection, roll 4140.

[35]*Documentary History*, p. 802.

Contributors

Jean H. Baker is professor emerita of history at Goucher College. She has published several books including biographies: *James Buchanan* (Times Books, 2004), *Mary Todd Lincoln: A Biography* (W. W. Norton, 1987 and 2008), *Margaret Sanger: A Life of Passion* (Hill and Wang, 2011), and *Stevensons: The Biography of an American Family* (W. W. Norton, 1996). Several of her books deal with politics: *Politics of Continuity; Maryland Political Parties from 1858 to 1870* (Johns Hopkins University Press, 1973), *Ambivalent Americans: The Know-Nothing Party in Maryland* (Johns Hopkins University Press, 1977), and *Affairs of Party: The Political Culture of Northern Democrats in the Mid-Nineteenth Century* (Cornell University Press, 1983).

Jenny Bourne is the Raymond Plank Professor of Incentive Economics at Carleton College in Northfield, Minnesota. She previously held positions at St. Olaf College, George Mason University, and the U.S. Treasury Department. She is the author of *The Bondsman's Burden: An Economic Analysis of the Common Law of Southern Slavery* (Cambridge University Press, 1998), and *In Essentials, Unity: An Economic History of the Grange Movement* (Ohio University Press, 2017). Her current research includes a study of the relationship of income to wealth for the very rich and an analysis of the progressivity of the U.S. tax code.

Paul Finkelman is the president of Gratz College in greater Philadelphia. Before coming to Gratz, he was the John E. Murray Visiting Professor of Law at the University of Pittsburgh School of Law, and also held the Fulbright Chair in Human Rights and Social Justice at the University of Ottawa College of Law. He has been a senior fellow at the Program on Democracy, Citizenship, and Constitutionalism at the University of Pennsylvania and a scholar-in-residence at the National Constitution Center. In 2016 he held the Ariel F. Sallows Chair in Human Rights at the University of Saskatchewan College of Law. He is the author of more than fifty books and two hundred scholarly articles.

Guy Gugliotta spent sixteen years with the *Washington Post* as a science reporter and political and domestic policy correspondent. He began his career at U.P.I. and the *Miami Herald* covering wars, crises, and policy issues in Latin America and elsewhere around the world. Since leaving the *Washington Post*, he has had a successful career as a freelance science journalist writing for the *New York Times*, the *Washington Post*, *Smithsonian*, the *Atlantic*, *Wired*, and other publications. He is coauthor with Jeff Leen of *Kings of Cocaine: Inside the Medellin Cartel* (Simon and Schuster, 1989) and author of *Freedom's Cap: The United States Capitol and the Coming of the Civil War* (Hill and Wang, 2012). A former swift boat officer in the Vietnam War, he is a coeditor with John Yeoman and Neva Sullaway of *Swift Boats at War in Vietnam* (Stackpole Books, 2017).

Daniel W. Stowell was director and editor of the Papers of Abraham Lincoln from 2001 to 2016. He also served in a similar capacity on the Lincoln Legal Papers from 2000 to 2008. From 2011 to 2015, he was also director of the Center for Digital Initiatives, Abraham Lincoln Presidential Library and Museum, and senior editor of *The Journal of the Abraham Lincoln Association*, 2013 to 2016. His publications include *Rebuilding Zion: The Religious Reconstruction of the South, 1863–1877* (Oxford University Press, 1998) and as editor of *The Papers of Abraham Lincoln: Legal Documents and Cases*, 4 vols. (University of Virginia Press, 2008), as well as numerous articles, reviews, and digital media.

Peter Wallenstein is professor of history at Virginia Polytechnic Institute and State University at Blacksburg, where he specializes in the history of the U.S. South, Virginia, civil rights, and higher education. He is the author or editor of more than a dozen books, including *Cradle of America: A History of Virginia* (2d ed. rev., University Press of Kansas, 2014), *Blue Laws and Black Codes: Conflict, Courts, and Change in Twentieth-Century Virginia* (University of Virginia Press, 2004), *Tell the Court I Love My Wife: Race, Marriage, and Law—An American History* (Palgrave Macmillan, 2002), and *From Slave South to New South: Public Policy in Nineteenth-Century Georgia* (University of North Carolina Press, 1987).

Jennifer L. Weber is associate professor of history at the University of Kansas, where she specializes in the Civil War and Abraham Lincoln. Her work takes a holistic approach, examining how military, political, and social forces affected each other during the war. Her first book, *Copperheads: The Rise and Fall of Lincoln's Opponents in the North* (Oxford University Press, 2006), looked at the antiwar Democrats in the North and the political pressures that Lincoln faced. Her second book, *Summer's Bloodiest Days* (National Geographic, 2010), a children's book about the Battle of Gettysburg and its aftermath, was named a notable book of 2011 by the National Council for the Social Studies. Professor Weber is currently working on a biography of the agency that administered and enforced the Union draft, and what that bureau's experience illuminates about the growing size and power of government during the war.

Index